Christian

— Family —

In the world, but not of it

To God's glory! Cindy & Jim

By James & Cynthia McDermott

Salt Christian Press

Published by Salt Christian Press
2131 W. Republic Rd. #177
Springfield, MO 65807

The Christian Family:
In the world, but not of it

Marriage

2 My Dear Husband
3 An Anniversary Message, a Love Letter
5 How Do I Love Thee, My Husband?
8 A Man's Duty to Love His Wife
10 I Love You, Master
14 Oops!
16 Can't See the Burger King for the Road Block
18 My Obsessive Spouse
19 Birth Control: Leaving the decision with God
29 Working Wives: Should they or shouldn't they?
38 Reflections of this Working Mom

Children

40 Dear Baby,
41 Dear Josiah,
43 My Newborn, My Teacher
45 A Face Only a Mother Could Love
47 How Do I Love Thee, My Children?
50 Praying for Our Children
53 Fear in the Night
55 One on One in a Crowd
57 Boys!
58 Me & My Quiver: A mom's perspective ten children later
63 In Defense of Children
65 Farewell Address: To my oldest son on his graduation from homeschool

Parents

69 The Seasons of Life
70 The Season of Parenting
72 Fatherhood: Underrated and misunderstood
76 It's Not Just about Fatherhood
82 Now I Carry the Torch
84 Motherhood: Dirty diapers and child evangelism
88 How to be a Good Mother
91 Honoring Parents
93 I Appreciate You, Mom
95 Dad

Child Discipline

97 I'm Only Thinking of You (Not)
99 What Does "No!" Really Mean?
101 I'll Give You a Lollipop
104 Maybe it's Not the Strong Willed Child: Introducing the weak willed parent
109 The Habit Makers
113 Praise the Permissive Parent?
118 War of the Siblings
121 Balancing the Rod
127 Lost Children (part 1)
136 Lost Children (part 2)

Keeping the Home

146 Distracted!
148 A Mother's Work ... (part 1)
151 A Mother's Work ... (part 2)
153 Before You Start Organizing
156 Lessons on Household Organization from a Chronically Disorganized Man
160 Confessions of a Pack Rat
162 Stockpiling
164 99's the Limit!
168 Land of the Misfit Socks
170 That Silly Sock Saga
172 Chores for All
175 Kid Work
178 Our Family Vacation
181 The Unvacation
185 It's His Time
190 Managing the Home: Time
199 God's Economy
205 Managing the Home: Money
211 Frustrated over Money?
218 Bankruptcy, Anyone?
222 A Tip from a Cheerful Giver
225 Why Home Based Businesses Fail!
234 13 to 2 (People to Rooms)
238 Bittersweet: Moving can be such sweet sorrow

Courtship

241 The Birds & the Bees: And the need to know
244 Absolute Purity
249 Marriageable Age!
259 Preparing Sons for Marriage

265 Is Your Daughter Ready for the Wedding?
269 Finding a Mate
274 Choosing a Wife
277 Choosing a Husband
280 Who Should Pay for the Wedding?

Counter Culture

285 Garbage In – Garbage Out
287 What About Harry Potter?
293 On the Feminine Side
295 The Doofus
297 The TV Commercial Dilemma
299 The Super Bowl: A new low
303 Modesty is the Best Policy
312 Friends Unequally Yoked
314 The Difficult People at the End of the Bell Curve
318 Keeping the Family Together
324 Just Leave Me Alone
326 Please, Come in

Inspiration

329 The Urgency of Eternity
330 Stressed!
334 No More Locusts
336 Consider Job
338 All Things Are Possible
340 I Have a Dream, Too

Preface

In April 1983 I was in Cincinnati, Ohio, suffering the consequences of rebellion against my parents and against God. The choices before me were to undergo at least temporary homelessness or swallow my pride, go back home, and make a fresh start. Like the Prodigal Son, I came to my senses and returned to my father and my God.

I deeply appreciated God's grace and wanted to serve Him whole-heartedly. I was willing to go anywhere God wanted me to go and to do anything God wanted me to do.

In January 1984 I went to Concordia College in Wisconsin. I was hoping to turn the world upside down for Christ. I had considered renouncing marriage and I had considered missionary service. I enrolled in the pre-seminary program and thought I was on my way.

But the week I arrived at school I met Cindy Juedes and my life was never the same. By the end of the year my main focus was trying to figure out how to get this girl to marry me as soon as possible. How I got the Martin Luther High valedictorian to marry a poor guy like me before she graduated from college is a mystery, but love makes people do all kinds of crazy things.

Neither one of us, however, knew what God had in store for us. We were unified in our desire to live for God and the first major result of that desire was the decision we made to forego birth control. This culturally radical decision was followed by decisions to pursue a home business and to homeschool our children. And it seems like every couple years there is another issue that catches our attention: modesty, courtship, family integrated worship, and so on.

These life-changing decisions seem to make life more challenging than it might have been. We now have eleven children, who are all priceless but who are also a lot of work and very expensive. We have had financial struggles, children who were regularly in the emergency room for asthma, a child with chronic seizures, job disappointments, an encounter with Social Services, eight children with the flu on Christmas Day, business failures, and interstate moves. Needless to say, we did not write this book from the perspective of the chronically successful. However, the rugged terrain of the road less traveled has produced a beautiful and satisfying journey.

The purpose of this book is certainly not to condemn those who have chosen a different path, but to share with you how the Christian family looks from that less traveled road – the road God chose for us.

What follows are articles we have written over the last five years that relate to the family and living the Christian life. Some of the articles are practical, some discuss controversial issues, some are emotional, some are inspirational, and some contain a dose of humor.

Our prayer is that God will encourage and challenge you through what we have written and that your family will be blessed through the process.

-Jim

As I write this, Jim and I have just celebrated our nineteenth wedding anniversary. It is so exciting to spend every day with my best friend and to walk through life together. One of the greatest joys we share is raising our children. I'm reminded of the story in Genesis 33 when Jacob met Esau after many years of being apart. Esau looked at all the women and children with Jacob and asked, "Who are these with you?" Jacob responded, "The children whom God has graciously given your servant." That's exactly the way I feel about our children.

We have come to be known by many as the couple "with eleven kids". Although that is a type of identity for us, we rejoice even more in our identity as children of God. He fills our lives with purpose, joy, and hope. We can never thank Him enough.

We pray that God will use these humble words to His glory.

-Cindy

Dedicated to our parents Paul & Elizabeth Juedes, and the late Rev. Donald McDermott & Anita McDermott Contois. Of all the things you've given to us, we regard our spiritual heritage the most precious.

Marriage

For this reason a man shall leave his father and his mother, and be joined to his wife; and they shall become one flesh.
(Genesis 2:24)

My Dear Husband,

This is our eighteenth Valentine's Day together and our nineteenth as a "couple." When you're young and you get married you feel like you have an automatic sixty years to spend together. I know I did. I guess the years have given me some wisdom, because now I realize that you aren't guaranteed anything on your wedding day – not sixty years, or even eighteen. So I humbly thank God for each of the years He has granted us to be together.

I haven't always understood this Valentine's holiday. It seems so many people are grasping for the true meaning of the occasion – trying to give and receive heart shaped boxes of candy and red roses, looking for or hoping for a date. Through misfortune or choices of their own they have but a shell and lack the substance. But I get to be with my Valentine every day. What a precious thing that is.

I wish that hidden somewhere in this message was an invitation to a Valentine Hawaiian get-a-way. I wish I could give you a new car or even a mortgage paid in full. I wish I could wipe away the concerns and toils of your days. But you and I both know we have more of a fish-and-chips than a surf-and-turf sort of life. So here I give you what I can, something I too often don't make time to express - my appreciation and my commitment.

Thank you for loving the Lord and trying to follow Him day by day. By watching you walk with Him, I have been encouraged in my own relationship with God. I have seen you read your Bible and have heard you pray. I know that the desire of your heart is to use your life to serve Him. I have seen you confess your shortcomings and ask your children for forgiveness for your mistakes. You have been a spiritual leader to this family by your example. There's no greater thing you can do for us.

Thank you for your kindnesses to me. I know you love me by the things you do – but thank you for being willing to tell me, too! I have seen you make things harder on yourself so that things would be easier for me. I've seen you do things you don't really want to do (like going shopping!) so that I don't have to. I have seen you get less sleep so I can get more. I've seen you give up your wishes and preferences so that I can have mine. You have sincerely complimented me, lovingly encouraged me, and humbly led me. I want you to know that I see those things.

Thank you for being willing to lead this family. We know that it is not a position of power, but one of responsibility before God. Thank you for making the tough decisions and being willing to bear the responsibility for them. Thank you for all the times you told me not to "worry about it" because you had it under control. At the same time, thank you for valuing my opinion and asking for my input. Thank you for the times you've given me room and lee-way when you could have just as easily controlled it all yourself. Thank you that you have been a godly, humble leader instead of a leader of the type we so often see today.

Thank you for loving our children and being excited with the coming of each child. Your happiness and excitement in this area means more to me than if the whole world was happy for me and you were not. Thank you for your strong convictions in raising this family, and for being true to God's calling for us, rather than being concerned about what is acceptable in the eyes of others. Thank you for caring so much about being together as a family and doing things as a family. Thank you for your involvement in our children's education, spiritual training, discipline, interests, and future. Thank you for tickling the girls and playing football with the boys. Did you ever think there would be so many tea parties?

So what can I give you this day? Today I affirm the promise I made nearly eighteen years ago – to forsake all others and be bound only to you. I will undertake to be a good helper to you – one with a gentle and uncomplaining heart. I will regard as important those things that are important to you. I will allow you to lead and I will allow you to make mistakes. I will rejoice with you in your victories. I will attempt to show you half of the kindnesses you have shown me day by day. I will pray for you.

We've been through many things, these years of ours together. I have never regretted marrying, nor marrying when we did. After all this time, I still get excited when you call me from work or I hear the car drive up to the house! We've had some challenging times, but we've also experienced God's blessings, provision, and joy. He has helped us grow as individuals, and has helped us grow together into a unit, a couple, a team. I pray that God would use us together to accomplish His purposes for His Kingdom.

What have I missed in this letter? I'm sure there must be something I've forgotten. But I hope this covers it all –

"With this love we can live, but we can't keep it to ourselves. He is mine and He is yours, and we can spend our lives in telling. I give my heart, I give my soul, I give you all my worldly goods. Two in one, one in two, that's the way it's got to be. I will cling to you, you will cling to me, and in the shadow of the cross we'll live on bended knee..." (Pat Terry, "That's the Way," *Word Music*, 1974)

Love and forever, Me

An Anniversary Message, a Love Letter

"Arise, my darling, my beautiful one, and come along! O my dove ... let me see your form, let me hear your voice; for your voice is sweet, and your form is lovely." Song of Sol. 2:13b

Cindy, My Love,

Our 19th anniversary has just passed and I can honestly say that I love you much, much more now than I did on our wedding day – and I was crazy with love on my wedding day.

You've handled hard times and hard work with grace, charm, and faith. Remember the overdue bills, the water turn-off notice, the middle of the night trips to emergency rooms, car problems, basic training, long shifts at the hospital, and the 4 interstate moves? Remember when our budget allowed dessert – ice cream – only once a month? Remember the 11 births, the 2 miscarriages, the sleepless nights with babies, and the days alone with our first six children when the oldest was 7 years old? Remember the entire year we didn't get out of the house by ourselves even once? And yet, I remember all our years as happy years because no matter what life was dealing us, you were almost always happy and always affectionate towards me. You never blamed me for our troubles even when they were my fault and you were very rarely discouraged even when our situation seemed hopeless. Your love for me has been sorely tested, but it has proven to be extraordinarily strong and pure. How could I not love you?

But the good times have been more than the bad. Remember how happy we were when we were first married? (I guess you don't need a car, a phone, or your own kitchen to be happy.) Remember sitting up late with our older children and laughing about everything? Remember the precious newborns? Remember the baby snuggles and the toddler giggles? Remember sneaking out for Frapuccinos? Remember seeing the Golden Gate Bridge, feeding the sea lions, walking on the boardwalk in Ocean City, or actually getting to Washington, D.C. when the cherry trees were blooming? Remember the Turkish Restaurant in Georgetown, the bed and breakfast on the Chesapeake, the outdoor theater in Branson, and walking the Inner Harbor in Baltimore together?

And as I look around and see the women of our culture, I know that only a rare and fine woman would let her husband continue to lead when he hasn't always made good decisions. Only a rare and fine woman would allow her husband to make his dreams a reality when no one else on earth seems to believe in those dreams. Only a rare and fine woman would continue to encourage her husband to succeed in high-risk ventures when past ventures have made life so hard. Only a rare and fine wife would consistently advise her husband to do what's right even when it didn't seem to be in her best interest. Only a rare and fine woman would be so generous when she isn't so wealthy (in worldly goods).

But I suppose in God's economy, I may have more wealth than Bill Gates. You Cindy, my godly wife, are worth more than all the money in the world and the 11 children you bore me are all of incalculable value as well. How many men have been blessed by God as I have been?

My anniversary prayer for you, then, is that God would help me to lead our family well. I pray that God will prosper us and that you will enjoy a time of refreshing and rest. I pray that God will give you the desire of your heart to leave the hospital and be home with your children full-time. I pray that our children will all grow up to be strong in the Lord and that all of them will hear, "Well done, good and faithful servant," when their lives are done. And I pray that God would help my love for you to resemble more and more Christ's love for the Church.

Thank you for an inexpressibly wonderful 19 years and I pray God will give us many more. –Your Loving and Grateful Husband, Jim

How Do I Love Thee, My Husband?

"Fiddler on the Roof" is one of my favorite movies. It is profound, yet still entertaining and humorous. In one scene the wife and husband are doing some innocent bantering back and forth. Then the wife mutters under her breath, "You can die from such a man." (It is at this point in the movie that I characteristically look at Jim and smile. Jim insists I enjoy that line too much!) Later on in the movie the husband asks his wife, because of their arranged marriage, if she loves him. In song she begins to recall their twenty-five years of marriage and how she bore his children, milked his cow, "worked with him, starved with him" and then concludes, "If that's not love, what is?" How do you define love? How can we show our husbands that we love them?

We can love our husbands first of all by letting them be the heads of our families. I know this is a volatile issue in our society. I think that those who are opposed to this do not fully understand the Bible verse: "Wives, be subject to your own husbands, as to the Lord. For the husband is the head of the wife, as Christ also is the head of the church, He Himself being the Savior of the body. But as the church is subject to Christ, so also the wives ought to be to their husbands in everything." (Ephesians 5:22-24) This is the way God ordained marriage to be. It's His idea. Some women find it difficult to allow their husbands to make the final decisions in the home. But it doesn't mean that women are inferior or less intelligent. It just means that God chose the husband to have that position and *bear that responsibility*. How many top bosses do you have at your work? Only one, right? When there are disagreements there has to be someone to make the final decision and bear the responsibility for that decision. Furthermore, verse 25 in the same chapter of Ephesians states, "Husbands, love your wives, just as Christ also loved the church and gave Himself up for her..." Our husbands are not to rule as tyrants in our houses, but to lead us lovingly. They are to love us as much as Christ loved the Church. If our husbands love us that much, we are in a very good place.

What does this have to do with loving our husbands? We want to show our husbands that we respect and accept their authority. Why should we want them to experience stress and discord in their own homes? We want to make it easy for our husbands to perform their role in our families. Our husbands must stand before God to answer for how their households were run. If we love our husbands, we want to make that a pleasant experience for them!

In relation to that we should stand behind our husbands in the decisions that they make, even if we don't agree with them. We can follow their lead with a good attitude despite our disagreements. We will do what is asked of us. We will refuse to speak badly of them in front of our children. We will remain a unified front before the children. We will not blame new rules on the father, but enforce them as a team. Furthermore, we can allow our husbands to make mistakes without throwing it in their faces and then reminding them of it again and again. We love our husbands in spite of their mistakes and their weaknesses.

We can love our husbands by serving them and our children well, and with a happy heart. Sounds like another controversial topic! The truth is that we were made to be helpers for our husbands. Genesis 2:18 reads: "Then the LORD God said, 'It is not good for the man to be alone; I will make him a helper suitable for him.' " It was then that God created Eve for Adam. Serving our families is not demeaning. There is actually great nobility in serving others. Jesus told His disciples, "If anyone wants to be first, he shall be last of all and servant of all." (Mark 9:35b) Jesus, though God, came to earth to serve and to help. We should follow His example – not only in His serving, but also in His willingness to do so. Would we want someone to help us begrudgingly? We should strive to make our home, both physically and emotionally, a place that our husbands hate to leave and can't wait to come back to.

We should treat our husbands as our soul mates. I've seen women who run to their mother or best girlfriend at the first sign of personal triumph or defeat, joy or grief. I do not believe this is the way God intended marriage. We are a couple, a partnership. We are one flesh, remember? Our husbands should be our first line of defense, our number one fan, our biggest shoulder to cry on, our most enthusiastic cheerleader. It should be you and him against the world. How would you like him to confide in his college buddy before you? We show our husbands how important they are to us and how much we love them by turning to them first to share our joys and sorrows. It shows we value their presence and their viewpoint. It shows that we desire them to have an active part in our lives. In the process we make our relationship stronger.

You don't feel like he's your soul mate? He won't be if you place him on the perimeter of your emotional life.

We can love our husbands by being considerate of their needs and wishes. One way to do this is by making what's important to them, important to us. Support him in his goals and help him if possible. Listen to what he has to say. Allow him to dream – and dream with him. This can apply to little things, too. Just like you don't want to get a chain saw for Christmas, he probably doesn't want crystal for your anniversary or to go window-shopping on your next date. Surprise him with an unexpected outing, a hidden note, or a special treat. (Whatever *he* would like!) Remember, "little things" can mean a lot. Our thoughtfulness should even extend to being "generous" in our physical affection towards our husbands. The bottom line: we shouldn't be selfish. Even if they let us get away with it, we needn't take advantage of our husbands' love for us.

Our husbands will know we love them if we encourage and praise them. It's a tough, unfeeling world out there, and our husbands need us to be *their* fan, cheerleader, and admirer. They need to know they are not alone and that we appreciate their hard work for us and our children. There may be no one else who will appreciate who they are and what they do, or to encourage them when things aren't going well. Even if all the world supported our husbands, it may mean nothing to them if we don't.

We also show our love by being a Proverbs 31 wife to the best of our ability. She is confident and hard working. She is competent to perform her tasks. She is compassionate towards others. She is an asset to her family. She is a woman of "noble character." She is wise and shares that wisdom with others. Above all, she fears God. My guess is that most men would love to have such a woman by their side.

Finally, if we love our husbands, we will want to pray for them. We will want to pray for their health, their happiness, their wisdom, their walk with God, and any specific needs that they may have. Our husbands may not know we do that, but "when you pray, go into your inner room, close your door and pray to your Father who is in secret, and your Father who sees what is done in secret will reward you." (Matthew 6:6)

Next to Jesus, my husband is the most precious thing to me. I love him with all my heart and forever. And I'm going to try to make sure he knows that.

How do I love thee? Let me count the ways, my love!

A Man's Duty to Love His Wife

Have you ever heard a man say, "I *have to* get my wife something for Valentine's Day," or, "I *have* to think of something to do for our anniversary"? What do you suppose is forcing these men to do nice things for their wives, since they feel they *have to* do them? I believe Valentine's Days and anniversaries have been established for the man who otherwise would never break the daily routine to make his wife feel special. That's why he *has to* get his wife something for Valentine's Day and he *has* to do something nice for her on their anniversary.

Some misguided folks believe Valentine's Days and anniversaries are mainly for courting and newly married couples, but that is ridiculous. Everyone knows that courting and newly married girls don't need a silly holiday to get gifts or dinner invitations. After a girl is married a few years and gets stuck on her 29th birthday, a transformation takes place in many men. The tangible signs of affection he willfully and obsessively showered on her when they first became a couple slowly diminish until the man considers signs of affection an awkward duty reserved for Valentine's Days and anniversaries.

Most people would define duty as something you do because you have to and not necessarily because you want to. If we say, then, that a man has a duty to love his wife, it would seem that loving one's wife may be an unpleasant but necessary task. Apparently the problem of men needing to be compelled to love their wives goes way back. Paul, led by the Holy Spirit, had to command the men at Colosse to love their wives. (Col. 3:19) But something about the Ephesian men made Paul command them not once, but three times to love their wives. (Eph 5:25, 5:28, 5:33) Maybe the men of Ephesus weren't even observing their anniversaries.

But loving one's wife wasn't supposed to be a burden. The Bible says to the man, "Rejoice in the wife of your youth. As a loving hind and a graceful doe, Let her breasts satisfy you at all times; Be exhilarated always with her love." (Prov. 5:18b-19) God, speaking to Ezekiel of his wife, called her the delight of his eyes. The Lover in Solomon's Song of Songs says of his bride, "How beautiful you are, my darling, how beautiful you are!" His beloved replies, "How handsome you are, my beloved, and so pleasant! Indeed, our couch is luxuriant!" (Song of Sol. 1:15-16) In the beginning God created Eve to be a suitable helper for Adam and his life-long companion. Adam sure didn't seem to be complaining when he called Eve, "Bone of my bones and flesh of my flesh." It seems, then, that God didn't intend married life to be a burden, but a source of life-long companionship and pleasure. After all, marriage was instituted before the fall when Adam and Eve lived in the Paradise of God.

If that is the case, why was it necessary for Peter and Paul to command husbands to love their wives? The reason, of course, is that after the fall both men and women became sinful. In the Garden Adam was the perfect lover and Eve perfectly lovable. After the fall, perfection was lost, but some men became especially unloving and some women became especially unlovable. Now, instead of excitement and joy, the man says, "My wife is a nag," and the woman says, "That irresponsible slob!"

As a result of the fall, my greatest enemy could be my own wife. But that does not excuse me from loving my wife. The Bible commands us to love our wives and to love our enemies. If my enemy and my wife are the same person, I can efficiently keep both commands by loving one person. More pleasant, however, is the knowledge that a man who loves his enemy receives a reward from the Lord. (Prov. 25:22) Our love for an unlovable spouse will not be in vain, even if he or she remains a difficult spouse till the end.

When we love our enemies, however, we run the risk that our enemy will love us in return. Therefore, if a man loves his unlovable wife, she may stop being unlovable. When a man loves his unlovable wife, he becomes like Christ in his own home. For Christ loved us first when we were unlovable, and we ought to initiate and sustain a love relationship with our wives as we reflect the love of Christ. And, as Christ's love changed hearts and caused formerly hostile men to respond with everlasting devotion, so we may eventually soften the hearts of our unlovable spouses if we continue to love them.

Many of us, however, have loveable spouses who we don't love as we should. They are not hostile, but we are selfish. Or perhaps, we love our wives, but don't do a very good job at showing it. Men in these situations just don't know what they're missing. For a lovable woman who is regularly showered with tangible signs of her husband's affection is likely to make him feel like the luckiest man on the face of the planet. (I know this from personal experience.) For those unromantic types who need help, tangible signs would be putting your wife's interests ahead of your own, but it would also include gifts, surprises, and romance.

The point that men have a duty to love their wives is a terribly unromantic theme for Valentine's Day. In my defense, however, I'll guess that most men who read this message and begin surprising their wives with chocolates in their shirt pockets, roses for no particular reason, love poems, and romantic get-a-ways will find that loving their wives is a very, very pleasant duty – and the fringe benefits are amazing.

I Love You, Master

Our family doesn't watch much TV, but recently we have seen some of the later episodes of "I Dream of Jeannie" – the ones after Jeannie marries her master. Most of the time she still referred to him as "Master." "Why does she still call him "Master" even after they are married?" I wondered to myself one day. The thought barely finished when I remembered the verse, "For in this way in former times the holy women also, who hoped in God, used to adorn themselves, being submissive to their own husbands; just as Sarah obeyed Abraham, calling him lord, and you have become her children if you do what is right without being frightened by any fear." (1 Peter 3:5b-6) My, now that was pretty convicting.

Now please don't stop reading out of anger or fear. I'm not advocating calling our husbands our masters. (Although it must not be a bad thing, since Sarah was commended for it.) It just seems interesting to me that in times past those who were submitted to were called "Master." That's what this article is really about: submission.

The Bible mentions submission in many ways. We are to submit to God (Hebrews 12:9), to the governing authorities (1 Peter 2:13-14), to our leaders (this may mean our spiritual leaders – see Hebrews13:17), and even to other Christians (Ephesians 5:21). We are generally pretty agreeable to these, but perhaps the one women have the most difficulty with is submission to their husbands.

The Bible is so clear on wives submitting to their husbands:

Ephesians 5:22: "Wives, be subject to your own husbands, as to the Lord."
Ephesians 5:24: "But as the church is subject to Christ, so also the wives ought to be to their husbands in everything."
Colossians 3:18: "Wives, be subject to your husbands, as is fitting in the Lord."

1 Peter 3:5: "For in this way in former times the holy women also, who hoped in God, used to adorn themselves, being submissive to their own husbands…"

That pretty much answers the question as to "why" we should submit to our husbands. The Bible says we should! It is not an option, but a command. It doesn't say we should submit only when our husbands are being nice, or only if they're being reasonable. It just says to do it – go and submit! Unfortunately, though, that's not always good enough for us Christian women. We are sinful in nature and have been so influenced by our culture that sometimes we have to fight with ourselves to follow God's plan and command. Although God's command alone should cement the issue, let's look at some other reasons why we should submit.

We submit because it "is fitting in the Lord." Let's say that Prince William decided to forsake his heritage, move to Iowa, marry a peasant girl and work the soil for a living. Perhaps we can hear the Queen saying, "But that is not the way a Windsor should act!" Likewise, it is not right, fitting, or appropriate for us Christian women to refuse to follow our husbands.

We also do not want our lack of submission to give a bad name to God or those of the faith. "They [the older women] may encourage the young women to love their husbands, to love their children, to be sensible, pure, workers at home, kind, being subject to their own husbands, so that the word of God will not be dishonored." (Titus 2:4-5) If we call ourselves Christian and then disrespect, speak badly of, and refuse to follow our husbands, what will non-Christians think? If we truly love God, would we want to do anything that may defame His name?

It is also important for us to submit to our husbands so that our children, and especially our daughters, can see how a biblical marriage should work. Our older daughters know that wives are to submit, but they will understand that better when they see it lived out in practical ways. I do not want my daughters to detect even a hint of nonsubmissiveness from me. That requires a special vigilance on my part. For example, if I disagree with my husband I try to share my concerns and suggestions with him in private, or phrase them in question form if the children are present (depending on the specific situation). I certainly am not resisting his leadership in that instance, but I do not want my daughters to misunderstand that and think that I am rejecting his authority. Not only can our words betray our submission, but also sighs, frowns, and rolling of the eyes. Even private, playful jokes between spouses can be misinterpreted by naive children.

The way I treat my husband can largely influence the way my children treat him. Years ago we knew a couple who were having marital problems. One day their young daughter stated, "We don't need Daddy." Now, where do you suppose she got that from? That's an extreme example, but if I do not respect my husband or follow him, why should my children? Wouldn't it be sad if our children scorned their fathers on the account of our behavior?

We should also want to submit to our husbands to make their job easier. Why would we want to make his role in the family a burden and a trial rather than a joy? Don't we love this guy that we married? Our husbands did not take on this job as leader themselves; *it was given to them by God*, and someday they will have to stand before God and take responsibility for what went on in our families. I want to make that day as easy as I can for my husband. Submission can be a function of the love we have for our husbands!

Finally, submission makes us beautiful in the eyes of God (and of our husbands). "But let it [your beauty] be the hidden person of the heart, with the imperishable quality of a gentle and quiet spirit, which is precious in the sight of God." (1 Peter 3:4) Don't we want to be beautiful in God's sight?

Now that we've explored *why* we should submit, let's consider *how* we should submit. The verses mentioned previously from Ephesians 5 state we should submit to our husbands "as to the Lord" and "as the church submits to Christ." What does that mean? When we submit to the Lord's leadership in our lives we are to submit to him *fully*. That means every area of our lives – completely. Not only part of our lives or only part of the time. All of our lives all of the time in the way that God desires. That's how we should follow our husbands.

I personally believe that it also means we should submit willingly and happily. Don't you think it would be hard to be a leader of someone who is grouchy and unyielding in spirit? Don't you think that would make the leader feel bad? It would be good if we submit not only in our actions but also in our minds and spirits. We should portray a spirit of submission to our husbands and before our children. For example, let's say that Jim and I are leaving a store and walking to the car holding hands. If Jim would say, "We are going in this direction," that's the direction I go in order to be submissive. Or maybe he just leads me a certain direction by the hand. He hasn't demanded my submission, but I follow because I have a submissive spirit. Now say instead that he says and does nothing in particular so I head in a certain direction to get back to the car. That is not being resistive to his leadership. But perhaps even better in that situation is waiting for him to lead. That shows a true spirit of submission.

Maybe you think I'm getting mighty particular about things. I'm just trying to make a point with a practical example. We should be submissive in our spirits and not just in our actions. Our submission should be more than just following kicking and screaming. It should be more than, "OK, I'll do it, but only if you tell me to."

I know that women have a lot of concerns about all of this, such as: "My husband isn't a Christian." That doesn't seem to make a difference. 1 Peter 3:1-2 says, "In the same way, you wives, be submissive to your own husbands so that even if any of them are disobedient to the word, they may be won without a word by the behavior of their wives, as they observe your chaste and respectful behavior."

"What about women who are in an abusive situation?" I'm not getting into that topic in this article. Let's not get distracted. The fact is that most of us are not in such a situation, and the fact is that most of us can improve in submission towards our husbands.

"My husband does stupid things." Most husbands will do some stupid things – especially new husbands. (Just like wives.) Submission involves letting our husbands make mistakes and fail. And we need to let them fail *gracefully*, without words or attitudes of "I knew it would happen!" It'll be OK. You are doing what God wants you to do. He will take care of things.

"I'm more intelligent than my husband." That may be true, but you are still not the leader of the household. There can be only one person in charge - the one who makes the final decision when there is disagreement, and the one bears the responsibility before God. God gave that role to the husband, regardless of his IQ.

"I just don't agree with his decisions." That's bound to happen. I think it's OK to share our concerns, but then that's the end of it. It's our role just to accept his decision, even if we think it's a mistake. We shouldn't be whiny or moody about it. That includes the little things, too. We know that sometimes it's the little things that bug us more than the big things. Suppose the children want to stay up late and you think it's OK because there's no school tomorrow or whatever, but your husband says they must go to bed on time. It's not a big deal. Our husbands have more than the right to make that decision. The little things just don't matter. And the big things we need to let God take care of.

"God gave me a strong and decisive personality." That may be true, too, but you are still not the leader of the household. You can use the personality He gave you to glorify Him, but that is not by usurping your husband's authority. Being wives doesn't mean being passive and apathetic. We must be decisive with our children and strong in our role as wife and mother. We can respectfully share our insights and opinions with our spouses. Most husbands would like their wives to do such things.

"Submitting is hard!" The right thing is not always the easy thing. We can ask God to help us and to change our hearts and minds. And that is where this all ends. Submission – especially in spirit – isn't easy because it is contrary to our sinful nature. But it is God's will and command that we submit, and He will help us please Him in this. It is also by our joyful submission that we show our God and our husbands just how much we love them.

Oops!

The other week Jim and I decided to go out on a date for a couple of hours. We wanted to eat dinner, but didn't want to spend much. Living in a new city, we figured we'd be a little adventurous and explore a section of the city we weren't familiar with. Before long we found a nice restaurant. We parked the car, and since it was rainy and cold, we made our way rather quickly to the entrance. Jim took a quick glance at the menu posted on the window. "Look, it's upside down," he said. But he had seen enough of it and we headed on in.

The restaurant had been open only for a few minutes. We were the first customers of the day. The dining room had a rugged sort of look to it. The waiting staff were neat and clean, but not in a fancy sort of way. They led us to our table. I barely noticed the linen napkins. I began wondering when the wine list was actually more of a book. My creeping suspicions were confirmed when I looked at the menu. On the left were offerings such as "wild boar." (McDonald's doesn't serve wild boar!) On the right were prices a good $10-$15 more than we had planned. I guess if the nicely dressed patrons had arrived before us, and the window menu had been right side up (so the appetizer prices hadn't been mistaken for the entrée prices), we would have known what lay ahead – and turned in the other direction! But here we were, sitting near the back of the dining room with our sodas in front of us. Not a good time to exit. "Well, we're here. You might as well enjoy yourself," were Jim's instructions to me.

And so we made the best of an unexpected situation. Not that it was difficult. That was one of the more favorable problematic situations to find ourselves in! Marriage in this crazy world seems to be a series of unexpected situations. As a couple we have faced new babies, illnesses, accidents, miscarriages, isolation, relocations, job changes, and financial challenges, to name a few. How we react to those situations as a couple is very important, and indicates a great deal about the way we view our marriage, our spouse, and ourselves.

I think the bottom line is this: Do we view our marriage as a partnership, two people bound together in order to accomplish the same goals? Or is our marriage more like two people in the same house, each with his own agenda? "And the two shall become one." Those are powerful words and they can mean a lot. We have become one in setting priorities and goals. We work together. We evaluate events not by how they affect "me," but by how they affect "us." Together we discuss how we can solve the problem at hand. This may be easy when the event is out of our control. But what happens when the event is the direct result of a mistake made by our spouse? This is when our love for our spouse can really show through. We can realize it really was an accident, a mistake. We can treat our spouse the way we would want to be treated – not with accusation or blame, but with understanding. There need be no attempts in a marriage to lie or cover up anything. We are one.

Jesus prayed for unity for His disciples because He knew that by unity they could accomplish God's purposes. Relationships of love are a good witness to the love of God. Unity provides focus, and without focus it is difficult to accomplish anything. Unity also makes us feel safe and loved.

I'm not saying that once we are married we lose our personal characteristics and preferences. What I am trying to say is that we see ourselves in the light of the bigger picture of our marriage and family. I'm also not saying that we do away with the biblical plan for marriage. The husband is still the head of the family and final decision maker. That still stands.

I believe that God created the marriage couple to be a powerful force in accomplishing God's plans for His Kingdom. In oneness and solidarity we can get past all the "oops" that happen and get on with serving God – one in mind and determination of will – for the glory of God.

Can't See the Burger King for the Road Block

Recently they constructed a large shopping center near our house. It's of the strip-mall variety with other clusters of stores on a big parcel of land. Jim and I were out by ourselves for a little while and we decided to stop at the Burger King in this center. He began to turn down one of the small streets, as he could see the Burger King in plain view at its end. I suddenly told him to stop. Right in front of the road was a concrete barrier with no possible way to get through. He hadn't even noticed it.

We still laugh about that because it's a perfect illustration of our two individual personalities. Jim is the one with the vision and grand ideas. He sees the goal, the outcome – the Burger King, so to speak. I, on the other hand, more readily see the possible problems that we might encounter to getting there – the road blocks. Jim sees the big picture and moves along quickly. I see all the details and move at a slower rate. Was this a match made in heaven or not?

They say that opposites attract. I guess that might be true to only a certain point. It's necessary in a marriage to have a common ground and a similar way of looking at the world. How else will you decide on family priorities and goals? How will you raise and discipline the children? How important is religion in your married life? But it's not just the big issues. How will you spend your money? What will you do together on your day off? Where will you go together on vacation? Married couples need to share a common way of thinking. Otherwise, they are not a couple, but two individuals struggling to keep their separate agendas from clashing.

Beyond that common worldview, however, I guess a lot of opposites do attract. Maybe we admire in our mate what we do not find in ourselves. Maybe we wish we were brave and daring like our spouse rather than being the timid and fearful person that we are. While before marriage that opposite personality may seem so intriguing and attractive, after marriage it may turn into a source of frustration and disagreement. The cautious me may not appreciate my fearless spouse motorcycling or sky diving. In the day-to-day life of marriage that opposite personality has taken on a different meaning – and not a particularly good one.

I do not believe it needs to be like that. First, I think we need to be respectful of the differences in our personalities. It may drive me nuts if my spouse is an early bird instead of a night owl, but that's just the way he was made. That's him. I can be respectful of his traits and his preferences. They are not worse than mine; just different. I don't need to degrade him or speak negatively of him. Along those same lines I can allow him his choices without playing the martyr. I can do that out of kindness, just because I love him! It doesn't need to be me, me, me. Second, we can use our differences to our mutual advantage. Jim and I have learned to yield to each other's strengths when it is advantageous to do so. For example, if detail is not important but speed is, I let Jim do what he needs to do and I don't think about it. At other times, when detail is more important, Jim slows down and allows me to tend to the nitty-gritty. Say we're leaving home on a two-week vacation. It's going to save us hassle and money if I can make sure everyone has the proper clothes and medicine. We also do this in regard to the chosen course of our family. He leads the way, but is appreciative of my input and observations. Without him, I may never think to go to Burger King. Without me, he might run into a couple road barriers on his way to get there.

Yes, I do believe this was a match made in heaven – orchestrated by God who brought us together at just the right time in our lives. We are stronger and more effective as a couple than as individuals. God can use our joint strengths in order to accomplish His will for His Kingdom. That's the purpose of our marriage. I'm looking forward to getting to

Burger King. And I bet Jim is looking forward to getting there with a few less dents in the car.

My Obsessive Spouse

My husband likes to describe himself as an "eccentric Christian husband." He's pretty accurate about that. He is also somewhat obsessive. Generally he is very easy to live with, but there is that one area...

It just happens to be our SALT Magazine. Every aspect of its production is a matter of care and concern to him. It is a topic of great discussion in our household. And because it is important to him to get the issues out in a timely manner, he keeps very close tabs on where we are in the process. This includes watching how much has been written day by day – in order to keep us on schedule. I get daily updates usually two or three times a day. (No, that sentence was written exactly like I meant it!) Not only can he tell me where we are and how much we've done for the day and gained for the week, but he can compare that to where we were at the same time for each of the last six issues. (God gave him a great mind for numbers.) In order to compare apples with apples, each of our budding manuscripts must be typed in the same way. I used to just sit down and type my contributions and be on my way. Then I would see Jim sit down and fix what I wrote to make it all uniform in font, margin size, etc. I didn't think Jim should have to do that all the time, so now when I write I make sure I'm in the right font and don't leave too many empty lines between articles. (Too many empty lines is more than one.) I also try to listen to his updates with interest. I can be sensitive to my husband's obsession and even make it easier and more pleasant for him. It's such a little, easy thing to do. I love the guy, so why not?

In all fairness to my wonderful husband, I must admit that I have a few obsessions, or quirks, of my own. One is that I prefer the toilet seat to be left in the downward position. I know that is an age-old point of contention between the genders, but it really does bother me. In the downward position it blends into the background of the bathroom and lends to a cleanly, peaceful atmosphere. Left open, it yells at me as I enter the room: "Hey! Look over here! I'm ugly! I'm cold! I'm....utilitarian!" But I don't give Jim (and the other males in my household) a hard time about it. It's too petty a thing. Maybe the issue is a personal problem I have, but it doesn't have to become Jim's problem. I can be sensitive to Jim's quirks without demanding that he be sensitive to mine.

I believe that one of the key ingredients to a happy, satisfying marriage is kindness. We have a sort of "me" oriented society. I have my rights. No one should get in my way. I should never feel the least bit inconvenienced or wronged – even if it was an accident. These philosophies edge themselves into marriages, and are compounded in many relationships by the call for "equal rights for women." Many women demand their husbands go out of their way to do this or that or not hurt their feelings, but will not return the favor. Love should not be about tallies and rights, but about building each other up and being kind and sensitive to one another.

So in kindness to my husband I will not only "put up" with his little idiosyncrasies, but I will be gracious – even supportive – in doing it. Yes, my spouse is obsessive. But so is my husband's.

Birth Control: Leaving the decision with God

When Cindy and I decided to allow God to decide how many children we would have, we hadn't really thought the issue through. We had been married less than a week when we first discussed birth control. We had gone to pre-marital counseling with Cindy's pastor and he said that we still needed to resolve exactly how we intended to support ourselves and what we were going to do about birth control. The money issue was resolved to our satisfaction – we had a budget of less than $600/month, which was supplied by the full-time job I had as a grill cook at Hardee's. We had no car, no phone, and no health insurance, but we were so in love that none of that mattered. We both still had one year of college left to go. Cindy would get her nursing degree first and go to work so I could get my bachelor's degree in theology. The following year we were to head off to the seminary and I would either become a church pastor or a Wycliffe Bible Translator. After the schooling was completed, we would have four or five kids and live happily ever after. So you see, the money problem was resolved assuming no major illnesses or a baby. Birth control was assumed except for the method.

When we first discussed birth control, I assumed Cindy would be taking the pill, which to my surprise she was very much opposed to. She talked about the negative side effects and suggested we look into another method. As we started to think about the problem, we both had pangs of conscience at the thought of any form of birth control. So we quickly came to the decision that we would leave the baby issue up to God. Cindy found and taped a little red sign on the wall that said, "God gives His best to those who leave the choice with Him."

I would like to say that our decision was based on an exhaustive search of the Scriptures and of all the issues associated with birth control. I would like to say that we had taken a great deal of time applying biblical principles to those issues, but we didn't. We just decided that children were always a blessing in the Bible and that our consciences didn't appreciate the thought of limiting the size of our family. We concluded that God would provide for us somehow if we were trying to do the right thing, so the decision was made.

The first baby came two days after our first anniversary and just a couple of weeks after Cindy's graduation. The second baby came 14½ months later. We just celebrated our 19th anniversary. Our children and their ages are: Michael 18, John 16, Shannon 15, Meghan 13, William 12, Kathleen 11, Keenan 9, Heather 7, Bridget 5, Kelly 3, and Josiah 1.

The birth control debate

As you can see, we have had a few years to mull over the issue of birth control and haven't changed our minds. We are convinced that God commanded us to be fruitful and to multiply. (Gen 1, Gen 8-9, Gen 35, and more.) Having children is, therefore, one of the primary purposes of marriage. Malachi writes, "Has not the LORD made them one? In flesh and spirit they are his. And why one? Because he was seeking godly offspring." (Mal. 2:15, NIV) Everywhere in the Scriptures children are considered a blessing and large families are considered a special blessing. Abraham was considered blessed because God promised him, "Indeed I will greatly bless you, and I will greatly multiply your seed as the stars of the heavens and as the sand which is on the seashore; and your seed shall possess the gate of their enemies." (Gen. 22:17) The Israelites were told that faithfulness to the covenant would be rewarded by an increase in the fruit of the womb, while disobedience would mean the fruit of the womb would be cursed. (Lev. 26:9, Deut. 27-8)

Men like Heman and Obed-Edom were considered blessed because of their many children. The Scriptures reveal that Obed-Edom had eight sons and this comment is made, "God had indeed blessed him." (1 Chron. 26:5) "Of Heman, the sons of Heman: Bukkiah, Mattaniah, Uzziel, Shebuel and Jerimoth, Hananiah, Hanani, Eliathah, Giddalti and Romamti-ezer, Joshbekashah, Mallothi, Hothir, Mahazioth. All these were the sons of Heman the king's seer to exalt him according to the words of God, for God gave fourteen sons and three daughters to Heman." (1 Chron. 25:4-5) Psalm 127 says, "Behold, children are a gift of the LORD, the fruit of the womb is a reward. Like arrows in the hand of a warrior, so are the children of one's youth. How blessed is the man whose quiver is full of them." The message in Psalm 128 is similar: "How blessed is everyone who fears the LORD, who walks in His ways. When you shall eat of the fruit of your hands, you will be happy and it will be well with you. Your wife shall be like a fruitful vine within your house, your children like olive plants around your table. Behold, for thus shall the man be blessed who fears the LORD."

I just don't find the reasons people give us for limiting the size of their families very convincing. Allow me to list the reasons most people give to justify their use of birth control:

1. We can't afford children – From a biblical perspective, there is no reason to believe God wouldn't provide for the children He creates. Jesus said, "For this reason I say to you, do not be worried about your life, as to what you will eat or what you will drink; nor for your body, as to what you will put on. Is not life more than food, and the body more than clothing? Look at the birds of the air, that they do not sow, nor reap nor gather into barns, and yet your heavenly Father feeds them. Are you not worth much more than they? And who of you by being worried can add a single hour to his life? And why are you worried about clothing? Observe how the lilies of the field grow; they do not toil nor do they spin, yet I say to you that not even Solomon in all his glory clothed himself like one of these. But if God so clothes the grass of the field, which is alive today and tomorrow is thrown into the furnace, will He not much more clothe you? You of little faith! Do not worry then, saying, 'What will we eat?' or 'What will we drink?' or 'What will we wear for clothing?' For the Gentiles eagerly seek all these things; for your heavenly Father knows that you need all these things. But seek first His kingdom and

His righteousness, and all these things will be added to you." (Matt. 6:25-33) Likewise, David said this: "I have been young and now I am old, yet I have not seen the righteous forsaken or his descendants begging bread." (Psalm 37:25)

God will, therefore, see that we have everything we need, but that doesn't mean God will give us everything we want. The problem many of us have is that we consider the following as needs: air conditioning, cable television, two cars, new clothes, vacations with hotel stays, convenience foods, restaurant food, a large home, and a new car. These are not needs, but many of us give them a higher priority than having children – using them as an excuse for not having children.

When our life is over, God will judge our work by His own standard. Paul writes, "Each man must be careful how he builds ... for no man can lay a foundation other than the one which is laid, which is Jesus Christ. Now if any man builds on the foundation with gold, silver, precious stones, wood, hay, straw, each man's work will become evident; for the day will show it because it is to be revealed with fire, and the fire itself will test the quality of each man's work. If any man's work which he has built on it remains, he will receive a reward. If any man's work is burned up, he will suffer loss; but he himself will be saved, yet so as through fire." (1 Cor. 3:10b-15) What does this have to do with having children? My house, my car, my air conditioner, my computer, and my new clothes have this in common: none of them will survive judgment day. On the other hand, we can be certain that the souls of our children are eternal. Now then, if I limit the number of children I have so I can watch television, play computer games, eat convenience foods, or avoid sweating in the summertime, I have invested my money foolishly. In the eternal sense, I have given away gold and exchanged it for straw.

Martin Luther put it this way: "But the greatest good in married life, that which makes all suffering and labor worth while, is that God grants offspring and commands that they be brought up to worship and serve him. In all the world this is the noblest and most precious work, because in God there can be nothing dearer than the salvation of souls. Now since we are all duty bound to suffer death, if need be, that we might bring a single soul to God, you can see how rich the estate of marriage is in good works. God has entrusted to its bosom souls begotten of its own body, on whom it can lavish all manner of Christian works. Most certainly father and mother are apostles, bishops, and priests to their children, for it is they who make them acquainted with the gospel. In short, there is no greater or nobler authority on earth than that of parents over their children." (The Estate of Marriage, 1522)

If only we all had such an exalted view of raising children, but as it is we often despise this noble right by selling it for a new car, a vacation at the beach, or a new wardrobe. We are like Esau who sold his blessing for a bowl of stew.

2. We can't handle the kids we have now – Most of these people can be divided into two categories. First are those who are doing a poor job raising their children. In this case having more children really isn't the problem – it just exacerbates a deeper problem. The solution in this case is to search God's word and pray for the wisdom to discern the biblical principles for raising children, and for a spirit of obedience that will see that those principles are implemented. Since all of us are sinful, we all struggle with poor parenting in varying degrees. However, the solution is not to accommodate our sin but to overcome it. We should urgently seek to manage our families well whether God gives us more children or not.

Second are those who really are struggling because their children are especially difficult for some reason. Our first child was the most difficult and time-consuming child we had until our tenth. He didn't seem to need more than half a night's sleep and he was very strong willed. With our first, Cindy wasn't working at all and I can remember coming home one night to find Cindy with large black rings under her eyes and tears rolling down her cheeks. Our oldest had simply left her worn out, sleep deprived, and discouraged.

Eventually, however, Cindy made it through and God gave us the grace to survive every additional child He gave us. We survived the lost sleep (I must confess that Cindy lost more than I did), the diapers, the disobedience, the expense, the extra work, and the loss of our freedom. But our life has been easy compared with those who have children with serious chronic illnesses or handicaps. Sometimes God gives people seemingly impossible circumstances, but even then they usually manage to survive. The bottom line is that we are sinful and our kids are sinful and a lot of work besides. Therefore, having more children means that the sin and the work are multiplied.

Even the most extraordinary circumstances we can imagine, however, are nothing compared to the life of suffering Jesus endured on our behalf, and we ought to have the same attitude toward suffering that Jesus did. Paul writes, "Have this attitude in yourselves which was also in Christ Jesus, who, although He existed in the form of God, did not regard equality with God a thing to be grasped, but emptied Himself, taking the form of a bond-servant, and being made in the likeness of men. Being found in appearance as a man, He humbled Himself by becoming obedient to the point of death, even death on a cross." (Phil. 2:5-8)

The reason so many of us "can't handle" our children is because we don't have a Christ-like attitude towards suffering. We want parenting – and the rest of our Christian walk, for that matter – to be without suffering. We expect that the Christian life should be one long series of easy victories. Paul, however, understood that the Christian life wasn't supposed to be painless. He compared our life to that of a soldier or an Olympic athlete. Jesus painted a more painful picture when He told us to pick up our crosses daily and follow Him. Even so, Paul could write, "May [I] know Him and the power of His resurrection and the fellowship of His sufferings, being conformed to His death; in order that I may attain to the resurrection from the dead." (Phil. 3:10-11) The writer of Hebrews wrote, "[Jesus], who for the joy set before Him endured the cross, despising the shame, and has sat down at the right hand of the throne of God. For consider Him who has endured such hostility by sinners against Himself, so that you will not grow weary and lose heart." (Heb 12:2b-3)

As parents, then, we should endure the hardships of parenting for the joys of sharing our faith and the Christian life with our children. We can handle having as many children as God gives us because parenting gives us a chance to humble ourselves and suffer for the sake of our offspring. In this way, we share in the sufferings of Christ, but these sufferings are nothing compared with the joy we will have before Christ when He comes in His glory.

Nevertheless, there will still be times when it seems to us we can't handle another child. If God gives us another child anyway, we can be sure that He will give us all the strength we need to do the task. Isaiah says, "Do you not know? Have you not heard? The Everlasting God, the LORD, the Creator of the ends of the earth does not become weary or tired. His understanding is inscrutable. He gives strength to the weary, and to him who lacks might He increases power.

Though youths grow weary and tired, and vigorous young men stumble badly, yet those who wait for the LORD will gain new strength; they will mount up with wings like eagles, they will run and not get tired, they will walk and not become weary." (Is. 40:28-31) Perhaps in our own power, then, we cannot handle another child, but those who trust in the Lord will have a joy and a strength that will overcome the hardships.

3. I'm not going through that again (the painful process of giving birth) – Our discussion of suffering is relevant to this topic as well. The pain – as severe as it may be – is to be endured for the joy of giving birth. Jesus once said, "Whenever a woman is in labor she has pain, because her hour has come; but when she gives birth to the child, she no longer remembers the anguish because of the joy that a child has been born into the world." (John 16:21) This is a real test of a woman's attitude towards suffering. Can she endure the suffering of childbirth for the joy of giving her baby life? Didn't Christ suffer infinitely more so that we could have life?

Yes, it is hard to convey to a man the pain involved in childbirth – Carol Burnett compared it to taking one's lower lip and wrapping it around one's head – but that pain has been overcome by women since the days of Eve. Instead of focusing on the pain, the woman should be a willing vessel – as Mary was when she was chosen to give birth to Jesus. Mary said, "Behold, the bondslave of the Lord; may it be done to me according to your word." (Luke 1:38) What would we think of Mary today had she said, "But God, I can't do that because it will hurt too much."

4.We're not ready yet – There seems to be a belief – even among Christians – that a couple should wait a few years after they are married before having children. I can think of two ways in which a couple would feel unready to have a child. The first is financial. Waiting would give husband and wife a chance to save a bit of money before the children start coming. This is really the "I can't afford it" excuse in disguise.

The second reason is that the couple must "mature" a little before becoming parents. It seems to me, however, that putting off responsibility is the worst way to foster maturity. One of the reasons modern young people are so immature compared with the youth of centuries past is because we have moved back the age of personal responsibility ten years. A boy who would in times past have been apprenticing for a trade at age 12 is now getting ready for his first real job at 22. The result of this delay and coddling has not made for better parents. People who are old enough to be married are old enough to have children.

5. My wife/husband doesn't want another one – If the husband wants a child and the wife refuses, she is not acting in biblical submission to the husband's authority. If the husband says to his wife, "The Lord commanded us to be fruitful and multiply, the Lord made us one because He wanted godly offspring and in the Bible children are always considered a blessing," the wife has no right to deny him. She is to be in submission to her husband. The Scriptures say, "In the same way, you wives, be submissive to your own husbands ... For in this way in former times the holy women also, who hoped in God, used to adorn themselves, being submissive to their own husbands; just as Sarah obeyed Abraham, calling him lord, and you have become her children if you do what is right without being frightened by any fear." (1 Peter 3:1a, 5-6)

What should be the case if it is the wife who wants more children and the husband does not? In this situation the burden and the responsibility of birth control should fall on the man and not on the woman. The woman is to be subject to her husband, but not if obeying her husband would require her to disobey the Lord. If the husband wants to reject God's command to be fruitful and to produce godly offspring, let the birth control method be inflicted on his body. The wife should not be complicit in his rebellion.

6. God has given me a choice and a brain – The argument goes something like this: "Modern medicine has given us the ability to determine if and when we will have children. God made me a rational being and I will use my human reason to effect the best possible outcome."

The first problem with this is that modern medicine has given us means of birth control that may result in the death of the baby. The most obvious is surgical abortion, but the IUD and the pill may also induce the body to abort after conception by not allowing the fertilized egg to implant in the mother's womb. (For information on this topic see www.backlife.org/birthcontrol/ and check out the article by Randy Alcorn.) What disturbs me is that after being confronted with the truth about the pill, many Christian women choose to continue using it. How is this possible when the consequence of using the pill may be the death of their babies? The possibility of an "unplanned" baby is so frightening to many Christian women that they refuse to consider any evidence that would take away their ability to limit their family size. We know there have been over a million legal surgical abortions a year in our country since Roe v. Wade, but only God knows how many legal chemical abortions have happened since the introduction of the birth control pill. We may call using the pill "using our brains," but any method of birth control that risks the death of a child is wrong. If the baby actually dies it is murder.

Of course, there are other methods of birth control that don't harm a baby after it is conceived – like the condom and "natural family planning." What are we saying, though, when we limit the size of our families in this way? We may be saying that we refuse God's command to be fruitful and multiply and we scorn His desire for godly offspring. We may be saying that children aren't really a blessing – that they are more trouble than they are worth. We may be saying that we don't believe God will provide for us and our children, and we may be saying that our comfort and ease are more important to us than having and raising godly children.

Yes, natural family planning is birth control and is contrary to the will of God. Paul said, "Stop depriving one another, except by agreement for a time, so that you may devote yourselves to prayer, and come together again so that Satan will not tempt you because of your lack of self-control." (1 Cor. 7:5) Paul did not say: do not deprive each other except by agreement and for a time, so that you may avoid having unwanted children. In fact, natural family planning was what Onan, Judah's son, practiced in Genesis 38 when he refused to have children for his brother. The Scriptures say, "But what he did was displeasing in the sight of the LORD; so He took his life also." (Gen. 38:10)

So then, using our brains is all well and good, but we should use them to determine God's principles from His word and apply them to the issues of our lives. Human reason must never be used to trump God's word or as a cover for disobedience.

How have we been affected by our decision?

The decision to forgo birth control has defined me in the eyes of other people. I realize that my decisions to follow Jesus Christ and to marry Cindy were the two most important decisions I ever made, but I am known to most as "the guy with eleven kids." I can't begin to count the times I've been asked, "Are you Catholic?" "Are you Mormon?" "Have you figured out what causes that?" How often have we seen people visibly nudging each other as we walk by? How many times have I been asked, "Are these all yours – I mean yours and hers together?"

I'm not really surprised at the reactions of other people. I think most of us react to people who are different. Let's face it, in a culture that considers three children a large family, we look strange.

Sometimes I think it would be fun to turn the tables on those who find us so peculiar. I could stare at the family with two children as they walk by and say, "Are you secular humanists? Are these all you have, or are the rest at home? Do you have a medical situation?" It would be rude if I asked all these questions, but if two-child families were confronted similarly on a regular basis they would get used to having to explain the number of children they have as I must do now.

Children are time-consuming and expensive. The number of children we have has made me regret my days as a prodigal son, because we have struggled more financially than was necessary. I am convinced, however, that God used our financial struggles to mold us into the people He wanted us to become and to protect our children from some of the negative influences that turn many children away from the Lord.

So what is it like having eleven kids? I hear "Daddy's home" whenever I walk in the front door. People are always hugging me and jumping on my back. Somebody always wants to play with me or talk with me about something. We usually have thirteen people at our dinner table and there is almost always some noise in our house. We drive an old rusted 15 passenger van and the average bedroom in our house has three occupants. More important is that God has filled my life with purpose by giving me eleven children who need my help to become the zealous, spiritual, loving people of faith He wants them to be. My relationship with Cindy has grown deeper and stronger as we have struggled together to overcome the challenges of managing a large household. My life has been filled with inexpressible joy over what God has done for me through this experience.

I'm not saying God has called all of us to have large families. God has called some – like the Apostle Paul - to a life of singleness. God has called others – like Zechariah and Elizabeth - to many years of childlessness. What I am saying is that married couples should let God determine for them how many children they will have. We need to appreciate God's purpose for marriage and His desire for godly offspring. We need to believe that children are always a blessing and that God has promised to provide for the children He gives us. Finally, we need to set aside our desire for personal comfort and our aversion to hard work and suffering, and make it our goal to sacrifice our lives to teach God's word and way to as many children as God sees fit to bless us with.

God gives His best to those who leave the choice with Him.

Working Wives: Should they or shouldn't they?

The issue of women working outside the home is one that elicits emotional responses from liberal feminists to conservative Bible-believing women and just about everyone in between. Women often pour out their hearts on Christian radio programs agonizing over their decision to work or their decision not to work. While I suppose hearing other women struggling with the issue may be encouraging and educational, the heart of the issue is often missed.

Many churches and radio ministries rarely, if ever, discuss the core biblical principles involved in the woman's decision to work outside the home (too divisive, too judgmental). However, they are more than willing to help the woman succeed in the decision she has made - no matter what that decision is or why it was made. Everybody is pacified. This week there will be help for professional women and next week for housewives. This month there's a program on helping our daughters adjust to college life; the month after there'll be one on women leaving their careers to be at home.

This approach is backwards. What good does it do to discuss how to make the best of a course of action before discussing which course of action is best? If I don't know whether I should work outside the home, why would I want advice on how to successfully juggle a job and a family? The heart of the matter is discerning God's purpose for women. The agnostic feminist and the Christian woman would not agree on their purpose in life, so they will not agree on what they should do with their time. A woman must understand her purpose to understand her role, and she must understand her role to determine what her priorities are, and she must understand what her priorities are before she can decide where she should labor. And the only way a woman can know God's purpose for her life is by understanding what the Scriptures say about it. Too many Christian women don't know, don't understand, or don't agree with what the Scriptures say about women. In other words, women are getting a lot of emotional support but not enough truth. Ironically, when a woman settles on the unemotional truth of her biblical purpose and role, the emotional difficulties are greatly diminished. Much of the anguish women feel about this issue is doubt and guilt.

What, then, do the Scriptures say on this issue? Regarding God's purpose for women, we read in Genesis 2, "Then the LORD God said, 'It is not good for the man to be alone; I will make him a helper suitable for him.'" (Gen 2:18) We see two purposes for women in this verse. Women were created to provide companionship and help for their husbands. This is abhorrent to our feminist culture, but even Paul writes, "For man does not originate from woman, but woman from man; for indeed man was not created for the woman's sake, but woman for the man's sake." (1 Cor. 11:8-9)

We also read in Genesis 2, "For this reason a man shall leave his father and his mother, and be joined to his wife; and they shall become one flesh." (Gen. 2:24) This shows us that the companionship and help the woman was to give the man was in the context of the marriage relationship – a relationship of unity with one man that included physical intimacy. Thus, Paul commands the married Corinthians not to deprive each other. He writes, "The husband must fulfill his duty to his wife, and likewise also the wife to her husband. The wife does not have authority over her own body, but the husband does; and likewise also the husband does not have authority over his own body, but the wife does. Stop depriving one another ..." (1 Cor. 7:3-5a)

Certainly, the physical union of man and wife fosters companionship and unity, but God had an additional purpose in mind. Malachi writes, "Has not the LORD made them one? In flesh and spirit they are his. And why one? Because he was seeking godly offspring." (Mal. 2:15a, NIV) In Genesis 1:28 God says to Adam and Eve, "Be fruitful and multiply, and fill the earth." God told the same to Noah and his sons. (Gen. 9:1) The Psalmist writes, "Behold, children are a gift of the LORD, the fruit of the womb is a reward. Like arrows in the hand of a warrior, so are the children of one's youth. How blessed is the man whose quiver is full of them." (Ps. 127: 3-5a) It is also written, "How blessed is everyone who fears the LORD, who walks in His ways. When you shall eat of the fruit of your hands, you will be happy and it will be well with you. Your wife shall be like a fruitful vine within your house, your children like olive plants around your table. Behold, for thus shall the man be blessed who fears the LORD." (Ps. 128:1-4) Children are considered a blessing and having many children an honor and reward.

If a woman, through the use of birth control, overrides her ability to have children, or, even worse, kills the baby God creates in her womb, she denies her husband part of his godly heritage, his reward, and his blessing. (Ps. 127-128) God equipped only women's bodies to bear and nurse children, yet many women resent the limitations this places on them for work and ministry outside the home. Others consider childbearing too painful to suffer again or just too expensive. Women, as well as men, need to realize that we are not put on this earth to pursue our own agendas or to avoid pain. Jesus, too, had a purpose that required that He undergo pain infinitely more severe than childbirth. Yet, He set the example for the rest of us when He prayed to the heavenly Father, "not as I will, but as you will."

To summarize, then, the woman's purpose is to provide companionship so the man won't be alone, to help him in his work, to unite with him in body, and to bear him children. This determines her role. Since she is to help her husband and since she was made for him, it is only fitting that he would have headship and that she would be in submission. Paul writes, "Wives, be subject to your own husbands, as to the Lord. For the husband is the head of the wife, as Christ also is the head of the church, He Himself being the Savior of the body. But as the church is subject to Christ, so also the wives ought to be to their husbands in everything." (Eph. 5:22-24) Peter adds, "In the same way, you wives, be submissive to your own husbands so that even if any of them are disobedient to the word, they may be won without a word by the behavior of their wives, as they observe your chaste and respectful behavior. Your adornment must not be merely external – braiding the hair, and wearing gold jewelry, or putting on dresses; but let it be the hidden person of the heart, with the imperishable quality of a gentle and quiet spirit, which is precious in the sight of God. For in this way in former times the holy women also, who hoped in God, used to adorn themselves, being submissive to their own husbands; just as Sarah obeyed Abraham, calling him lord, and you have become her children if you do what is right without being frightened by any fear." (1 Pet. 3:1-6) The woman is not the head of the family nor does she reign as family co-regent – sharing headship with her husband. No, the woman's role is to accept her husband's leadership and submit to him.

Since this is a sensitive issue, let me say that I don't equate submission with inferiority. The woman is equal to the man in her humanity but is nevertheless subject to him. The woman's position of submission to an equal is similar to Jesus' submission to the Father. Jesus is equal with the Father in His deity but still willingly submits to Him. Paul writes, "Have this attitude in yourselves which was also in Christ Jesus, who, although He existed in the form of God, did not regard equality with God a thing to be grasped, but emptied Himself, taking the form of a bond-servant." (Phil. 2:5-7a) Paul summarizes the issue this way: "But I want you to understand that Christ is the head of every man, and the man is the head of a woman, and God is the head of Christ." (1 Cor. 11:3)

Now that we understand a woman's purpose and her role, what does the Bible say her priorities should be? Consider these verses: "A widow is to be put on the list only if she is not less than sixty years old, having been the wife of one man, having a reputation for good works; and if she has brought up children, if she has shown hospitality to strangers, if she has washed the saints' feet, if she has assisted those in distress, and if she has devoted herself to every good work." (1 Tim. 5:9-10) "Therefore, I want younger widows to get married, bear children, keep house, and give the enemy no occasion for reproach ... If any woman who is a believer has dependent widows, she must assist them and the church must not be burdened." (1 Tim. 5:14,16a) "Older women likewise are to be reverent in their behavior, not malicious gossips nor enslaved to much wine, teaching what is good, so that they may encourage the young women to love their husbands, to love their children, to be sensible, pure, workers at home, kind, being subject to their own husbands, so that the word of God will not be dishonored." (Tit. 2: 3-5)

From this we see that a Christian woman should cultivate high standards of character, but we also see more clearly how she should live. Her good deeds should include bringing up children, being busy at home, managing her home, showing hospitality, washing the feet of the saints, helping those in trouble, and taking care of widows. Certainly, these Scriptures do not prohibit women from working outside the home, but we can see that this list of good deeds is more easily accomplished as a housewife than as a high-powered attorney, a TV anchor, a traveling salesman, or even a full-time grocery clerk. It should be evident to all that bringing up children, being busy at home, managing a home, and taking care of widows is more difficult for a woman who spends most of her time and energy working outside the home.

Let us now consider the "wife of noble character" in Proverbs 31. We read, "An excellent wife, who can find? For her worth is far above jewels. The heart of her husband trusts in her, and he will have no lack of gain. She does him good and not evil all the days of her life. She looks for wool and flax and works with her hands in delight. She is like merchant ships; she brings her food from afar. She rises also while it is still night and gives food to her household and portions to her maidens. She considers a field and buys it; from her earnings she plants a vineyard. She girds herself with strength and makes her arms strong. She senses that her gain is good; her lamp does not go out at night. She stretches out her hands to the distaff, and her hands grasp the spindle. She extends her hand to the poor, and she stretches out her hands to the needy. She is not afraid of the snow for her household, for all her household are clothed with scarlet. She makes coverings for herself; her clothing is fine linen and purple. Her husband is known in the gates, when he sits among the elders of the land. She makes linen garments and sells them, and supplies belts to the tradesmen. Strength and dignity are her clothing, and she smiles at the future. She opens her mouth in wisdom, and the teaching of kindness is on her tongue. She looks well to the ways of her household, and does not eat the bread of idleness. Her children rise up and bless her; her husband also, and he praises her, saying: 'Many daughters have done nobly, but you excel them all.' Charm is deceitful and beauty is vain, but a woman who fears the LORD, she shall be praised. Give her the product of her hands, and let her works praise her in the gates." (Prov. 31:10-31)

Here we have a seemingly superhuman example of womanhood. We can see that the "wife of noble character" was fulfilling her biblical purpose. She helped her husband. She brought "him good, not harm, all the days of her life." She bore her husband children. In fact, they "arise and call her blessed." She was busy at home. She got up while it was still dark and did not "eat the bread of idleness. " Her lamp didn't go out at night. She took managing her home seriously, for she watched "over the affairs of her household." She also helped those in trouble, for she opened "her arms to the poor."

Did "the wife of noble character" work outside the home? If what you mean is whether she held a paying job working away from home for someone else, the answer is no. If what you mean is whether she did any work outside the home, the answer is probably yes. One would think that considering a field and buying it would require her to leave her own property. She may also have left home to select wool and flax, deal with the clothing and sash merchants, and buy food for her family.

Did the "wife of noble character" make do on her husband's income? No. She sold clothing and sashes to the merchants and she planted a vineyard from her earnings. The Bible says her trading was profitable. She made important financial decisions such as the purchase of property. She even had servant girls to help her with the work. The "wife of noble character" was commended for her contributions to the family economy and would probably have represented a two-income family. (I say probably only because we have to assume the husband also had an income.)

It is probably true, however, that most of her work occurred at home. And this portion of Scripture emphasizes how all of her work benefited her household or revealed her godly character. We don't see her trying to secure world peace or ridding the world of injustice. We don't see her running the country or taking her seat at the city gate among the elders of the land. Instead, she is focused on the welfare of her household. Therefore, her family is prepared for winter hardship and she can "smile at the future." And her faithful service does not go unnoticed, for her children and her husband praise her.

Where does this leave us in our discussion about working wives? First, some Christians are too dogmatic on this issue and others are inconsistent in their positions. We have no Scripture that prohibits a woman from working outside the home. Some who oppose a mother working for pay at the grocery store because it takes her away from her family will support a woman with a home based business that requires her to keep appointments and attend functions away from home. And even those who oppose a two income family - an unsupportable position if we accept Proverbs 31 as a model – will allow their wives to do non-income producing work outside the home. Grocery shopping, running errands, helping at church, and other activities will take the housewife without a job away from her family. Almost every woman - like the "wife of noble character" – does some work outside her home.

The question, then, should not be whether the woman can do work outside the home or whether she can make money. She can. The question the woman should be asking is whether the work she does outside her home is the best way for her to fulfill her God-given purpose. It is difficult to provide companionship to her husband, to help him in his work, to become united in body and spirit, to bear and raise children, and to manage a home when she spends most of her time at her place of employment. On the other hand, developing an income that demands she spend some time away from home may give her family the resources to prepare for the future or perhaps merely to subsist in the present. It would seem ridiculous for a family to miss meals or lose its home because the woman wouldn't spend a few hours a week away from home. Part of raising children and managing a household is seeing that basic needs are met, and, if the Proverbs 31 woman is an example for us, the woman can help her husband by producing income.

Under ideal conditions it is probably best if the woman does not work for another outside the home if she has children at home. The man who makes more than enough to meet the financial needs of his family is a blessing indeed, for he makes it easier for his wife to do the work God intended women to do. Even so, the Proverbs 31 woman, whose husband was a respected leader in the community, still blessed her family by producing income. Being in a good situation, then, does not preclude the woman from blessing her family by making money.

However, many women do not enjoy ideal conditions. Some women are widowed, some have been divorced, some have husbands who have become physically incapacitated, some have husbands who work hard but do not earn an income sufficient to provide for the family's basic needs, and some are suffering the ongoing consequences of poor financial decisions made in the past. In cases like these, her family's survival may require the woman to work outside the home.

What we see in our culture, however, are women who work outside the home to escape their responsibilities at home. We see women abandoning their children in order to maintain a needlessly expensive lifestyle. And we also see women falling in love with their careers to the detriment of their families.

The answer is not a prohibition against working mothers. That goes beyond what is written in Scripture. Rather, women should be striving to fulfill their God-given purpose, which will certainly keep them from straying too frequently or too long from home.

A Personal Postscript

So as not to be open to the charge of hypocrisy, I will explain how this issue has played out in our family. As many of you know, Cindy has been working full-time as a registered nurse for a number of years. This is true despite the fact that we have 11 children and homeschool. Believe me, Cindy would like nothing better than to quit her job and dedicate herself full-time to her children, her husband, and managing our home.

Why have I failed (so far) to bring Cindy home? First, as a prodigal son I squandered my best chance to develop an income adequate to support a large family. So when I married at age 24, I was a full-time grill cook with one year to go for a degree in theology. (As Mottle said in *Fiddler on the Roof*, "Even a poor tailor is entitled to some happiness!")

Second, unforeseen events changed my plans after we were married. I was studying theology with hopes of becoming a church pastor or missionary. After completing the theology degree I decided I didn't belong in the denomination whose school I had just graduated from. This caused me to pursue missionary work through Wycliffe Bible translators, but the medical problems of my first three children led Wycliffe to discourage me from missionary service.

Third, I made poor financial decisions such as buying a house and two new cars on credit.

Fourth, God blessed us with many children, which increased our financial needs.

Eventually, it got to the point that Cindy's income was over twice my income and through normal career choices, I could never hope to get Cindy out of her job. Thus, I pursued home-based businesses because they had at least some chance of creating an income that would get Cindy home.

The point I am trying to make is that I have been working for many years to bring Cindy home. I believe what I have written about women working outside the home. I appreciate Cindy's full-time income, but the children and I would appreciate Cindy's full-time presence much more – and as long as God gives me strength I will continue to pray, plan and work to free her.

It discourages me sometimes that God seems slow in granting me the desire of my heart. It is humiliating for me to have my wife have working so hard outside the home when she has so much more than most to do inside the home. And Cindy has been such an incredible blessing to me (many women have done noble things but she surpasses them all!) that it pains me not to be able to give her the desire of her heart to be home full-time with the children.

So I have become compassionate towards families who want to bring the wives home but haven't found a way. I think some one-income families unintentionally look down on us. I have also become painfully aware that sin – even forgiven sin – may continue to have future consequences. The time I squandered as a young man made it more difficult to provide for my family. This struggle has also revealed a weakness in my own character. I have needlessly caused myself pangs of anguish and resentment towards imaginary others who judge me or perceive me as weak for struggling financially and having a wife who works. And finally, I have become more aware of how God works through our struggles to mold our characters. I can honestly look back on the last 13 years and say that God has used this issue to teach us patience and to make us all better than what we otherwise would have been.

Still, God is able to "make up to you for the years that the swarming locust has eaten." (Joel 2:25) He has the ability to get Cindy out of her job today. There is no scarcity of resources in God, and He is good and merciful. Cindy, with God's help, this will be your year.

Reflections of this Working Mom

Sometimes I feel suspended between two worlds.

I am a statistic. I work full-time outside of the home. The thought that I fall into this category seems strange to me. I don't really feel a part of that world. But the 32 hours that I work each week definitely qualifies me.

Fortunately, the 32 hours I work are crammed into just two days on the weekend, making me a full-time, stay-at-home mom the rest of the week. For five days a week I can concentrate on nothing but diapers, meals, housework, schooling, and loving and serving my family. These five days seem to go quicker than the other two, perhaps because home is where my heart is.

It is sometimes a strange existence, hopping between these two worlds. Each carries with it its own burdens, triumphs, and challenges. Each requires its own mindset. But in one I feel a stranger and visitor; in the other I feel at home.

Don't get me wrong here. I take my job very seriously, for I am well aware of the responsibilities I assume when I begin my workday. I work hard and feel satisfaction from a job well done. I believe my work is essential and worthwhile. And I hope I am not kidding myself when I believe I have made a positive impact on people's lives. Yet I don't always feel like the people I meet in the workplace truly understand me. I have no desire right now to earn higher degrees or assume higher positions. I don't care for vocational status. And I can't count how many times I have heard, "So you come to work to get a break from the kids, huh?" But I try not to be hard on them. I'm just different than so many of the people I meet.

My "career" life has not been without blessing, however. I have learned a great deal about my chosen line of work. This knowledge has even helped me in taking care of my family. My "career" has provided some much-needed income with little disruption to the family. I have learned about people. I have helped people. And I have grown greatly in my character.

Yet, again, my heart is at home with my husband and those young people who will forever be my babies. Yet even here I sometimes feel out of place. Do my stay-at-home counterparts really understand me? Do they understand that what they cram into six days I must cram into four? (Allowing a day of rest.) Do my decisions and time commitments seem strange or wrong to them? Do my methods of doing things (or not doing things) make sense to them? Are my priorities a mystery to them?

I do not believe that working outside the home is inherently bad, as long as the motives, methods and results are in line with God's will. I do believe full-time motherhood is best if at all possible. But here I find myself with one foot in both places. I realize this has given me the opportunity to understand some of both worlds. How can God use this for His good? I wonder what exactly it is that brought me to this point. Human error? God's plan? Some sort of combination of factors? (I don't know much about such things.)

Whatever it is, God is able to bring good out of it for me and glory for Himself. It is our hearts' desire, though, for me to be home, and to that end we pray and to that end we work. But why is it that He has not yet fulfilled this desire? He has His reasons. God sees the whole picture and how the threads are so delicately and intricately intertwined. I see just one small square. I rest in knowing that God knows the situation quite well and has it all under His control. And He cares about this family a great deal.

I know that God can work through me in both these worlds in which I find myself, and I do believe He does. I will continue my tasks as one working for Him, which is really the case, and not just as one working for the boss or the husband or the children. I will fulfill the roles He has called me to in this place and time.

Perhaps someday God will pave the way for me to fulfill my heart's desire and find myself only at home. Should He see fit, it will be just another way in which I will be forever indebted to Him.

Children

How could you have too many children? That's like having too many flowers.
(Mother Teresa)

Dear Baby,

It's been just a few days since we found out about you joining our family. I was almost nervous to find out whether we were expecting, because I knew I would be disappointed if we weren't. But God was gracious to me and granted me my heart's desire: He gave me you. You know, it seems like I think about you all the time.

Dad is so excited, too. You are blessed to have a dad who thinks of you as a blessing and as a gift of God – who considers it an honor to be a father. He asks about you constantly.

What a family you have joined! Your brothers and sisters are happy about your coming. Already you have so many people who love you and can't wait to see you. Sadly, it is not like that for every baby. God has been good to you.

We love you dearly. But love without commitment is meaningless. So I want you to know that we are committed to you. It doesn't matter whether you are a boy or girl. It doesn't matter whether you are sick or healthy. It doesn't matter what kind of personality you have. We are committed to you because you are a McDermott. You are part of this family. You are one of us.

We are committed to meeting your needs. Not only your physical needs, but your needs of support and encouragement and companionship. No matter how old you are, you never need to feel alone! We want you to be happy.

We are committed to teaching you about God. We want you to know Him and what He has done for you. We want your goals, desires, passions, and principles to be fueled by your love for God. Life without God is without meaning or purpose. Without God, there is no hope for the future. We want God to look upon you and say to you, "Well done, good and faithful servant." And when the time comes for us to leave this earth – whether together or one by one – we want to be together in heaven. We want to spend eternity with you. What a joyous time that will be!

Finally, I want you to know how much God loves you. I want you to feel and understand His deep, never ending, sacrificial love for YOU. Things may change around us, but He does not. Our love may not be perfect, but His always is. He is a good GOD.

So, my little one, may God be with you, watch over you, and protect you. I commit you to His care, for you are safe within His hands. We pray for your daily. And we look forward to the time when we can celebrate what will truly be your first birthday. -Love, Mom

Dear Josiah,

The last time I wrote you a letter it was addressed simply, "Dear baby." We had just recently found out you were on your way, and we didn't know exactly "who" you were! It seems as though those days and weeks when you were being knitted in darkness went so fast. We thought about you and prayed for you so very much. Yes, we even worried about you sometimes. How special it was for me to know that God had you in His hands and that He loves you and us so very much. These words were a comfort to me: "For You formed my inward parts; you wove me in my mother's womb. I will give thanks to You, for I am fearfully and wonderfully made; wonderful are Your works, and my soul knows it very well. My frame was not hidden from You, when I was made in secret, and skillfully wrought in the depths of the earth; Your eyes have seen my unformed substance; and in Your book were all written the days that were ordained for me, when as yet there was not one of them. How precious also are Your thoughts to me, O God! How vast is the sum of them!" (Psalm 139:13-17)

But now those days of waiting and wondering and watching are past, and here you are! I look at you and hold you and wonder why it is that God has been so good to me to give me all you children! You all will probably never understand how precious you are to me!

I am so excited to have my Josiah Luther. It was thrilling to see you on the ultrasound when you were just six months old and to watch your heart beat. I got excited every time I felt you move inside of me. Seeing you for the first time was such a joyful moment. It didn't matter that

I've had other children; each time is so special. I'm telling you this because a lot of people will look at the sixth or eighth or eleventh baby and say that he or she is "just another" baby. You will never be "just another" baby to me. You are an important part of this family. You are an individual with your own strengths and talents and interests, created by God to do the work He has for you to do. God has something special for you to do for His kingdom, Josiah.

The name Josiah means "fire of the Lord." Josiah was one of the few good kings in Judah amid many evil ones. During his reign they discovered the Book of the Law in the temple and Josiah led the people in renewing their commitment to God. 2 Kings 23:25 says, "Before him there was no king like him who turned to the LORD with all his heart and with all his soul and with all his might, according to all the law of Moses; nor did any like him arise after him." The name Luther means "famous warrior." Besides your dad, the "other" Luther was the leader of the Reformation, teaching and reminding the people that it is only by God's grace we are saved. These men had a great love for the Lord. That is what we want for you, Josiah. To know God personally, to love Him with all your heart and soul and strength and mind, to be passionate in your service to Him. Nothing else really matters.

But today you are not even three weeks old, struggling to straighten out your days and nights, and capturing the attention of everyone in the house. I believe you are such a handsome baby. Of course, I am your mom, so I'm a little bit biased. I will always be biased – biased enough to be always cheering for you, biased enough to be like a mother bear protecting and providing for her cubs. But I will also try to be objective – objective enough to discipline you when necessary, objective enough to help you see your weaknesses and shortcomings and learn to overcome them. It's sort of a balancing act, but I'll try to do my best. I know that you are not really mine, but a gift and trust endowed me by God.

And one more thing, Josiah: happy birthday. Your momma adores you, you know.

My Newborn, My Teacher

Our little Josiah is now nearly three months old. He is just delightful to have around. He is quite handsome (remember, this is a mother talking here) and becoming charming with his toothless grins. It is fun to watch him reach his baby milestones. His siblings like to hold him and play with him. He is still the most popular person in the house.

For all of his cuteness, however, he has one major flaw: he has his days and nights mixed up. It's not that he doesn't sleep well. It's that he sleeps well after 3 a.m. He somehow got it into his newborn brain that the day ends at 3 a.m. – unless he wants to stay up late. Then it ends at 4 a.m.

I know people have ways of getting babies to sleep at the right times, but I think those ways are usually ineffective on two month olds. One thing I've learned from having children: if babies want to sleep, there's not much you can do to stop them. If they don't want to sleep, there's not much you can do to convince them otherwise. They either have incredible stamina or they are incredibly stubborn.

Josiah's sleep habits have created a bit of havoc on the family. He has greatly reduced the number of hours of sleep that this family gets. We older ones take turns being up with him. That way we can share the joy of sleep deprivation. We are getting less done because either our day is starting later or we are walking around tired. More than once I have heard the question, "Mom, why is it that we keep him?"

I have asked myself that same question. I've also asked Josiah that question. Of course, we aren't serious about it, but it does make one contemplate the bigger issues of life and family and Christianity.

The first thing I tell my children is that we keep Josiah because he is one of us. He is a McDermott. He didn't do anything to become part of our family. But on the day he was born we welcomed him with open arms. How excited we were the moment we first saw him! And because he is one of us, we love him and are loyal to him.

And that is just how God treats us. God loves us because we are part of *His* family. We didn't do anything to become God's children. Through the death and resurrection of Jesus Christ God opened His arms to us. How excited He was when we became His children! Jesus said in the parable of the lost coin, "In the same way, I tell you, there is joy in the presence of the angels of God over one sinner who repents." (Luke 15:10)

I also tell my children that we keep Josiah because of grace. Because of grace we accept him with kindness and love, patiently putting up with his weaknesses and needs. He doesn't deserve it. He doesn't do any work around here and he's not a very good conversationalist. All he does is require constant attention. He is a drain on the resources of this family. That's why it's grace.

And that is also the way God treats us. We have done nothing to deserve God's kindness. In fact, we have done everything *not* to deserve it! We have defiantly turned our backs on God. "But God, being rich in mercy, because of His great love with which He loved us, even when we were dead in our transgressions, made us alive together with Christ (by grace you have been saved)." (Ephesians 2:4-5)

Another reason we keep Josiah is because he is God's gift to us. Each child in this family is welcomed as a gift from God. God didn't have to grow this family. It is only by His kindness to us that He has! One of my daughters said to me, "We have too many girls!" I told her that we absolutely did not! We have the exact number of girls God wants us to have at this time and I wouldn't give a single one back! Children in this household are desired and loved and accepted. Without conditions.

Jim likes to remind us that the way we treat Josiah is the way we live out our faith. In Matthew 25 where Jesus talks about the final judgment He says, "The King will answer and say to them, 'Truly I say to you, to the extent that you did it to one of these brothers of Mine, even the least of them, you did it to Me.' " Now, I don't know if Josiah is the least of them, but it reminds us that we are really serving Christ. Dealing with the dirty diapers, sleepless nights, and fussy cries are just some of the ways that we can serve our King. "Whatever you do, do your work heartily, as for the Lord rather than for men, knowing that from the Lord you will receive the reward of the inheritance. It is the Lord Christ whom you serve." (Colossians 3:23-24)

Finally, we also remember the "Golden Rule": "In everything, therefore, treat people the same way you want them to treat you, for this is the Law and the Prophets." (Matthew 7:12) I know that if I was needy or in trouble, I would like someone to come alongside me and help me with gentleness and a good attitude – even if I wasn't particularly considerate or fun to be with. We treat Josiah well because that is how we want to be treated.

Ruth Tuttle Conard writes in *Devotions for New Moms*: "...And He never goes to sleep. When you are bending over this soft little bundle in the night to lift her, comfort her, diaper her, or feed her, remember that your heavenly Father is bending over you." Josiah has taught me once again that in all things God deals with me according to His grace. Caring for Josiah is just passing along the kindness that God has given to me.

(In case it concerns you, Josiah is now going to bed 3 hours earlier and sleeping through the night.)

A Face Only a Mother Could Love

On Friday, April 6, God blessed us with a beautiful baby daughter, Kelly. Through the last nine months I have once again seen God's goodness, faithfulness, and mercies. I have been blessed to have given birth and begun to raise ten wonderful children. Why is God so good to me?

I could happily regale you with labor stories and tales of quick trips to the hospital - stories of interest only to me and perhaps to a few other mothers. (Do you have a minute?) But instead it is more important to share with you something that I learned anew this past weekend - something you can ponder, whether you're a parent or not.

After Kelly's first night in the nursery, the nurse came and told me how "good" she had been that night. Of course, that's the stuff that every mother thrives on, but I also thought to myself, "Well, we'll see how she does tonight at home!" Like I said, Kelly is beautiful, but she's also a baby and I've learned from experience that those sleepy, "good" brand-new newborns often come home and turn into fussy insomniacs, making you question if someone had switched the name bands at the hospital. We would soon see what Kelly had in store for us.

So we brought home our new little one that Saturday and what a good baby she was – until about midnight. We soon found out that Kelly would indeed sleep for us – but only in someone's arms. As everyone went to bed, I was left with a sleepy baby who turned on me the minute I laid her down. I tried everything I could think of. I swaddled her, rocked her. I patted her. I made sure she was fed, changed, and warm. I talked to her in soothing mother-tones. I tried the bassinet, the playpen, and the infant seat. I even laid her down and let her cry a handful of minutes. All to no avail. If she was by herself, she cried. Finally, near dawn the two of us snuggled on the couch and slept a couple hours. I didn't want her to get into any habits difficult to break, but you know the old saying – fatigue makes cowards of us all.

What a sweet baby she was all of Sunday. Her mom was tired, but still thrilled with this little creation. But as the day turned into night, I quickly realized we were to relive our previous night together. She thought the best place to be was in someone's arms – awake or asleep. We had made a little progress, however. She could now tolerate being in her bed fifteen or twenty minutes before beginning to fuss. I believe in power naps, but not in the middle of the night. What were we going to do with this little girl?

What's significant about all of this is that even amid the fatigue, the frustration, and the confusion, my love for her did not waver. I still spoke to her sweetly, held her tightly, and let her know how sweet I thought she was and how she's my favorite Kelly in the whole world. No regrets on this path of motherhood. I was still in love with her, despite her behavior. Why is it like that? I often kid with people that God made babies cute so people will put up with them. After all, babies are a hard bunch. They are not productive members of society. They make a lot of noise and eat an awful lot. They fuss over their easy life. They demand a lot of time and energy. They are selfish and believe the world revolves around them. They don't care if you feel sick or tired or that other people or matters demand your attention. They want their needs – and their desires – to be satisfied immediately. If they were adult strangers, we'd kick them out. But not our babies. We still love them.

I began to wonder why that is. I love Kelly (as I do all my children) unconditionally. I love her just because of who she is, not because of what she does or doesn't do. I have never felt an emotion as intense as motherhood. Maybe it is because in some small way I had a part in her being here, and in her still being here – sustaining and nurturing her. Perhaps this is just a glimpse into God's love for us. After all, we all are a hard bunch to deal with. We are often slow to serve God. We, too, make a lot of noise and complain about our lot in life. We are selfish and unconcerned about others. We believe the world should revolve around us. We, too, want our needs and even our desires met quickly, and we often become bitter and frustrated when they are not. But God does not treat us as we deserve. He still loves us with an unwavering, unconditional love. He loves us because we are His and He made us. He loved us so much that when we were still ugly with sin, He sent His Son Jesus to save us.

Of course, my love for my children isn't a perfect love like God's is. I must struggle with selfishness on my part, but God's love for me is complete, unending, sweet, and strong. I'm so glad, since I have a face that only a Father could love.

How Do I Love Thee, My Children?

The emotions of motherhood have been unlike anything I have ever experienced. For me they have been immediate, intense, and constant. I liken them to a mother bear with her cubs. How can I take these strong emotions and express them in a practical way? How can I love my children?

The most basic way is to care for their physical needs. This one's a given, and you may be wondering why I even mention it. It may be the most basic, but it is often the most tedious, unexciting, and least stimulating. Maybe that's why being a mother has gotten such a bad reputation in our modern day society. After all, who can't change diapers – and who would want to? For that reason we need to remember that this is indeed part of loving our children. We punch in the time clock because we love them. We drive in rush hour traffic because we care about their needs. We make meals, clean floors, wash little bodies, and do all those other myriad of things because we love our children and want them safe and healthy. That brings a whole new meaning to the tasks. These things are truly a labor of love. So, mom and dad, when you're up half the night with a sick child or a hungry baby, do not feel discouraged or inadequate when you can't get a lot done the next day. You've already done much important work before the sun even rose.

The most important way to love our children is to nourish their spiritual life. Do we not care where our children will spend eternity? We need to instruct them in the words of God. "You shall therefore impress these words of mine on your heart and on your soul; and you shall bind them as a sign on your hand, and they shall be as frontals on your forehead. You shall teach them to your sons, talking of them when you sit in your house and when you walk along the road and when you lie down and when you rise up." (Deut. 11:18-19) In our houses, faith should be a natural part of ourselves and of our daily lives. Our faith is who we are. We will want to instill in our children good habits of, and a love for, daily prayer, praise, and Bible reading. We will also want to foster good character traits within them.

Closely related to this idea of fostering their good character is the concept of disciplining our children. We need to be consistent in making rules, setting consequences, and following through. We need to discipline when necessary, even if we don't want to. We aren't being loving parents if we allow our children to grow up to be disobedient and undisciplined. Their life will be more difficult because of it. "Foolishness is bound up in the heart of a child; the rod of discipline will remove it far from him." (Proverbs 22:15) "Do not hold back discipline from the child, although you strike him with the rod, he will not die." (Proverbs 23:13)

In our quest to discipline our children we should guard against being too harsh. "Fathers, do not provoke your children to anger, but bring them up in the discipline and instruction of the Lord." (Eph. 6:4) "Fathers, do not exasperate your children, so that they will not lose heart." (Col. 3:21) This does not mean that we refuse to discipline or instruct our children because it makes them feel bad. Discipline must create conviction and discomfort before the child changes. It is like that in our walk with God. Paul wrote to the Corinthians: "For though I caused you sorrow by my letter, I do not regret it; though I did regret it – for I see that that letter caused you sorrow, though only for awhile – I now rejoice, not that you were made sorrowful, but that you were made sorrowful to the point of repentance; for you were made sorrowful according to the will of God, so that you might not suffer loss in anything through us. For the sorrow that is according to the will of God produces a repentance without regret, leading to salvation, but the sorrow of the world produces death." (2 Cor. 7:8-10) So our children will need to feel bad before they change, but if we discipline in an unkindly, unrelenting or harsh manner, or if the discipline is not warranted at all, the child may become bitter. They may no longer respect us or be receptive to our instruction. It may encourage them to head in the wrong direction. If they feel they can never please us or that we don't have their best interest in mind, they may stop listening to us or trying to change. Let us raise our children with instruction and discipline, but not with regret.

It will be easier for our children to be self-disciplined, godly men and women if they can see us living that way. There is a good chance that they will develop good character traits and values if they see them in us. They should be able to see not only what we value and believe, but also how we apply our convictions to our daily lives.

Loving our children will include loving our spouses. We want our children to grow up in a home that is a refuge and safe place from the world outside. It should be a place where they can feel happy, helped and secure. Our homes should not be filled with unrest and discord, but with unity and peace.

Our children will know that we love them if we spend time with them. "Quality" time is important, but there's something to be said about quantity, too. It's good for our kids to see that we can put other things aside to listen to them or do something with them. Put the paper down when they tell you about the show they just watched. Accept the invitation to a tea party. Play a game of football. Read Dr. Seuss yet again. We will want to be interested in what interests them and to encourage them in their pursuits. They need to know that we are on their side in spite of the way the world may treat them. "You know how we were exhorting and encouraging and imploring each one of you as a father would his own children, so that you would walk in a manner worthy of the God who calls you into His own kingdom and glory." (1 Thess. 2:11-12)

It will also help us to keep things in perspective. It doesn't really matter if their coats are "coated" in mud from playing football. It was fun, you know. And when they're getting on our nerves, we should ask ourselves: are they doing something unsafe or disobedient, or are they just being kids? The house will become quiet soon enough. In the meantime, they'll respect, and appreciate, the fact that we're tough when we need to be, but not when we don't.

We will be better parents if we grow in our relationship with God. He will create in us the fruits of the Spirit, making us more loving, gentle, and patient. He will give us the wisdom we need to raise our children if we will ask Him for it. He will supply us with whatever we lack.

Our children will also know we love them if we make sacrifices and perform our duties as parents with joy. A complaining spirit and heavy heart may make them feel like an inconvenience to our lives. Rather, we want them to feel that they are the treasure that they are – a treasure worthy of our time, talents, and resources.

Finally, we need to pray for them. It is really only God who can enable us to love our children, and it is really only His work that can protect, save, and nourish them. So much is out of our control, but it is all within His. "All your sons will be taught of the LORD; and the well-being of your sons will be great." (Isaiah 54:13)

I know that I can never love my children as much or as perfectly as God loves them, or me. But I hope that when all is said and done they will know that I've tried really hard. And I also hope that deep down they know that I love them with all my heart.

Praying for our Children

Sometimes as parents we feel very much in control. We fill our cupboards and refrigerators with healthy foods so that our children receive a balanced diet. We take our children to church and read the Bible together so that surely they have good spiritual training. We make sure they never miss a physical or dental checkup to maintain their good health. We monitor what they see on TV or hear on the radio so they are not exposed to any bad influences. We take note of who they play with. Then all of a sudden, or off and on, we feel pretty powerless, as if our efforts are merely stabs in the dark. We're not sure where our children are headed or if we're accomplishing anything. These feelings may become more profound as our children get older or as they are exposed more and more to the world outside our four walls. Maybe they're eating cookies all day at grandma's house. Maybe the neighborhood kids aren't Christian. Maybe they are diagnosed with a chronic sickness. Maybe they stumble on to things on the internet that they should not see. The scenarios are endless. We are not as much in control as we thought. We realize our neediness and pray for wisdom and strength for ourselves as we raise our family. At the same time we should be praying regularly and fervently for each of our children.

I begin praying for my children before they are born. I pray that as they grow in the womb they will be healthy, if that's His will. I pray that in a way beyond my understanding they would already be His, and be His forever.

The physical health and safety of our children is a constant prayer. Even with the best of health care our children's physical well-being is ultimately in God's hands. Four of our children have a chronic sickness. One of our children we nearly lost to an asthma attack, and there have been many scary trips to the emergency room. Our children may or may not grow out of these conditions, but I certainly pray that they do. I do not want my children to have to deal with the impacts of these sicknesses on their daily lives. I realize at the same time, however, that complete healing may not be God's will. We all have certain burdens we have to bear and this may be one of theirs. I will pray for their healing, but I will also place them in God's hands and trust Him to take care of them.

Perhaps of greater importance is prayer for their spiritual health. What they believe about Jesus Christ will determine their eternity. We do not want them only to be believers, but also to be fruitful for God. We can pray that they will be faithful in Bible reading, church going, and Christian fellowship. We can pray that they will understand what they read and accept only the truth of what they hear. We can pray that our children will love and serve God above all else. These things only happen by God's grace. "Open my eyes, that I may behold wonderful things from Your law." (Psalm 119:18)

I pray that my children will turn to the Lord for wisdom as they are faced with choices in their day-to-day lives as well as when they have to make decisions regarding their futures. They need God's wisdom to steer away from temptation and to choose wisely from among the different paths before them. I pray that God will help them make proper priorities and seek to serve Him in all things.

I also pray that they will be teachable. I want them to learn the easy way – from our mistakes – instead of making the mistakes themselves. I want them to get the most out of their education. Above all, I want them to be open to the spiritual instruction we give to them. I also pray for the growth and maturity of their faith and their character. Maybe this is a hard prayer to watch God answer! As parents we want things to go smoothly and easily for them. We want them to experience only joy and peace. We want them to win their games, do well on their tests, place highest in their competitions, and get in the college of their choice. We don't want them to feel left out or hurt by their friends. We don't want them to feel the disappointment of unfulfilled dreams or desires. But we know that people grow and mature best when they are faced with difficulty or disappointment. The struggles and challenges help us focus on God, learn what is important, and become people of strong belief and character. Our children may not become what God wants them to be if they do not experience hardship. They may not fulfill the plan God has for their lives if they do not experience difficulty. They may not truly know the love and provision of God if they do not face fear or hurt. We can pray that things go well for our children, but most of all we should pray that they will mature in Him, that whatever happens may teach them and draw them closer to God and closer to being the people He wants them to be.

I have heard people talking about praying for the future spouses of their children. That is something I had not thought of but that seems quite wise. I have begun praying for my children's future spouses – that they will be teachable and grow in the knowledge of the Lord. I pray that they will commit their lives to Jesus Christ, keep themselves pure, and be ready to assume the role of a godly spouse. I also pray for their parents, that they may have wisdom in raising them. Finally, I pray for their individual, present needs. Our children are all so different

– each with unique strengths and weaknesses. Each one is at a different place and a different stage in his life.

A few years ago I asked my mom how she (and Dad) raised us kids. I was a captive audience and she could have told me anything. She didn't share with me her personal philosophy on child-raising. She didn't tell me the do's and don'ts of disciplining. She didn't instruct me on priorities or balancing a mother's many duties. Her response was a simple four-word sentence: "I prayed a lot." She chose from all the wisdom she had gained from her child raising years and directed me to God. So as I now approach God on behalf of my children, I remember that He is the Father of us all, and that He loves these children of His, whom I call "mine," with an awesome, powerful, limitless love. They are secure in the hands of their – our – Father.

Fear in the Night

That Friday night began just the same as the others. It was 10:30 p.m. and the house was quieting down. Even I, the night owl, was getting ready to go to bed, since I was scheduled to work in the morning. Shannon left our room after talking and laughing with us to get a breathing treatment, so she could sleep well in spite of her cold and asthma. Thus began an experience we had never thought we would encounter.

Following her breathing treatment, Shannon came in our room, breathing hard, saying the breathing treatment hadn't worked. With twelve years of dealing with asthma behind us, we were concerned but in familiar territory. We gave her some prednisone and started another treatment. Half way through, with Shannon still struggling and her nail beds turning dusky, we called 911. Before they arrived, Shannon collapsed and stopped breathing. We have never been so terrified. I immediately began mouth-to-mouth resuscitation. Between breaths I called out to God, "God, my baby, my baby!" Jim ran out to flag down the ambulance. Aren't they here yet? Where are they? Within a short time (although it felt ever so long), the paramedics arrived.

Surrounded by four paramedics in her small room, it was difficult for us to see her. "Is she alive, is she alive?" my husband called out. Some of our other children were scattered about. Did I look as frightened as they? The paramedics instantly put a tube down her throat and into her lungs, forcing air into her limp body. As a nurse, I knew that was what they were going to do, and of course that is what I had wanted them to do (there was no other recourse), but the reality of it shook me and validated my fears. This was really happening. They stabilized her and carried her outside to the stretcher. There in front of my house were two ambulances and a fire truck, all with their lights flashing. On the sidewalk stood a group of people here and a group of people there. The sight surprised me, for I had forgotten that there was a world outside my four walls. We made our way carefully – quickly – with sirens and lights to the nearest hospital. After a couple of hours in the ER we were transferred to a pediatric ICU at the University of Maryland Hospital in Baltimore. Watching my daughter heavily medicated and on a ventilator, all because of that menace called asthma, was surreal. But God was gracious. By Saturday afternoon the ventilator came off. She was transferred to a regular unit Sunday afternoon and came home on Tuesday. She is on medication and will be followed by a specialist, but she is doing so well.

So how is one affected by such an experience? Once again I see that our lives can change on a moment's notice, and no one is exempt from that. I encountered first hand the goodness of so many people, and they have my gratitude. Their competence and kindness were reassuring. I especially think of the paramedics. They worked quickly, calmly, and competently. While only God can grant and sustain life, their work saved my daughter, and their kindness to me afterwards was touching. I will always be thankful to these men and women who, for that time, allowed my priority to become their priority. I felt the concern of family and friends, who called day after day to check in on all of us. I am also reminded about the priorities of life. That night it didn't matter that I had so many things to do, that my carpet needed cleaning, and that our food bills were going up. All that mattered was that my daughter would breathe again. And I hope when life throws its bumps and curves I remember that night and what it taught me. I'm reminded that my children are truly not my own, but God's and that they are a precious gift.

I'm realizing, too, that I cannot go on from here more fearful or cautious than what a parent should be. Our days and our times are in God's hands. As He sustained us and went before us that night, so He will continue to do, no matter what happens. Parents should do the "worrying" for their children, and I need to let my heavenly Father do that for me.

Finally, I saw again just how good and gracious God is. The experience was frightening, but I can see His provision in it all. I am so grateful that both Jim and I were with her when it happened. He gave us the sense to do what we needed to do for her. He brought the ambulances (both which had been on other calls and which were from neighboring cities) to our house at just the right time. He surrounded us with wise and caring medical personnel. He spared us sorrow and granted our daughter her life and health. She became well so quickly. I can never thank God enough for His undeserved kindness to us.

It is late as I write this. There is a full day ahead of us tomorrow. There is teaching to be done. We have chores to do. And then there are the errands. I noticed that our water bill is going up and that the car is making a funny sound. But we are a family, and we are together. God is ever so good.

"You will not be afraid of the terror by night, or of the arrow that flies by day." (Psalm 91:5)

One on One in a Crowd

The funny thing about being a large family is that we sort of resemble a crowd – especially to those who aren't familiar with children, or at least so many children. I imagine that we are quite a sight walking down the street or into restaurants. While we don't feel like a crowd to ourselves – it's just who we are and anything different wouldn't be us – we do face some challenges numbering so many. We know that it is important to spend quality time with our children. While that is easy to do in groups of two, three, or more children, it remains more of a challenge to do it with just one child. The problem is not only finding the opportunity to spend time with just one child, but also then finding even more time to be able to do it with each one. Smaller families can face this problem, too, as the busyness of life fills our day with commitments and errands, leaving little time for one on one interaction with our children.

Sometimes the opportunity won't come unless we purposely and thoughtfully create it. Jim and I have made the effort to take each of the older children out individually. Jim and I usually do these outings together. We go get some fast food or just go to a place to get a dessert or drink and talk. We want to create a discussion-type atmosphere with the older ones. We want to have a chance to talk to them about their problems, needs, and future. We want to give them a good chance to bring up whatever they feel they want to talk about.

With the smaller ones we do it with two children at a time. The younger ones just want to have fun and play! They still get some special attention, which they enjoy, and this solution helps us with our time issues.

Spending time alone with each child every few months is not enough, however. That's why impromptu, informal moments with our children are so important. We can have our children be a part of our everyday lives and activities. We can ask one to go grocery shopping with us and another to help us with dinner. We can ask for their help in an area of their expertise. We can even join with them in *their* work, helping them to get it done and providing a time together.

We can also make sure that every day we touch base with our children individually. I don't mean reminding them to do their chores or checking their schoolwork. I mean asking them about their hobbies or experiences. How is their story progressing? Did practice go well? What did they think of the youth group meeting? What do they think about the story they read or the show they watched? The interaction doesn't have to be deep or intellectual. And it certainly doesn't take a great deal of time, but it shows that we take interest in their lives and it keeps us connected with them. This may be especially meaningful to them if they see that our time is limited because of our many children or many responsibilities.

We don't want to have our children grow up and feel like we don't really know them. We don't want them to grow up and regret the time we didn't spend with them. We don't want them to grow up and wish we had spent more time teaching them, listening to them, and laughing with them. We need to make it a priority, do the best we can, and let God take care of the rest – even if we have to interact one on one in the middle of a crowd.

Boys!

I had just gotten home from the supermarket with a bunch of things that needed to be kept frozen. Our small freezer above the refrigerator was fairly full. I began the task of trying to stuff everything in – a war I usually can win but only with great difficulty.

It's amazing how sometimes we forget what's in our freezer. (It's equally amazing how unfrozen foods are clearly recognizable, but not their frozen forms! But that's a different issue.) Anyway, as I was rummaging through the freezer, I noticed a small plastic container. I didn't remember that in there, so I opened it up – only to find a wasp! "Who put this in here?" I shouted. "Is it really necessary for us to keep this?" The perpetrator, my second son, just happened to be traveling through the kitchen during my little discovery. "We found it dead and stuck it in there," he explained. "We wanted to petrify it. It's the biggest wasp I ever saw." Well, I sure couldn't debate that. It *was* the biggest wasp *I'd* ever seen. I closed up the container and put it back in the freezer.

I kid my husband a lot about what we're going to do with all these boys. I never mention that about the girls, even though we do have seven girls and only four boys. Boys are just different than girls, which has been a great source of amusement to me over the years. If you have boys, you know what it's like. For instance, it seems I rarely see the floor of my boys' bedroom, although I'm sure there was one there when we moved in. They are refreshingly (but sometimes frustratingly!) unconcerned about their clothes and their appearance. "Do you have enough socks?" I may ask them when shopping. The answer will probably be "yes," but there's a good chance I'll find out later that the socks they have are full of holes. Why don't holey socks drive boys nuts? Then there's the way boys play. Boys just play rougher than girls. It used to be that I couldn't tell the difference between roughhousing and fighting, but now my ear has been trained and I can tell pretty well, blood or not. Boys can be very meticulous about organizing and taking care of their football cards, but clean laundry piles tend to be sloppy and dishes half-washed. They also have tremendous appetites. At 2 or 3 gallons of milk a day, I'm wondering what restrictions our county has on owning cows. And don't forget that they don't care about mud – whether it's on their shoes or their feet or their clothes. In fact, you gotta realize that football is much more fun to play in the rain than on a sunny, 70-degree day. Sports is a big thing – whether you play it or watch it. William Shakespeare? They may not be able to tell you what he wrote, but you can be sure they know that the other Shakespeare played with the Steelers in 1934. Did you know that George Washington played safety for Denver?

Of course, I'm just generalizing. Each boy has his own personality and strengths and weaknesses. Boys may share some characteristics, but they are still individuals. I find great joy in discovering their differences and watching them grow.

I do figure that boys are just like husbands – you can find some use for them. I love having older boys because they're great at moving furniture and taking out the garbage and lugging things into the attic. I know they make great bodyguards for their sisters even now, and I'm sure they'll protect them from all the nasty boys who will come courting in the years ahead.

But with all kidding aside, I feel so blessed to have my boys. The house would be so empty and the family so incomplete without them. They each have a wonderful soft side, too. I look forward to watching them grow into tall, mature, godly men. At the same time, I sure will miss them when they leave. I pray to God that I can be a good and wise and fun mother to them.

Recently my son showed me the newest addition to his collection: a dragonfly. I have to admit again that it's the biggest one I've ever seen. I wonder what will become of these bugs. I won't wonder too hard, 'cause I don't suppose my sons are too worried, either. That's just the way boys are.

Me & My Quiver: A mom's perspective ten children later

"They will be such a blessing to you when you're old."

"They will, but they're also blessings now!"

This is part of the conversation I had with a couple I had just met. Standing around me were my ten children, a sight that usually sparks a myriad of facial expressions and comments. This gentleman was positive, but I respectfully had to add my comment about my children being blessings to me even now. I didn't want my children to entertain the thought that they weren't blessings. I also wanted the gentleman to know how much I treasure my children even when they're young and "high maintenance." When I was first married I believed children to be blessings. Sixteen years and ten children later, I still feel the same way.

When people learn of the number of children I have, they often ask if I am Catholic or Mormon. (I'm neither.) The decision, to let God determine the size of our family, was certainly a religious one, but not one connected with any church group. When we first got married, Jim and I began to consider the issues of children and birth control. We wondered what God thought and what the Bible had to say. Scripture states that children are blessings (see Psalms 127, 128). First off, I don't think I should really argue with God, about this or anything else! If God says they are blessings, then they are. Secondly, why would I want to turn down God's blessings? Most people probably think that money is a blessing, but I've never heard anyone say, "God, I know that money is a blessing, but please stop sending it!" I'm going to accept whatever blessings God wants to give me.

Birth control is really an effort to turn down or limit God's blessings. I'm not about to say that there is never a good reason to use birth control (although I think such an instance would be rare), but I do believe that people should be honest with themselves about why they want to use it. Could birth control be a form of selfishness? Do couples want to limit the amount of money or time they invest in children so they can keep more for themselves? Could it be a form of mistrust? Do couples believe they will not have enough resources or energy or wisdom to raise (more) children? Do couples believe that *they* must provide these things, instead of relying on God for them? God did promise we would have all we need, and He does love our children more than even we possibly can.

Finally, we are here to be servants for God. He has a plan for our lives, for the way He wants us to serve Him. If that means no children or a dozen, so be it. "Behold, the bondslave of the Lord; may it be done to me according to your word." (Luke 1:38)

My purpose here, though, really isn't to go into a theological discussion about these things. I simply want to share my perspective, one born of conviction and seasoned with time.

The decision we made regarding children has given a type of unity to me and my husband. Together we face the challenges of raising the children God has given us, not that we chose to have. Together we enjoy the blessing that they are. Together we evaluate and confirm our decision in the midst of criticism from people and from the society around us. There is no disagreement between us because one wants another child but the other doesn't. There are no times of indecision or uncertainty because we don't know whether we should have more children or not. That decision is safely in God's hands, the best place of all. And together we have the excitement of wondering what God's will is and when our next child (if God so deems) will come. Allowing God to determine the size of our family has given us a freedom we didn't realize when we first made that decision over sixteen years ago.

This decision has also required us to yield our plans for our lives to God. Accepting the children God wanted to give us has required a great investment of time and resources. Our emphasis on family and raising our children has affected the types of careers we chose, the amount of time we put into them, and the status we've achieved. It has affected what we do with our money and our time. It has also affected the possessions we've acquired. When others our age are retiring, we will probably still be raising and releasing our children. But that's OK. I'm not here to please myself. If I must work until the day I die, that's fine, because I will have an eternity to have fun! Of course, there are other factors besides children which affect our lives, but the impact of ten children is great.

Being the mother of ten children has taught me many lessons – about myself, about child rearing, about God. I've had to frequently evaluate my priorities and values. I've had to sort through all the messages that this society throws at me about what is important and decide for myself what is truly important and worthwhile in God's eyes. Additionally, I've learned that you really need fewer things to raise children than what you think you do. All this "stuff" that our society says we need for child rearing is nice, but not really needful. Most important of all, I've learned that sometimes I must be different than those around me, not for the sake of being different, but for the sake of being true to my conscience and to the word of God. There are no regrets.

Allowing God to determine the size of our family has also given me many joys and blessings, more than I expected. I enjoy my children and watching them grow. It is fun having them around. They also fill my days with a higher purpose than just myself. And I suspect that I won't have much of a space between children and grandchildren. I feel that if I had limited myself to just one or two children, I would have also limited the joys that I now, and will, experience.

Of course, having many children has made my heart vulnerable. Like any mother, I have concern over my children's physical and spiritual needs (multiplied by 10!). I do not know what lies ahead. I may suffer hurt or fear or heartbreak over my children. Is there injury or illness ahead for them? Will they devote their lives to God? But I am just called to be a faithful servant to God. God will take care of us.

Being willing to have many children for God has made me vulnerable in another way - vulnerable to the tactless remarks of others. I have been told (by acquaintances, family, and often strangers) that I am selfish (I still haven't figured that one out), wasting the earth's resources, wasting my own potential, or crazy. People have told me to my face that I have too many children. Others have told me that I should stop having them. One woman told me she feels sorry for me. Sometimes people even have the boldness to tell me these things in front of my children.

It is difficult to be on the receiving end of such comments. I have often felt misunderstood or mistreated. Comments like those used to upset me, even to the point of making me want to cry. But that usually doesn't happen anymore, because going through this has made me stronger. When you are faced with opposition to what you are doing, I figure you have one of three options. You can look at those around you and consider what you believe and what they believe, and say, "They're right and I'm wrong, so I'm going to change what I'm doing." The second option is to say, "I'm right, but I can't stand being different, so I'll just do what everybody else is doing." The third option is to decide, "I know I'm doing the right thing, and so I will be faithful and continue the course, regardless of what people will do or say to me." I still don't always know the best thing to say to these people, but my conviction is as strong – actually stronger – than ever.

Being willing to have many children for God has also made me vulnerable to the encouragement of others. I hear not only the tactless remarks of people, but also the sweet encouragements of people I meet. Those kind and heartening words, both from Christians and nonChristians, have been like salve on a wound. They have warmed and encouraged my heart.

I remember when we were newly married and had just made that decision. We met an older couple at our college who were not using birth control. They had three children at the time. They felt that even without birth control, no one would end up with a dozen children. In the years since, their family has grown by one and ours by ten. The thought makes me chuckle. Anyhow, I believe very strongly that God can limit or expand our families by the way He sees fit. Nothing, either way, is guaranteed. I'm also acutely aware that at any time God may say we have enough, and our last child will certainly be our last. When that day comes, I will feel a sense of sadness. What will I do without little ones around? But I trust that God will gently lead me into the next season of my life, and there I will also find blessings.

I've had people tell me that I have courage, having all of these children. But I don't look at it like that. I'm not courageous, just obedient.

"He tends his flock like a shepherd; He gathers the lambs in his arms and carries them close to his heart; He gently leads those that have young." (Isaiah 40:11, NIV)

In Defense of Children

Washington State Representative Maralyn Chase is sponsoring a bill which would require the state health department to distribute a pamphlet talking about the purported benefits of having two children or less. The bill does not limit the number of children a family can have, but its purpose, Chase states, is to promote "population sustainability." This is certainly stirring up a controversy. But right now I don't want to talk about the political ramifications of such a bill. I don't want to argue their assumptions. And I don't want to discuss the potential economic and social results of the legislation. All I want to do right now is talk about the children. The children!

The mother of eleven, I have very strong feelings about children. I'm very well aware, however, that not everyone shares those feelings with me. Often I've heard the statement, "So, you come to work to get away from the kids for awhile!" I'm very familiar with looks of disdain or quizzical, raised eyebrows concerning my children. I even had one woman look me straight in the eye and say, "I feel sorry for you!"

I feel sorry for her! And for all those who share such a view of children. Was their personal childhood so bad? Is parenting so difficult for them? Perhaps some of their feelings would change if they could just spend some time alone with the children – away from the trials and difficulties of day-to-day life. Or maybe if they would just look deeply into the eyes of the children. The children!

I just love being around my children. I love all the activity in the household. I love hearing all the busy sounds, the chattering, the laughter, the play. And while sometimes it would be nice to finish one thought or say one complete sentence to Jim, I know that the silence would ring too loudly for me in a house without children.

The distractions are endless. In the time it's taken me to write these few paragraphs, I've made two pony tails, deciphered a two-year-old's complaint, worn Groucho glasses for the four-year-old, and gave instructions about the baby to an older child. But I'm tending to the children. The children!

I'm not the least bit naïve about it all, and I know full well that without children I could have a prestigious, successful career. I know that my standard of living would be much higher. I know that my circle of friends would be larger. I know that my life "experiences" would be broader. I know that daily life would be less complicated and complex. But life is so much bigger than all of that. Those things don't even matter to me. My children have given my life a high and noble purpose. It is a purpose of eternal magnitude. What else could be more important? I'm playing a part in molding the future of the world and of my children. The children!

My children have taught me many things. I've learned that some things are very important, and most things aren't. I've learned that there's a place to draw a big, fat, black line over which no one should pass, but that we can range free elsewhere. I've learned that it's OK just to sit down and play sometimes. I've learned to get away from myself and focus on others. I've learned God makes us individuals. I've learned about grace. And I've gained a little insight into the character and workings of God. All because of my children. My children!

My children have filled my life with joy. Their antics, their words, their thought processes can just make you laugh. There's nothing more engaging than a baby's smile or delightful as his first giggle. There's nothing cuter than a three-year-old. There's nothing sweeter than a child's embrace. There's nothing more gratifying than watching your children enjoy and help each other. There's nothing more enjoyable than talking to your teens as they evolve into adults. There's nothing more satisfying than seeing your children grow in the Lord. All of this joy because of the children. My children!

I set out to talk about "the" children and have talked about "my" children instead. I'm still on the same subject, though, because children are children. They are little people with thoughts and feelings, growing into adults with their own strengths and gifts and purpose – while giving us a whole lot of love and joy and lessons along the way. They are the creation and favor of God. So now I've come back to the bill. It's a bad bill because it devalues children. It sends the message that whatever the benefits of children may be, they are outweighed by the costs. It means they're not worth it. It reduces them to a mere cost analysis. Which child would we give back? Ours? Our neighbor's? The kid across the country? It shouldn't matter. Could Ms. Chase look a child in the eye and tell him he shouldn't have been born, that she wishes he weren't here? If she could, that would be truly sad, indeed.

Farewell Address: To my oldest son on his graduation from homeschool

My son, my heart is full and I wish to share so much with you as you prepare to enter a new phase of life that will see my role in your life begin to diminish. I am happy for you that you have come this far and hope you will become the man of God you were called to be. I want you to work hard in the calling God has assigned to you. I want you to find a godly wife who will help you and bring you joy. I want you to diligently teach your children the word of God, the Gospel of Jesus Christ, and the Christian life.

More than anything, I want you to hear, "Well done, good and faithful servant," when your life is over. Yes, my son, your future is before you and I wish only God's best for you. I suppose when you have time to ponder your life you tend to dwell on the future. You must forgive me, however, if this occasion makes me reminisce about days gone by. I remember how helpless you were the day you were born. I remember how you used to stand up on your toes so you were able to look over the back of your crib and see your mother and I. We could only see the top half of your face. I remember when you first learned to walk. I still needed to carry you around when we needed to get anywhere in a hurry. I remember teaching you to read and to play baseball and football. Yes, I'm sure I think about your childhood more than you do - or at least remember it more fondly.

Since I have seen you from the beginning, perhaps I have a much better appreciation for how far you've come in the 16 years you've been with us. As you ready yourself for college next fall, my thoughts are also drawn back to my own past. When I was your age I squandered my time and my opportunities on foolishness - as young people are in the habit of doing. I remember the meeting I had with my parents in the principal's office in the spring of my senior year of high school. He told me I was failing three classes and if I didn't improve my grades I wouldn't graduate. An end of the year surge lifted my GPA to 1.2 for the semester - bad, but just good enough to graduate. Two years later I flunked out of college to become a full-time dishwasher. I gladly associated with the wicked and if it wasn't for the grace of God, I would have certainly destroyed myself. Although God forgave me for the sins of my youth, those sins have had consequences that are still with me today. I beg you to learn from my mistakes and make the most of the time you now have.

Now that I'm done talking about the past, I'd like to look into the future with you and tell you what I see. Young people spend too much time thinking about the immediate future and not enough time thinking about their eternal future. You will be spending an eternity in the kingdom of Jesus Christ - surrounded by all the saints and God's holy angels. Please prepare for those days now. Before you enter eternity you will stand before God and give an accounting for the life He has given you. If you always remember that, you will be able to resist the temptations of youth. You will not waste your days in idleness or immorality, and when you get a little older you won't waste your early adulthood chasing dreams of selfish ambition that will leave your soul empty even if you succeed. Instead, make it your ambition to be the best servant for Jesus Christ you can be. Ask God to direct your ways so that all the talent, skill, and resources God has given you can be used for God's glory and for the advancement of His kingdom. If you make this your ambition you will be opposed and persecuted by men and by demons, but the work will give you a tremendous sense of fulfillment and peace of mind.

I realize that a young man who is consumed with pleasing his Lord and considers the eternal consequences of his present deeds will not be popular with many people his own age. You will see the fun and the companionship the worldly are having and may at times wish your path wasn't so hard and so lonely. Nevertheless, you must be strong. In the end, the fun the worldly are having will be a source of sorrow and regret. Therefore, don't seek out worldly youth to fulfill your need for companionship. Instead, patiently seek out the young woman God is preparing to be your lifelong companion. Let her be the one who will satisfy your desire for intimate friendship and help you with your life's work.

Since we are on the subject of life's work, don't despise the importance of your family or of raising children. For most people, raising children is the most eternally significant thing they will ever do. Always consider children a blessing and take as many of them as God sees fit to give you. Diligently teach your children God's word through which their souls will be saved and their characters molded. See that they read their Bibles in the morning and at night – as you have been trained to do. The Holy Spirit through the Scriptures will teach your children what their frail and sinful parents have neglected to teach them. I know this from personal experience.

Show your love for your children by enjoying them and desiring their company. Play games with them, tell them stories, and include them in as many of your activities as possible - including your work. Do not be harsh with them and do not demand of them more than is reasonable given their age. On the other hand, do not spoil them. Do not allow them to challenge your authority or to willfully disobey you, and do not let violent behavior go unpunished.

If you do these things, your godly children will be your glory when you enter eternity. Even so, remember that even the children of godly parents are saved by God's grace alone - you cannot save your children no matter how effective you are as a parent - so pray for the salvation of your children regularly. You may be wondering what all this has to do with your graduation. Why haven't I been saying more about the importance of education? Why haven't I given you advice on how to succeed in college? The truth is that formal education and college aren't really very important in the eternal scheme of things - and even as it affects your career, education is highly overrated. A man of faith and character will be a success in God's eyes whether he finishes high school or not. A man who lacks faith and character will be a failure in God's eyes even if he has a Ph.D. from Harvard. If you concentrate on improving your character, the issues involved in getting through college will take care of themselves. An honest, diligent, disciplined, faithful, and loving man will succeed in getting through school, unless God wills it otherwise.

In conclusion, keep your eyes on the heavenly prize. Do not be distracted by the foolish and destructive desires of youth - learn from my experience. Don't fret if your

Christian walk makes you lonely. Instead, trust that God will bring you a godly wife. Treat the family God gives you as a precious and noble work that deserves your time and resources. And don't worry about getting through college nearly as much as you worry about developing a strong Christian character. This may be the last year you will spend most of your time in our home. Your mother and I will miss you more than you know. It is my experience that parents usually treasure their children more than children treasure their parents. Perhaps this was by design, as it reflects - rather dimly - the perfect love our heavenly Father has for us and how we His children take that love for granted. So, my son, we are proud of you, we love you, and we wish you all of God's blessings as you prepare to leave us. Remember that no matter where you are, we will always be thinking of you and praying for your welfare. -Love, Dad

Parents

I remember a great man coming into my house at Waltham, and seeing all my children standing in the order of their age and stature, he said, "These are they that make rich men poor." But he straight received this answer, "Nay, my lord, these are they that make a poor man rich; for there is not one of these whom we would part with for all your wealth.

Joseph Hall (1574-1656)

The Seasons of Life

The seasons have begun to change once again. It is time for me to put away the swimming suits and get out the sweatshirts and coats. It is no longer time for us to spend days at the beach; rather, we can pick pumpkins and jump in piles of leaves. In a way, we will be trading one fun for another.

And so it is with life. I used to hear people talking about the seasons of life, but I didn't really understand it. But time has passed, and as I have gained a fuller appreciation of what it means, I have experienced a type of freedom in the way I view my life and my service for God.

Right now I am in the season of bearing and raising children. By weekend, out of necessity, I am a nurse. By weekday I am a mother of ten, homeschooler of seven, and keeper of a busy household. Because of the activity in my house, I am very limited in the amount of time I can spend outside of the house. I used to feel upset, even guilty, that I couldn't do more. I wished I could invest more time working in the church or volunteering in my community, like I saw other women doing. But then I began to notice that these women were in a different situation than I was – and still am. Perhaps they have fewer children or send their kids to traditional schools. Perhaps their children are older or out of the house, or maybe they don't have children at all. They are in a different season of life than I am. Right now God has called me to take care of my young children; that is my first and foremost ministry. I have attended churches which downplay this ministry. Having a ministry to children is OK if you are helping out with Vacation Bible School or are teaching a Sunday School class. But if your work is towards *your* children at home, well, that's not really a ministry. Taking care of your children is getting in the way of your *real* ministry. I do not agree with this. My household is my ministry. I am caring for their souls, and in the process affecting future generations.

I will not use that as an excuse, however, for not being involved in church to the degree to which I am able. I may not be able to head the Sunday School, but I can be part of the prayer chain, or make meals for the new moms or grieving families, or substitute teach.

I used to think that our ministry to God was a static, unchanging thing. For instance, if we have the gift of music, we will spend our years playing the organ or singing in the choir. That may be the case, but I also think that God may call us to different ministries in the different seasons of our lives. I am caring for my children now, but I will enter into a new season and God will have a new job for me to do. My ministry and calling will change. I am now free from the guilt I used to feel. I will not feel bad that I cannot do what I see other people doing. I will not allow myself or anyone else to minimize my current work for God. The season will change, and I will have a new crop to nourish and a new fruit to harvest. But for right now I will be faithful to the call God has given me at this time.

I really enjoy summer. Each year as we head into fall I know I will miss the warmer temperatures and all the activities of summer. But as I stand in the apple orchard in the middle of fall, seeing the changing leaves and smelling the fragrances of autumn, I realize there is joy and blessing in this season, too. And so it is with the seasons of life. The freedom of my college years is past, but now I have the joy of my children and the fullness of purpose they bring. I know I will be sad when this season passes, but I trust that God will have new joys and blessings for me in the season ahead. In each season He will give me a purpose and a joy. The best place to be is always in the center of His will and His plan.

The Season of Parenting

"All that generation also were gathered to their fathers; and there arose another generation after them who did not know the LORD, nor yet the work which He had done for Israel." (Judges 2:10)

My Bible reading that day found me in Judges and the words just about jumped off the page at me. I read them again, incredulous. How could it happen that they did not know God? How could it be that they hadn't heard of the Lord? Could their parents watch the walls of Jericho fall down and not tell their children? Were they unaffected by how the fear of the Lord swept through Canaan before they even got there? Could they possibly have felt that the stories of the plagues, the Red Sea, the water from the rock, and God's judgments on the wrong doers were just too uninteresting or insignificant to tell their kids at bedtime? What had happened? Were they too worried about their enemies in the land? Had the foreign gods become a snare to them? Were they overcome by the bounty they now enjoyed? I was mystified. What a sad commentary on the effectiveness of the parents.

The task of parenting is certainly a daunting one. Our child's birth day signifies the beginning of a life-long journey filled with hopes, fears, and happiness. It is the most important and most challenging job we will ever face. We're concerned about their physical needs: should I take him to the doctor, is she gaining weight, it's time for their shots, he needs braces. We must make decisions about their education: what school should they go to, maybe we should try homeschooling, will this prepare them for college, what career should they pursue. We want them to be prepared for life: how can I teach them to make friends, do they know how to clean a bathroom, what about computer skills, I must teach him how to budget. We want them to be well rounded: I will take them to the theater, we'll listen to jazz, what extra-curricular activities will she like, let's see the historical sites. We fear for their physical safety: we need a car seat, "Buckle up," "Don't talk to strangers," "Wear your helmet." Then there's the logistics of it all: we need a van, the house is too small, the food bills are going up, where can I get a good deal.

And looming above it all is the knowledge that we and our children are engaged in a very real spiritual war. Our children not only need to know who God is, but what a relationship with God really means and really entails. We cannot control how our children respond to God's calling, but we can control the exposure our children have to God and His people, His word, and the example we set for them in our lives. May it never be said of this next generation that they do not know God or what He has done. But how can we accomplish so great a task?

Psalm 127 says, "Unless the LORD builds the house, they labor in vain who build it." We are not only building our own house, but are setting the foundation for the houses of our children. Without God, our building is in vain. We cannot hope to be effective Christian parents without God's help, strength and wisdom. It was never God's plan that we parent alone. They truly are God's children – given to us for only a short time.

God loves them more than we ever could and He will certainly help us teach and care for them. A Christian woman once sent me an encouraging note, which has been a comfort to me over the years. It closed with Isaiah 40:11 (NIV), which says, "He tends his flock like a shepherd. He gathers the lambs in his arms and carries them close to his heart; he gently leads those that have young." What a tender heart God has towards families! Not only does He carry our children close to His heart, but He gently leads us, their parents! We are not alone in our task. We have the mighty, loving God to lean on. He will lead us. Be encouraged. Take comfort.

Fatherhood: Underrated and misunderstood

Would you be more afraid to skip Mother's Day or Father's Day? I bet most people would be more afraid of their mothers. And why is Mother's Day a bigger deal than Father's Day? Is motherhood a greater honor than fatherhood?

Now, don't get me wrong. I'm not jealous of the attention my mother and the mother of my children get on Mother's Day. You must understand that Mother's Day is big because motherhood is extremely important to most women. We may, indeed, appreciate our mothers and our wives, but we also fear their reaction should we slight them on Mother's Day because we know that motherhood is so important to them. Women invest so much of themselves in raising their children that it is painful not to be remembered and appreciated for it. Indeed, mothers deserve even more honor than what most children give them.

That being said, I believe fatherhood is just as important and just as honorable as motherhood. Mother's Day is a bigger event – at least in part – because one gender does not consider fatherhood nearly as important as it should. And surprisingly, the guilty party is the men.

Consider this: Who are the men our culture honors most? Tiger Woods, Michael Jordan, Bill Belichik, Bill Parcels, Bill Gates, Paul McCartney, Mel Gibson, Tom Hanks, Steven Spielberg, Colin Powell, George Bush, Bill Clinton, Ronald Reagan, and Rush Limbaugh come to mind. Now, what do all these men have in common? They have distinguished themselves in the work they do outside the home to the point of being famous.

How many of these men have distinguished themselves as Christian husbands and fathers? I don't know, but I believe most people don't care. If you excel in your profession to the point of being rich and famous, very few people will hold you accountable for being an immoral man and a lousy father.

I'm afraid, however, that honoring the man who excels outside the home and downplaying a man's performance inside the home is all too typical among Christians as well. In our churches, who would receive more attention – an All-Pro football player who has struggled in his family life or a garbage man who has been faithful as a Christian husband and father? I suspect most of the congregation would consider themselves especially fortunate merely to have been in the presence of the professional athlete but very few would consider it any honor to have been in the presence of a faithful husband and father.

I know that I, too, have struggled with this issue. As a person who has struggled finding success in his career, I know that I have allowed myself to be needlessly miserable at times. The fact that I had a Proverbs 31 wife and eleven terrific children sometimes wasn't enough, in a down time, to keep me from feeling cursed compared to other men because I've had such difficulty finding my stride in the work-world.

This kind of thinking is ridiculous, but even worse it reflects the values of the world and not of God. It also gives insight into the reason Father's Day is not such a big deal. Too many fathers care far too much about the status of their temporary careers and far too little about the status of the eternal souls of their children. Men just get more excited over a promotion and a raise than they do about succeeding as fathers.

I'm sure this isn't a modern phenomenon. We can read about many men in the Bible who would have done well to invest more time in their families. However, modern life has exacerbated the natural tendency of men to abandon their families for glory outside the home. When the vast majority of men were farmers, the typical man did not spend the majority of his day away from his family. Although there may have been a distinct division of labor between husband and wife, the entire family worked together in an effort to make the family business successful. The father probably worked with his older sons in the fields and the daughters helped their mother around the house and in the barn. Therefore, if the children turned out to be lazy or dishonest, the father who employed his children would suffer financially – even as the children would suffer spiritually. Now that most men have been separated from their families by their jobs, fathers have less opportunity and less incentive to raise godly children. While many conservative Christians have idealized the return of the woman to the home and homeschoolers have brought children back into the home, only a few are calling for the men to come home.

I am not saying that it is wrong for a man to have a job that demands that he spend a significant amount of time outside the home. There are many necessary and honorable professions, such as the military, that require men to be away from their families for extended periods of time. I am also not saying that most men need to leave their jobs tomorrow and start home businesses. And I certainly am not saying that men should abandon their role as protector-providers and play Mr. Mom.

What I am saying is that a man should yearn to be a good husband and father. His mind should be occupied with the spiritual well-being of his children. He should be teaching, admonishing, disciplining, playing with, and enjoying his children. He should delight in them and help them on their way. If God has called him into the military and he can't physically be at home, his heart should still always be there.

However, I do believe that a man whose heart is always at home and who delights in his children will generally make a greater effort to spend more time with them. He will want to succeed at work, but so that his family will be provided for and not because it satisfies his selfish ambition. Assuming his family has enough, he may pass up promotions and transfers because his present situation is better for his wife and children. He may, indeed, figure out a way to work from his home or change his career to one that allows him more time with his children. The Bible has called him to be like Christ, who gave up His exalted position in heaven and gave up His life for us, His children. Do we men love our children enough to sacrifice our "exalted positions," if necessary, for them?

Raising children is not just "women's work." The man should be more than the person who provides enough money for the wife to raise the children by herself. In the book of Ephesians God told fathers to raise their children in the fear and admonition of the Lord. God told Eli to restrain his sons. The woman is the man's mate and his helper – not the one solely responsible for raising the children. Sometimes I think we men want our wives to be like Joseph, who managed all the affairs of Potiphar's household so that he only had to concern himself with the food he ate.

When the lives of men are judged in an eternal perspective, the most important thing most of us will ever do is raise godly children. The success of our business or job for many of us will have little eternal impact, but successfully launching a new generation of godly men and women who are taught to do likewise will have a great and lasting impact on eternity.

I say all this so that fathers everywhere get better treatment and better presents on Father's Day (just kidding). Rather, I'm reminded of John the Baptist, of whom the Bible says, "It is he who will go as a forerunner before Him in the spirit and power of Elijah, to turn the hearts of the fathers back to the children, and the disobedient to the attitude of the righteous, so as to make ready a people prepared for the Lord." (Luke 1:17) A holy people are prepared for the Lord when fathers turn their hearts to their children.

It's Not Just about Fatherhood

I think most wives appreciate and admire strong leadership skills in their husbands. Most wives wish their husbands were confident, competent, and willing to assume the responsibilities of family headship. Yet, we often discuss the tendency of modern women to think of submission as a dirty word – and I do think feminism has had a negative influence on Christian women in this regard. However, I think the primary cause of unsubmissive women is the absence of strong and principled male leadership. By saying this I am not absolving women from responsibility for their unsubmissive behavior. Everyone is responsible for his own sins and shouldn't blame them on others. I do believe, however, that if men were the kind of husbands and fathers God called them to be, Christian women would struggle a lot less with submission.

Areas where men have fallen short:

The truth is that men negatively influenced by the feminism of modern western culture are generally weak and timid. Since western culture is also secular and irreligious, it has produced men who exhibit both weakness and a lack of character – not a combination conducive to inspiring submission in the women and children who are called to follow them. Christian men should be strong men of character, but the truth is that sanctification is a painfully slow process and many men don't realize how far they have strayed from the biblical model until irreparable damage is done. Let us examine, then, the weaknesses of the modern husband, explore what God's word says about the problem, and pray that Christian men everywhere will commit themselves to strong and spiritual leadership before their weakness allows the devil to destroy the members of their unprotected families.

Problem #1 – Refusal to lead: I've heard too often of Christian wives who are struggling to submit to the leadership of their husbands, but their husbands refuse to lead. A husband who refuses to lead, to take responsibility for the direction the family is headed, to make sure the household is running properly, to oversee the family finances, property, and business, to make sure his children are disciplined properly, and, most important, to ensure that his family is being spiritually nourished and protected, is weak.

Such a man is weak because he cannot, for whatever reason, bring himself to exert the energy required to effectively lead his family. Whether the man is lazy, weak-willed, or ignores his family responsibilities to pursue other things, the result is the same – the family must find its way in a leadership vacuum. Sometimes the wife will make up for what the husband is lacking. Sometimes the wife will usurp the husband's role as leader of the family, sometimes the wife will leave, sometimes the children will become rebellious (for lack of proper discipline), and there is a good chance the children will grow up not understanding biblical gender roles. This makes it likely that family strife will be passed on from one generation to the next. In fact, only the grace of God will break the chain and save the family.

Why are godly men who are willing to exert strong leadership in the home so hard to find these days? First, the industrial revolution has taken men out of the home. It is much more difficult to set an example of strong fatherhood for the children when the father spends most of his time away from his wife and children. Second, modern technology has made it possible for women to leave the home as well. A wife doesn't need to be at home all day preparing meals and ensuring her family has clothing. Now she can stop at the cleaners on her way home from work and pop something in the microwave for dinner when she gets home. Thus, in many homes there is no one to teach or to set an example of what Christian adulthood should be like. Of course, even if the parents were home it wouldn't matter in most homes since the children are gone to school all day. Apparently, most of us have decided that it is more beneficial for children to associate with kids their own age than to associate with their parents. And most of us send our children to public school, which will ensure they are taught by example, if not overtly, that the feminist vision of gender equality is correct and that biblical gender roles are a discriminatory and shameful relic of our less enlightened past. Not surprisingly, the aggressive and active nature of boys – which if molded properly will prepare them for leadership – is suppressed and discouraged. The result of separated families and school-indoctrinated children is that the biblical concept of manhood is now rarely taught and even more rarely modeled to the children.

Given the upbringing of most boys, it is not surprising that we are a society noted for weak men. However, that does not excuse men from fulfilling their God-given responsibility to lead. God made the man to subdue and take dominion over the earth (Genesis 1), and He made the woman to be a suitable helpmeet. God chose the man to lead his family, and He called the woman and the children to be subject to the father's authority (Ephesians 5). God also called the man to love his wife the way Christ loves the church – by providing for and protecting her to the point of sacrificing his life if necessary. God commanded fathers specifically to see that their children are raised in the fear and admonition of the Lord (Ephesians 6). God called men to govern his people (Moses, Joshua, Saul, and David). God called men to govern his church (male priests, male prophets, male apostles, male elders).

Since the man's authority and command to lead are stated clearly and often in God's word, one would expect Christian men to eagerly and confidently lead their families. Yet, we continue to see Christian men who are loath to exercise their God-given authority. This can only mean one of two things. Either Christian men are so ignorant of God's word that they don't yet realize that God has commanded them to lead, or they do know God's word and have decided to be disobedient. Whether the man is lazy, irresponsible, busy with less important things, filled with feminist notions, or is unwilling to risk conflict with his wife and children is irrelevant. He is called to lead and if he chooses not to lead he is disobedient.

The bottom line is that men are called and commanded to lead. Since God has settled the issue for every family, there should be no argument or power struggle over who leads the family. It is the man of the house and he is responsible to see that his household follows the way of truth. As Joshua said, "Choose for yourselves today whom you will serve ... but as for me and my house, we will serve the LORD."

Problem #2 – Lack of character: We must admit, however, that there have been many men willing to lead their families who have been nothing but selfish tyrants.

Therefore, we must agree that deciding to accept leadership isn't enough. The man must also lead his family according to a biblical standard of godly leadership. The man isn't supposed to lead to benefit himself, but to benefit those under his care. The man isn't to lead in a cold and unfeeling manner, but in love.

It is far too common to see men watching TV and relaxing while their wives are cooking, cleaning, watching children, and changing diapers. It is far too common for men to waste an inordinate amount of time watching and reading about sporting events. It is far too common for men to work for their own glory and their family's comfort and not to further God's kingdom. It is far too common for men to be upset about every little thing that goes wrong instead of setting an example of faith and patience for their families.

The first character trait a godly man must have is a strong desire to forgo selfish ambition, greed, and pleasure and to turn his energies toward serving the Lord. It is extremely difficult for a man to crucify his flesh, but it is absolutely essential if he is going to lead his family where God wants them to go. A man who is living to please his flesh will never be the kind of husband and father God wants him to be.

A strong desire to lead his family in the direction God wants them to go is the first step toward strong Christian leadership. Every husband and family has a general command to serve the Lord, but God also has a specific work for each man to do – a work his wife is to assist him in as she is able. A man who knows what work God has for him to do – even if God has only shown him the work he must do today – can lead his family effectively. A man who is crucifying the flesh and trying to serve the Lord in the work God has called him to do deserves the confidence and trust of his family.

Sadly, many Christian men do not have a vision worth following or they have no vision at all. But this is inexcusable. Every man should have a vision to set an example of excellence and integrity in his work (no matter what that work is) so that he can be of service to others and be an effective witness for the Gospel. Every married man should have the vision to raise his children to be examples of godliness and usefulness to the Lord. If a man has a vision for these things it should stir him to action.

The man without vision will not act and the man who will not act will either be damned or enter heaven as one escaping the flames because his life's work had no lasting value.

The second character trait the godly leader must exhibit is love. Love distinguishes a godly leader from a worldly one. An ungodly man can lead his family with confidence and have a vision that spurs him to action. However, an ungodly man will never be able to love as the Spirit-filled man can love. The first fruit of the Spirit is love (Gal. 5). The man who loves will put the interests of his God, his wife, and his children ahead of his own. The man who loves will not treat his wife and children like servants but will set an example by serving them (as Christ did for His Apostles). The man who loves will actively discipline his children and see that they obey him, just as God disciplines those He loves. The man who loves will be considerate with his wife and treat her with respect (as Peter commands him). The man who loves will not be overly harsh with his children (as Paul commands him). And the man who loves will not care more about avoiding conflict than he does about the well-being of his wife and children. A husband who truly loves his family will oppose his strong willed, rebellious children and even his strong willed, unsubmissive wife if that is necessary.

Putting it all together: A man should be able to confidently and wholeheartedly assert his leadership over his family because God's word commands it. The man's authority should not be a debatable point. However, the man is himself under the authority of God. God has given him work to do and a family to raise, and the wife is to help him accomplish the work he is called to do. However, the man is not just called to lead, but to lead in the way God prescribes. The man is to love his wife and his children. He is to be an example of Christ-like leadership and lovingly serve those he is called to lead.

If the man isn't leading in his home, he should start immediately and he should expect conflict. It is difficult for those who have had to adjust to a man who wouldn't lead to then re-adjust. In fact, it is likely that after the husband has abandoned his responsibility for a long time, the wife and children may well be more capable of leadership than the father.

However, none of that should matter. God has called the man to head his family and the fact that his family will have to suffer through an adjustment period is no reason to disallow the man from fulfilling the job God gave him to do. And although it may be painful for the wife, who by this time may be seen as the head of the household and more capable than her husband, she needs to step aside and allow him to lead. While the wife should certainly be allowed and encouraged to advise and help her husband, she should not keep pushing her view at a time of disagreement until she gets her way. She needs to let her husband lead and let the family suffer the effects of poor decisions – as painful and frustrating as that may be. Most men will grow in wisdom as God is allowed to discipline them through the hardship their poor decisions bring to the family. When the wife will not allow the husband to make a mistake, she short-circuits the process by which he gains wisdom in leadership. And even if her submission causes her pain through which her husband does not grow, she should still be comforted by the fact that God cares for her and will reward her for her obedience when this veil of tears is lifted. She also sets an example of patient Christian endurance for her children and anyone else who knows her.

If the man is already leading his family he can always do a better job. Since perfection can never be achieved this side of heaven, a man's vision can always be more spiritual, he can always follow after God a little more closely, he can always be more holy, and he can always love more deeply. And since the man is responsible for his wife and children, there are always specks in their eyes to remove when the plank in his own eye is removed.

I listened to an interview with Bill Bright, founder of Campus Crusade for Christ. After hearing his words I was convicted by the lack of focus, vision, confidence, and peace in my own soul. We men are wasting the time and resources God has given us in order to live lives of selfish indulgence. Someday the Lord of heaven will return and judge the quality of our work with fire. What will last? It is certain that much of what we have strived for will be worthless on that day. Our houses, our jobs, our cars, our clothes, and the things we amuse ourselves with will be destroyed. The only things that will last are the souls of the people we have impacted.

We need to focus our families on impacting eternity for Christ. We need to teach and inspire the individuals under our authority to find the work in the body of Christ that God has assigned them to do and then to do it with all the strength they can muster. As long as our Master has not yet returned it is never too late to begin. A man who assumes his rightful place as the godly leader of his family should not be underestimated. God will use him to change the world.

Now I Carry the Torch

My generation has now become the mothers and fathers of society's young. The torch has passed to us, and what a task we face. Sometimes we feel overwhelmed, and we question ourselves and what we are doing. We search for answers to the ever-present challenges of parenting. And there's plenty of help out there. Books, tapes, and seminars abound on the subject. We look to our peers for advice and tips on how to be effective mothers. That is all well and good, but maybe we overlook the best resource of all: our own mothers. After all, they have traveled that road and have gained valuable wisdom and insight along the way. Maybe if we reflected more on all the things our mothers did right we would learn some lessons in parenting. Here follows my feeble attempt to do just that.

Thanks, Mom, for being a God-fearing woman. Because you revered God, you respected Dad's role in our family. There was no power struggle in our house. It was a peaceful, safe place. I saw how a biblical marriage should work. Because you revered God, you and Dad made the financial sacrifice to give us kids a Christian education. Because you revered God, you took us to church and kept our home free of questionable books and magazines and TV shows. Because you revered God, you had devotions and prayed with me as a young girl. The Christian heritage you gave me is the most precious and lasting thing you could have given me. It is the foundation for my life.

Thanks, Mom, for your servant heart. I never remember you complaining about doing the washing and the cleaning and the cooking and the shopping and the driving and the sewing. (And the list goes on.) Our needs were always met, and we never had to be afraid to ask you for what we needed. In a culture that encourages women to put themselves first, we saw an example of what it means to serve others, and to do it with grace.

Thanks, Mom, for your humility. I remember talking to you about raising us children, and you told me, "I prayed a lot." In that simple response you showed me the source of our power and success as mothers: our heavenly Father.

Thanks, Mom, for being a stay-at-home mom. You were always there when it was time for me to come home from school. I didn't have to be concerned about coming home to an empty house. If I woke up sick in the morning, there was no struggle about who was going to stay home with me. If I got sick at school, I knew I was just minutes from my bed because you were at home. And because you were at home, you were able to go on field trips, help at school, and take me to sports and music events. You showed us kids that we were more important than extra income or a personal career.

Thanks, Mom, for working hard. You taught me, by your example, what a good work ethic is, and how important that is in whatever we do – in the house or not.

Thanks, Mom, for letting me grow up. I never felt stifled, but I still felt protected. I remember flying (with layovers!) 2000 miles across the country by myself to visit my brother when I was sixteen. Later I went to Hawaii on a class trip. That's not to mention outings with my friends and college dorm life. Thanks for trusting me, and for trusting God even more.

Thanks, Mom, for caring about me even as an adult. I appreciate your packages of homemade soap and jelly and other stuff you send. Thanks for being faithful in calling and writing us. Thanks for praying for me and my husband and children, for I know how dependent we are on Him. And thanks for reminding me that God loves me and watches out for me. I guess daughters of all ages need to hear that sometimes.

Thanks, Mom, for the lessons in motherhood.

Motherhood: Dirty diapers and child evangelism

Everyone knows the emotional pull of a picture of a young mother loving her newborn. Motherhood in this form is soft and warm and beautiful. Your own skin can tingle as you see the innocent caresses. Your heart can melt when you see the protective affection in the eyes of this mother and the trust and contentment in the loving gaze of the child. Would you like a Kleenex now?

Unfortunately, motherhood isn't always so wonderful. Sometimes it's uncomfortable or even painful, but it always involves endless hours of what most people would call menial and humble labor. The new mother may get her first dose of reality when morning sickness comes, but she will progress to the fatigue and uncomfortable largeness that follows. This leads her to the pain of labor and delivery.

The joy that she has in bringing a child into the world may be followed by the pains of healing, the pains of a contracting uterus, the pains of her milk coming in, and the pains caused by a nursing baby. Before the pains involved in having a new baby have subsided, the drudgery begins. It is amazing how helpless God made babies. Everything must be done for them. Feedings, diaper changes, and holding the baby never seem to end – not even at night. The new baby may test the mother's ability at surviving long term sleep deprivation.

As the child grows, his mother becomes his best friend and he wants her to spend all day with him. She may spend her "leisure" time playing blocks or pressing the same button on the same toy 50 consecutive times. Since a crawling baby or toddler lacks any common sense, he must remain in her sight at all times so he doesn't walk into the street or stick his finger in an electrical outlet.

However, she cannot spend all her time "playing" with the baby. After all, there is laundry to be done, a house to clean, meals to cook, dishes to wash, and errands to run. And while a caring husband may reduce her workload, the work is never finished.

Eventually, the child will be able to use the restroom and dress himself, but by then the child will have a younger brother or sister. The process that begins with morning sickness must be repeated in its entirety, but this time with the added responsibility of caring for a two-year-old. Now there are two children in diapers and two children who cannot be allowed out of the mother's sight. The older child may not be as dependent as the baby, but he may be more dangerous. One short distraction can see the toddler disappear and a toddler left to himself for even a moment is capable of incredible damage to property and to himself.

Before the mother has a chance to catch her breath, she has become a tutor, the referee of petty arguments, and a disciplinarian. The doors of the homeschool are opened, the Scriptures are read and explained, and practical homemaking and home managing skills are taught. In the beginning, this process is frustrating. The dishes the child washes are greasy, and the laundry he folds isn't given to its rightful owner. Perhaps the lawnmower is destroyed for lack of oil, the garbage disposal ruined for the silverware thrown down the drain, the cookies get a cup of baking soda, or a gallon of milk is spilled when it is dropped on its way into the house. It seems the more helpers a mother has, the more work there is to do and the longer each job takes. Even so, more new babies may have come along – each child requiring of the mother pain, sleepless nights, and drudgery, but all in addition to the responsibilities that the existing children already demand.

When the children become trained and truly helpful, the mother can't relax because she must ensure that her children are ready for career and marriage. By the time the mother sees her last child out of the house and the bulk of her labor is finished, she may have changed considerably. The energy and beauty that were hers as she entered motherhood may have diminished. Her once flat tummy may now contain a permanent pouch from the stretching and restretching of pregnancy. She may have wrinkles, varicose veins, gray hair, and a less shapely appearance. She is now called a lady and no longer a girl. She may even be known to some as grandma.

Although motherhood is an instinctive longing for most girls, the hardships involved cause women to go to great lengths to avoid it. The typical woman may be capable of having at least half a dozen children, but the average woman has only two. Drugs and more awkward means are used by millions of women to stop their bodies from acting normally and naturally in order to keep themselves from having to go through motherhood again. Abortions are rampant because motherhood is considered by many a ball and chain so horrible that it justifies murdering the unborn baby. When women do plunge into motherhood they are often quick to get the children into daycare, which is followed by preschool and day school. Motherhood has become too hard in the eyes of many to make it a full time job. Is it true that a woman's instinctual desire for motherhood betrays her reason and makes her life unnecessarily hard? Are children really worth all the time and money required to raise them to adulthood? If the goal of life is pleasure or power, it may well be that children are a liability that should be accepted only in very small numbers – if they are accepted at all.

The Christian's goal, however, should never be pleasure or power. We say we want to set aside selfish ambition and serve the Lord out of thankfulness for His grace and mercy. We say we want to be molded into the image of Christ. We say we want to be useful to our Master. We say we want to be used to lead others to Christ. We say we are willing to suffer persecution and even death for the cause of Christ. We say all these things, but do we really mean them?

Consider what Christ did for us. He gave up His life in heaven and humbled himself – taking upon himself the form of a servant. He was willing to live 2000 years ago as the son of a carpenter. He didn't have air conditioning, modern plumbing, or central heat. There was no aspirin, antibiotics, or modern anesthesia. Insects and rodents were probably much harder to control. Death was probably a more common and imminent reality than it is for most of us in this time and place.

He chose a small group of men to train for the work that needed to continue after He returned to His Father in heaven. He protected these disciples and spent His life with them and taught them many things. Although Jesus was God, He put up with their human weaknesses, infirmities, and sin. He was willing to wash their dirty feet. He was even willing to suffer and die on the cross for the sins of His disciples and the sins of countless others. The price He paid and the punishment He bore was more than our human minds can fathom. Jesus submitted himself to the will of His Father although it demanded of Him so much sorrow and pain. In the end, Jesus' work was not in vain. His disciples turned the Roman world upside down – spreading the good news of forgiveness with great effect. They also trained and inspired others who were willing to carry on the work – work that continues today.

If a woman's greatest desire was to serve and emulate her Savior, wouldn't motherhood be an excellent means of doing so? A mother sacrifices a position of relative ease to bear and care for children. A mother cares for those who are ignorant, helpless, sinful, and who have done nothing to deserve her love. A mother is willing to do humble work like washing the dirty feet of her children. She protects and feeds her children. She suffers greatly for her children and sacrifices her own pleasures and ambitions, and she would be willing to sacrifice her own life if necessary for the sake of her children. She lives with them and teaches them so they can find the path to life and then spread the good news of salvation to a generation that will follow after she is gone.

Is a woman's career likely to affect the world as much as raising godly children? I wonder how many Christian women, professing to be willing to do anything for the sake of the Gospel of Christ, are loath to experience menial work, sacrifice, suffering, or drudgery on behalf of another person – even if the beneficiaries are her own children.

Our churches are full of women who are willing to attend Bible studies that include coffee and cake. They are full of women willing to sing in the choir. They are full of women willing to help plan the potluck dinner. But you know, as necessary as all those things may be, how many women attend these events looking for escape or for support in overcoming the trials of motherhood?

I'm not saying the church shouldn't minister to women or that a woman shouldn't be involved in her local church. What I am saying is that women should see motherhood as their ministry – as a primary purpose for their existence as long as God keeps children in their homes. How can a child make it in the world if his mother will not help him? Women should consider it an honor to have the opportunity to model the love of Christ to a child who needs her. They should understand that when a woman changes a baby's diaper, or holds her baby in the middle of the night, or cleans her child's dirty socks, or disciplines her child, or takes him to the doctor, it is as if she was doing these things for Christ himself.

Jesus said, "Then the King will say to those on His right, 'Come, you who are blessed of My Father, inherit the kingdom prepared for you from the foundation of the world. For I was hungry, and you gave Me something to eat; I was thirsty, and you gave Me something to drink; I was a stranger, and you invited Me in; naked, and you clothed Me; I was sick, and you visited Me; I was in prison, and you came to Me.' Then the righteous will answer Him, 'Lord, when did we see You hungry, and feed You, or thirsty, and give You something to drink? And when did we see You a stranger, and invite You in, or naked, and clothe You? When did we see You sick, or in prison, and come to You?' The King will answer and say to them, 'Truly I say to you, to the extent that you did it to one of these brothers of Mine, even the least of them, you did it to Me.' " (Mat. 25:34-40) How often do we pray for opportunities to be used of God and to minister the love of Christ when He has already given us many opportunities at home, and we have called them drudgery?

And although motherhood is a wonderful opportunity to humbly minister to the physical needs of children, that ministry also opens the door for opportunities to share the Gospel and disciple them in the ways of the Lord. When all is said and done, this is the highest calling of motherhood – to evangelize and disciple the precious souls God entrusts to the family. Indeed, the work many women despise as demeaning is truly a ministry of love and salvation.

How to be a Good Mother

Since it is Mother's Day month, I thought it would be good for us to offer an essay from a living example of excellent motherhood on how to be a good mother. I can't think of anyone more qualified to write on excellent motherhood than my wife Cindy, but she didn't want to. Of course one of the things that makes Cindy an excellent mother is her humble spirit, which is why she wouldn't tell you what makes her an excellent mother. In fact, she would never say she's an excellent mother. I realize my bias in all this, but since no one else volunteered to write this essay, who could blame me for writing it myself?

I think, sometimes, that we Christians have this picture of what an excellent mother is - something like a homeschooling June Cleaver with a superhuman spiritual life. The perfect mother always looks like she's ready to be seen in public. Of course, that's not just because she gets up early to ready herself for the day. She has the same thin figure she did when she was eighteen. She eats a healthy diet, exercises with Marine-like regularity, and her clothes are a statement of good taste no matter how casual or how formal the occasion. Her house is always ready for unexpected guests because it is always perfectly cleaned and organized. Her children are perfectly compliant and their defects are cute – merely the result of childish naiveté. Her children get along with each other and with their friends remarkably well. They never fight, cry, or raise their voices at each other. They are also always polite and friendly, conversing with confidence and ease around people of all ages. She teaches her children many hours each day, and they are academically sound and advanced for their ages. They all score over 95 percentile on every standardized test subject. By the way, her kids also excel in sports and music. She cooks superbly and she is more creative than Martha Stewart. More importantly, she lavishes ample time and attention on each child and still manages to attend every church function. She also is an intelligent, engaging companion to her husband and in her spare time spends time reading the Scriptures, praying, and making meals for families in her church. Oh, I almost forgot, she may have a job besides.

This perfect mother doesn't exist, but sometimes women feel a sense of failure when they fall short in any area. Raising a family is a messy business - especially if the quiver is full and the wife is like a fruitful vine (see Psalms 127 and 128). Babies cry, they ensure their mothers don't get a night of unbroken sleep, they want to be held all the time, and they go to the bathroom on themselves. Toddlers begin an ongoing process of testing parental authority. They are also mobile, but have no common sense. That's why you have to keep constant vigil to keep them from breaking things and from getting themselves run over. Pretty soon they need to be taught how to read and write, and then they want piano lessons or football spikes. Before you know it you're paying for braces and teaching them to drive the car. At every turn a mother is fighting the sinful natures of her children and the weaknesses inherent in their ages. The kids sometimes fight. Sometimes they are disobedient, sometimes they are lazy, sometimes they are selfish, and sometimes they are ungrateful. Meanwhile, she is fighting her own sinfulness and that of her husband even as she fights fatigue, overwork, boredom, and discouragement. Even this negative picture assumes she's not dealing with sicknesses, financial woes, loneliness, war, or death. Even in the best of families and under the best of circumstances, good mothering is just plain hard work.

Excellent mothering does not eliminate sin and human weakness, but it does mitigate the damage. Excellent mothering protects the child from the evils lurking outside the home. It purges the evil lurking within the child by disciplining, correcting, rebuking and teaching the child to do right. It is affectionate and nurturing so the child knows he is loved. Excellent mothering introduces the child to his Maker – teaching him to love God's word, to pray regularly and from the heart, and to seek God's favor. Finally, excellent mothering shows the child how to persevere with grace and faith through the drudgery and adversity of life.

This ability to persevere with grace and faith is what makes Cindy an excellent mother. She has given birth to our ten children. She has been pregnant or nursing most of our sixteen years of married life. She has endured many years of financial struggle. She has continued to work outside the home when she would rather not. Some of our children have chronic medical conditions that have been the cause of countless doctor visits. She has endured all night vigils at emergency rooms and over hospital beds. She hasn't had the time or the resources to clean and furnish her home the way she'd like to. She struggles to educate our children when it doesn't seem there are enough hours in the day. But through it all Cindy has generally been pleasant and relaxed.

When people hear that Cindy has ten children they are surprised. They expect her to be aging prematurely from the constant stress. Cindy doesn't let the stress of changing diapers and refereeing fights get to her because she keeps things in perspective. She knows that nothing God has given us is more precious or has more eternal significance than our children. She appreciates, therefore, the importance of raising children and she accepts that crying babies and dirty laundry are part of the job. She doesn't waste her time sulking about how difficult her life is - saving herself and everyone else in the family from needless stress. Cindy accepts motherhood humbly. Like Mary the mother of Jesus, Cindy sees herself as the Lord's handmaiden.

The excellent mother, then, is not consumed by adversity. Because of that, she is able to savor those special moments a mother experiences when her child giggles, gives her a hug, or says, "I love you, Mom." She is able to discipline her children when allowing them to do wrong would be easier. She also sets an example of self-control that will be picked up by her children. Being an excellent mother, then, is not about perfect mothers raising perfect children, but about persevering with grace.

Honoring Parents

Here we are in between Mother's Day and Father's Day - days which give us a special opportunity to appreciate and honor our parents. Of course, our parents should be honored throughout the year and not just on one day. This is an important point in God's eyes. God commanded in Exodus 20: "Honor your father and your mother, so that you may live long in the land the Lord your God is giving you."

This is a serious issue in our household. We feel that it is very important to teach our children to honor their parents. We don't do this because we are the ones who will be honored! Rather, we have much more noble and spiritual reasons for teaching our children this commandment.

First, we teach them to honor their parents because God commanded it! The issue is not only one of honoring their parents, but also one of obeying the God who commanded it. They need to learn the importance of obedience to God. They understand that they do not get to heaven by being good, but that our love for God and our devotion to Him will manifest itself in obedience. We read in 1 John 5:3-4a: "For this is the love of God, that we keep His commandments; and His commandments are not burdensome. For whatever is born of God overcomes the world." God rightly deserves our obedience and devotion, as He is our Creator and Redeemer.

We also teach them to honor their parents because children who do so will be teachable and open to instruction. Their young years are formative ones and we want to effectively teach them about God, people, and life. We don't want them to learn lessons the hard way. If they respect us they will be more willing to listen to us. This is to their life-long benefit. "A wise son accepts his father's discipline, but a scoffer does not listen to rebuke." (Proverbs 13:1)

Another reason honoring parents is so important is because of the effects it has on the entire family. Generally speaking, when children honor their parents there will be less discord and greater peace between family members. The home will run more smoothly as the children will be more obedient to their mothers and fathers.

Additionally, children who honor their parents will submit easier to other authority figures as well. The highest authority we have is God! Our children will also have human authorities over them all their lives. This includes teachers, pastors, the government, and later, husbands and bosses. Again, it is to their benefit to have a submissive spirit toward those who are placed over them.

It is well and good to teach children to honor their parents, but they need to be taught the practical application of this commandment. In day-to-day life, what does it mean to honor parents? To honor means to be respectful - which includes speaking and responding appropriately to parents. It means to be obedient: "Children, be obedient to your parents in all things, for this is well-pleasing to the Lord." (Colossians 3:20) This should include not only obedience, but complete and immediate obedience. Honoring also means to be considerate – desiring to please and help. Finally, it means to be humble – considering the parent greater and more worthy of respect. There may be others, but I believe these are the main ones.

The interesting thing is that as I teach my children and as I become honored on Mother's Day, I am still a child myself. I, too, have parents to honor. My age and the distance I live from my parents don't exclude me from that. God's commandment still applies to me. The Bible doesn't say, "Honor your father and your mother until you're 25" or "Honor your father and your mother unless you live more than 25 miles away." I believe that I am still to honor them. It is true that our relationship has changed a bit. For instance, as a married woman I must first obey my husband (after God) rather than my parents. So how do I honor them now, being older and living far away? I can honor them by respecting them with my words and actions. I can remember their special days and stay in contact with them. I can make a special effort to visit them. I can help them as they need it and as my circumstances will allow. I can make sacrifices to please them. I can listen openly to any advice they may share. I can recognize that as an adult I can still learn from them. I can treat them in such a way that they know they are respected, honored, and loved in my eyes.

We all are also children of our heavenly Father. Our relationship with Him as such will never end. Matthew 22:37-38 reads: "And He said to him, 'You shall love the LORD your God with all your heart, and with all your soul, and with all your mind.' This is the great and foremost commandment.' " We are to love God above all else and with our whole selves. He is truly worthy of the greatest honor.

As we remember our parents during this time of year, and as we give and receive honor, we also esteem and honor our heavenly Father and Lover of our souls. Happy Father's Day, God. We are forever your children.

I Appreciate You, Mom

"Your kids will never know what you do for them." Jim has told me that a number of times as he watches the things I do or the things I go through. It just may be, however, that as our children become parents they may have a better understanding of the things we have done for them. I know that after being a mother for sixteen years there are things that I appreciate now about my parents that I probably didn't when I was a child and teenager living in their house. So in honor of Mother's Day I want to share some things that it's taken me so many years to appreciate in my mom.

Sunday dinner. Every Sunday my mom was up early and had the meat in the oven before we left for church.

Right after we got home from church she was back in the kitchen preparing all the fixings for the meal. And so every Sunday we sat down to a wonderful dinner. I appreciate this because after getting up early and making sure everyone is ready to go on time and being gone all morning, I don't necessarily feel like cooking or walking into the kitchen! That Sunday dinner was a blessing to us!

"We have bread at home." Sometimes when we were out and doing whatever, my dad would suggest going out to eat, and sometimes this was my mom's response. I didn't exactly like that response, because I thought going to a restaurant was a super idea! The ironic thing is that I bet that my mom really thought it was a good idea, too. My guess is that it wasn't her love of bread that prompted that remark, but an inner desire to be a good steward and to be faithful with all that God had given us. There was something more profound going on than just deciding what to eat.

"We have to stop and get milk." I heard my parents say this one often! Again, I didn't much like this because I just wanted to get home and not make another stop! But now I hear myself uttering these same words, and now I understand! I don't always feel like stopping, but my "babies" need their milk and so I will make the stop.

Holidays. My mom spent a lot of time planning and preparing for holidays and special events. The cleaning, cooking, dishwashing, decorating, etc. and etc. took a lot of time and energy. Our holidays were always filled with good food, good company, and special traditions. Those things don't happen all by themselves.

Making sure we children had all the extra things we needed. Whether it was school supplies, treats for Scout meetings, a costume for the party, a special dress for band, or a ride to a function, there was never a question if we would have it and have it on time. I know it's not always easy or convenient to take care of children's needs, but our needs and extras were always provided.

Always being a mom. Moms can't very well take a day off, not for sickness or tiredness or not particularly feeling like doing whatever at a given moment. Even when you are gone or your children are gone, you can't help being a mom! Who would have known the physical and emotional and spiritual commitment involved in having children! As I once read, it's like "forever wearing your heart on your sleeve."

For loving God and bathing us all in prayer. For depending on God's strength and grace – for you and for us.

For childbearing and all that involves! Being the baby of the family, I can especially appreciate your willingness to go through all that "again" so that I could be here!

For having a servant heart – one that didn't complain or play the martyr, but was steady and dependable and content.

I'm sure there are things I still haven't thought of. Maybe I'll think of them by next Mother's Day and I can add them to my list. Until then, thanks for those things, too, Mom. May the grace and love and joy of God abound to you!

Dad

I came into this world without a thing to hold
Or a right to claim as my own.
But my dad took me, sheltered me and protected me
Because I belonged to him.
He sacrificed
So that I could live.
He shared with me riches,
Though they were rightfully his.

He gave his time to me, more than I could have known.
For he thought about me when my thoughts were far away.
He paved a way before me, and took note of where I'd been.
He taught me how to live,
And showed me the best paths to take.

When I was confused,
He spoke to me words of wisdom
But set me free to decide for myself.

He helped me build upon a firm foundation.
I can still hear his words to me, echoing in my mind.
I always knew I was loved.
I could always trust in him.

My dad:
A life of silent commitment.
And a commitment of unfailing love.
Dear God, who could have known that when I was looking at him,
I was really looking at you?

Child Discipline

Knowledge has outstripped character development, and the young today are given an education rather than an upbringing.
(Ilya Ehrenburg)

I'm Only Thinking of You (Not)

Way back when in college, Jim and I saw a play together. I couldn't tell you the name of it or even what it was about, but we do remember one line from one of the songs: "I'm only thinking of you." It was a comical song and this line was said rather sarcastically. It's kind of like a couple of weeks ago when Jim had strep throat. He wanted something really cold to soothe his throat and wondered if I would go with him to Starbucks for one of their Frapuccinos. Since this is the best cold coffee drink that I have ever tasted, he didn't have to twist my arm too much to get me to accompany him. Of course, though, I only did it for medical reasons for him. As I told him, "I'm only thinking of you."

We kid around with each other with that kind of thing, but it's no joke if it can be applied to how we discipline our children. Much has been said about the motives and emotions which fuel our discipline and rule-making, especially that of anger. But what about the motive of selfishness?

I think that sometimes parents discipline out of selfishness, even if they don't always realize it. Let's take the example of children playing nicely but somewhat noisily. The parent may yell at them for making so much noise. Now, the children aren't hurting anybody or breaking any rules. They are just acting like children and doing what children do. But the parent simply doesn't want to hear it and so the chastising begins. This may not be a perfect example because sometimes there may be valid reasons for the children to be quieter, but I think you can get the point of what I'm trying to say. The parent is yelling to suit his or her own desires rather than disciplining for the good or safety of the children, and it's fairly evident to everyone involved.

Selfishness can masquerade as kindness on the part of the parents. Consider this scenario: mom is busy preparing a birthday party for her daughter. Mom wants everything just perfect because she considers it her gift to her daughter. But mom's little girl wants to help decorate. Mom may want to tell her "no" for the reasons mentioned, but this is just another form of selfishness – the parent trying to please herself rather than acting on behalf of the child. If mom really wants the day to be special for the daughter, perhaps she should let the daughter decorate because that is what *she* wants. After all, the day is supposed to be for the child and not for the parent.

Additionally, the parent's selfishness can masquerade as being the best interest of the child – for his safety or character development. A parent may forbid his child to play outside in a light rain supposedly to keep the child from "catching cold," when in reality the parent just doesn't want to deal with the mess involved in having a child play in rain and puddles.

It's hard being a parent. We must sort through all the messages being sent to us by our culture and determine what is God's will for our family. We must train our children in the faith and ways of God regardless of the ways of those around us. We must lead our children by example. We must seek to help our children overcome their sinful natures through Christ to become all that God wants them to be. If all that wasn't enough, we must also overcome our own sinful natures and desires so that we can be God's effective vessels in raising His children. We cannot let our sinfulness and shortcomings stand in the way of the spiritual development of our children. We need to examine our motives before we act. Are we doing this for our children's physical safety? Are they breaking God's rules? Are they breaking the rules of our household? Are our rules fair, right, and necessary? Are we acting to further the character development of our children? Will our actions further their spiritual growth? Will what we do cause our children to become bitter or exasperated? Are our children just acting as children? Is what they are doing truly wrong or dangerous? Am I acting to satisfy my desires rather than acting for their good?

"We are taking every thought captive to the obedience of Christ." (2 Corinthians 10:5b) We need to take every thought and motive of ours and conform it to the character and will of Christ. We can then teach and discipline our children in ways pleasing to God and for their highest good. In that way our parenting can sincerely say to our children, "I'm only thinking of you."

What Does "No!" Really Mean?

"No" is usually one of the first words babies learn. "Stop" and "don't" are usually not far behind. This is partially because humans are born with a strong desire to stop perceived injustice when it is directed at them. Negative words like "no" give toddlers a way of verbally expressing their disapproval or their outrage at unfairness directed at their persons. Of course, to a toddler, a diaper change, a bath, or the snatching away of Grandma's best china can be perceived as acts of tyranny. Toddlers also learn the word "no" so quickly because their parents use it a lot. Children are born without manners or common sense and, frankly, they need to learn that much of their behavior is unacceptable. Crying every time you don't get your own way, eating chocolate as the main course for every meal, biting people who bother you, and stealing your little brother's toys deserve plenty of "stops" and "don'ts."

Now that we've determined that toddlers are uncivilized beasts and need to be tamed, we must be careful of how we use the word "no." If we use the word incorrectly, we may confuse our toddlers so that they don't really understand what "no" means. You may think that every human – even uncivilized toddlers – knows what the word "no" means. Since I don't want to confuse you, allow me to give you an example. Let's say you say to your toddler: "Unless you eat all your anchovies and bitter herb salad, you can't have any double chocolate chip double chocolate ice cream." When your toddler leaves the dinner table without having eaten any of his anchovies and bitter herb salad, what do you do when your toddler comes back for dessert? Do you give your toddler his dessert anyway? Perhaps you firmly say "no" to your toddler until he cries bitter tears, and then you change your mind and give him his dessert. Or, perhaps you firmly say "no" to your toddler even after he cries bitter tears, but when his tears, whining and pleading for double chocolate chip double chocolate ice cream continue, he eventually wears you out and gains your pity. Then he gets his dessert.

What, then, does the word "no" mean to the ignorant, uncivilized toddler? It wouldn't mean anything if the toddler came back for dessert and immediately got his double chocolate chip double chocolate ice cream. On the other hand, if he gets the ice cream after throwing a temper tantrum, he learns that the word "no" means "yes," but only after he makes a fuss. Alternatively, if he gets his ice cream after wearing his parents down, he learns that "no" means "yes" if he makes a fuss for a long time.

When a child translates "no" as "yes," it can cause big problems. It can be embarrassing when your uncivilized toddler begins tearing stuff off the grocery shelves and you say "NO!" and your toddler translates that as "yes, as long as I wail at very high decibels." It can even be dangerous when you tell your toddler not to run in the street or stick his finger in the electrical outlet.

Therefore it is un-good if your toddler translates "no" as "yes," but at this point, at least, he is not confused. He is quite certain that "no" means "yes." If you really want to confuse your toddler, change your responses when he challenges your "no." When he won't eat his anchovies and bitter herb salad and he comes back for his double chocolate chip double chocolate ice cream, you can give it to him immediately one time, after he bothers you all afternoon another time, and as soon as he cries bitter tears a third time. The next time, he won't have any idea what the price of turning a "no" into a "yes" will be. That will frustrate him, of course, but if you really want to confuse him, make "no" really mean "no" sometimes, and at other times let "no" be "yes." This works best if the "yes" is sometimes immediate, sometimes after crying loudly, and sometimes after being a long-term pest. After a time, your child will have absolutely no idea what the word "no" means.

Hopefully most of us don't confuse our children on purpose. Sometimes our pity for our children as they watch others eat double chocolate chip double chocolate ice cream overcomes our concern for their character. Sometimes we say "no" when we're grouchy and regret having said it. Sometimes we decide it is unreasonable to expect our toddler to eat anchovies and bitter herb salad. This should cause us to make sure we mean "no" before we say it. Once we say "no," however, it must be strictly enforced or our children won't know what "no" means. A child who doesn't know what "no" means is no picnic at the grocery store or anywhere else in public, but as he gets older the stakes get much higher. This can be hard for the child as he grows up and has to decide whether to cheat on his schoolwork, drink alcohol, smoke cigarettes, take drugs, or have a physical relationship with a member of the opposite sex.

God's word has many "Thou shalt nots" in it. God told us not to put other gods before him, not to murder, not to steal, not to commit adultery, and not to covet. We don't want our children growing up thinking "no" means "yes," or being confused in any other way of what the meaning of the word "no" is. When our children disobey God's prohibitions, they endanger their very souls. As the writer to the Hebrews says, "And to whom did He swear that they would not enter His rest, but to those who were disobedient?" (Hebrews 3:18) When we confuse our children about the meaning of "no," we teach them disobedience.

Not only will a child who knows that "no" means "no" be easier at the grocery store, he will know that if he wants double chocolate chip double chocolate ice cream he will have to eat his veggies. You'll be amazed when, instead of cries of woe and shedding of tears, you hear, "Please pass the anchovies and bitter herb salad."

I'll Give You a Lollipop

"I'll give you a lollipop if you're good in the store."

Many parents use this form of child training. I'm not one of them. In fact, I'm adamantly opposed to it. It may seem innocent enough, but I feel that it comes with long-term, negative ramifications. Some may call it an incentive. I call it bribery.

Parents do not need to resort to this. I can expect and demand obedience from my children because that is the authority that God has given me as a parent. "Children, obey your parents in the Lord, for this is right. Honor your father and mother (which is the first commandment with a promise)." (Ephesians 6:1-2) I have not given myself this authority; it comes from God. My children need to obey me because when they do that they are actually obeying God. If they refuse to obey me, they are rebelling against God because He has commanded that they obey me. It is vital that my children understand this. They are not left with a choice. They must obey. Therefore, I do not feel that I need to beg, plead, bribe, or negotiate with my children to get them to do what I say.

If my children respect my authority, they will respect other authority as well. This is an important life lesson. My children will always have an authority over them, whether it be an employer, a husband, the government, and, of course, God. They must obey that authority whether or not they agree with it or whether or not they feel that it is to their benefit. There will always be evil and rebellion in this world, but I venture to say that there would probably be fewer problems in the schools and on the streets if people were taught to respect authority as very young children.

My children also need to obey me for their own safety. Let's say that the ice cream truck is parked across the street. My child has it in his mind that he really wants ice cream and his few cents are just burning a hole in his pocket. So he takes off. In his zeal he doesn't see the car coming, but I do. "Stop!" I yell. My child does not have time to give the matter thought. He cannot take a moment to determine how badly he really wants that ice cream and if the treat is worth the negative consequences (Mom yelling). He doesn't have time because that car is racing down the street. All my child has time to do is hear my voice and obey. His well-being is at stake. In an instant he must hear me, trust me, and obey. He doesn't have time to wait for the lollipop.

Trading lollipops for obedience with our small children will have a negative effect on our older children, who probably aren't getting lollipops for obedience anymore. Our older children will think this isn't fair. "Why does he get a lollipop for picking up his toys? I clean my room... for nothing!" They will feel cheated and may be tempted to disobey and rebel. We will lose respect in their eyes. Any progress we may have made with our older children may be lost – all over a lollipop.

But let's say this isn't a problem because we are still giving our older children lollipops in exchange for their obedience – except maybe now the lollipops are bigger and more expensive, like new clothes or CDs. This situation is even more dangerous than the other. Are we going to teach our children to respect and obey authority or not? When are we planning on doing this? The longer we wait the more difficult it will be. In the long run, it is much easier to teach our children as toddlers. It is tempting to give them a lollipop because it makes things so much simpler – in the short run. But the confrontation, and the strength of will on the part of the parent, must come some time if we truly want our children to have obedient, teachable, humble spirits. It is easier on all involved if we don't change the game rules half way through.

I'm sure that some will say that the lollipop system is how the world is run, so there is no harm in it. Aside from all the arguments I just made, I still don't agree. That is not how the world is run. You don't get extra just by obeying the rules. I don't get a big bonus just for coming to work when I am scheduled. I don't get a raise just by fulfilling the basic conditions for employment. Our children won't get far by just showing up for work. But they will earn respect and admiration by first respecting and obeying those in authority over them. That is where it starts.

I am not saying that we shouldn't love and encourage and praise our children. Yes, we should. But that is not bribery. It is only bribery if they perceive it as such – if it is something they are expecting because it was held out to them as a reward before they were obedient. Teaching and then expecting our children to obey authority is not a harsh system. It is God's system. The system of a loving and good God.

"Which of you, having a slave plowing or tending sheep, will say to him when he has come in from the field, 'Come immediately and sit down to eat'? But will he not say to him, 'Prepare something for me to eat, and properly clothe yourself and serve me while I eat and drink; and afterward you may eat and drink'? He does not thank the slave because he did the things which were commanded, does he? So you too, when you do all the things which are commanded you, say, 'We are unworthy slaves; we have done only that which we ought to have done.' "
(Luke 17:7-10)

Maybe it's Not the Strong Willed Child: Introducing the weak willed parent

Some children have a very firm idea about what they want and they are willing to cry, argue, or even defiantly bulldoze ahead to get it. When a mother at the grocery store struggles with a screaming child who is distraught over not getting a candy bar at the check out aisle, she is likely to wonder why her child had to be strong willed. When a mother tells a child he can have no dessert until he eats his vegetables and the rebellious child throws his plate of food on the floor as the opening salvo of a temper tantrum, she is likely to wonder why she couldn't have gotten a compliant child instead. Parents are often wondering how to handle a strong willed child. Dr. Dobson wrote a best selling book on the subject that launched his public career. Everyone is always talking about the strong willed child.

I do recognize from having my own children that some children are more headstrong than others, but my experience also tells me that there is usually a greater problem involved in these situations than strong willed children. I would like to introduce you to the weak willed parent.

The weak willed parent is the one who at the beginning may appear to be the more compassionate one. She is distressed when the new baby cries and will do anything to quiet the baby down. Her natural instinct is to give the baby the desires of his heart. She is a pleaser and enjoys being liked. She wants to be loved.

When her children are new, the weak willed parent may seem to do just fine. The baby needs to be fed, changed, bathed, and held. As the baby grows, however, he becomes more accomplished in the art of evil. He learns to chafe under the boundaries set by his parents. He wants dessert without having to eat his carrots. He wants to stay up as late as he wants. He wants to color on the walls. He wants to play with the toy his sister is already playing with. He wants to watch TV all day.

At this point, the weak willed parent tries to muster her resolve but resolve is not her forte. She knows it is not healthy to eat junk all day, but she knows the carrots don't taste that great and what harm will be done if he gets dessert this one time? Bedtimes are just arbitrary anyway, and what will it hurt if her child is allowed to stay up awhile longer? The creative crayon art can be washed off the wall, you know. The boy's sister may be placated with a different toy – the least painful way to maintain the peace. And she knows it is not good for her son to watch TV all day, but what harm would there be in watching just one more show if it makes him happy?

The fact that she told her son he wouldn't be able to eat dessert until he eats his carrots, the fact that she told him he had to go to bed at 9:00 p.m. no matter what, the fact that she told him he would be spanked if he wrote on the walls again, the fact that he used force to take from his sister what didn't belong to him, and the fact that she told him he could only watch two shows a day disturbs her, but not enough to compel her to enforce the standards she set for her son.

The weak willed parent has deceived herself into thinking that these little crises are about food and toys. The second she set a standard for her son it became much more than that. In that instant, it became an issue of obedience vs. rebellion, respect vs. disrespect, and self-control vs. self-indulgence. Allowing the child to have his own way at this point will teach him that it is not necessary to obey the rules, that authority figures are not to be trusted or respected, and that selfishness is rewarded. The weak willed parent is destroying the character of her child.

The irony is that the weak willed parent – the one who most desires peace, who wants most to be loved, who has great affection for her offspring, and who wants most for her child to be happy - will find that her offspring will turn on her. In the end she gets turmoil, rebellion and tears. Even those considered compliant children in their early years may despise her in the end. Their rebellion may take a more passive form – lying, cheating, and hidden rebellion – but the weak willed parent will just wonder what ever happened to her once sweet child.

Furthermore, a weak willed parent is also liable to turn her children against the more disciplined parent as well. By not enforcing the rules of the stricter parent she is teaching the children that the parent who sets boundaries is an unloving, arbitrary spoilsport. Two strong willed parents who agree on the standards they set for their children will generally be able to overcome a strong willed child. After all, it's two against one, and the parents have authority and size. Consequently, when two strong willed parents present a unified front there is no way even the strongest of strong willed children can prevail in a struggle for power. However, one weak willed parent can give any child – even a child who tends towards compliance – a chance to win a power struggle.

What's a weak willed parent to do? The first thing a weak willed parent needs to do is acknowledge her weakness and pray to the Lord for the wisdom and the strength to discipline her children properly. As for wisdom, James writes, "But if any of you lacks wisdom, let him ask of God, who gives to all generously and without reproach, and it will be given to him. But he must ask in faith without any doubting, for the one who doubts is like the surf of the sea, driven and tossed by the wind." (James 1:5-6) In other words, God has promised to give us the wisdom we need. All we need to do is ask. God did not give us children and abandon us in our ignorance so that our children would be ruined. He is ready and willing to give us the discernment we need to discipline our children properly. Are we ready to ask in faith?

Second, the weak willed parent must acknowledge that parenting involves more than nurturing and comfort. Proverbs states bluntly, "Foolishness is bound up in the heart of a child; the rod of discipline will remove it far from him." (Proverbs 22:15) "Do not hold back discipline from the child, although you strike him with the rod, he will not die. You shall strike him with the rod and rescue his soul from Sheol." (Proverbs 23:13-14) The parent has the God-given responsibility to discipline the child – with physical force when necessary – so that folly, irreverence, and sloth are driven out of his character.

When we withhold discipline from our children we send the message – perhaps unintentionally – that we don't love or care for them. God doesn't withhold discipline from the children He loves and He doesn't expect us to behave differently toward our children. The writer to the Hebrews says, "My son, do not regard lightly the discipline of the Lord, nor faint when you are reproved by Him; for those whom the Lord loves He disciplines, and He scourges every son whom he receives. It is for discipline that you endure; God deals with you as with sons; for what son is there whom his father does not discipline? But if you are without discipline, of which all have become partakers, then you are illegitimate children and not sons. Furthermore, we had earthly fathers to discipline us, and we respected them; shall we not much rather be subject to the Father of spirits, and live? For they disciplined us for a short time as seemed best to them, but He disciplines us for our good, so that we may share His holiness. All discipline for the moment seems not to be joyful, but sorrowful; yet to those who have been trained by it, afterwards it yields the peaceful fruit of righteousness." (Hebrews 12:5b-11) God, then, is our example. His discipline is painful. He subjects us to hardship. But He knows that the pain He inflicts on us will produce a "harvest of righteousness." If we are unable to inflict pain on our children when they transgress God's law, we will reap a harvest of wickedness.

Eli the priest is a biblical example of a weak willed father who refused to discipline his sons adequately. Eli's sons served at the Tent of Meeting and treated God's offerings with contempt and slept with the women who served there. Eli knew about the wickedness of his sons and even rebuked them, saying, "Why do you do such things, the evil things that I hear from all these people? No, my sons; for the report is not good which I hear the LORD'S people circulating. If one man sins against another, God will mediate for him; but if a man sins against the LORD, who can intercede for him?" (1 Samuel 2:23b-25a) The Scriptures relate, however, that his sons "would not listen to the voice of their father."

The fact that Eli rebuked his sons was not enough to absolve Eli of responsibility for his sons' behavior. God said, "Why do you ... honor your sons above Me?" (1 Samuel 2:29) "For I [the LORD] have told him that I am about to judge his house forever for the iniquity which he knew, because his sons brought a curse on themselves and he did not rebuke them. Therefore I have sworn to the house of Eli that the iniquity of Eli's house shall not be atoned for by sacrifice or offering forever." (1 Samuel 3:13-14)

What was God's judgment on Eli's family? The Lord said, "Behold, the days are coming when I will break your strength and the strength of your father's house so that there will not be an old man in your house. You will see the distress of My dwelling, in spite of all the good that I do for Israel; and an old man will not be in your house forever. Yet I will not cut off every man of yours from My altar so that your eyes will fail from weeping and your soul grieve, and all the increase of your house will die in the prime of life." (1 Samuel 2: 31-33)

It is not enough, then, for the weak willed parent to rebuke her children. Parents have an obligation – even weak willed parents – to restrain and sometimes to inflict physical pain on their children sufficiently severe to ensure that the folly bound up in the child's heart is driven far from him.

Compassion is important, discipline must not be overly harsh, and love (not anger) should be the motivating force behind the punishment. It is not compassionate or loving, however, to allow a child's character to suffer because the weak willed parent cannot bear to inflict pain on her child.

Third, the weak willed parent should be sure that she is not setting standards for her child that she doesn't intend to enforce if her child rebels. It may be acceptable to allow a child to have dessert without eating *any* carrots when no standard has been decreed, but it is not acceptable to allow a child who has eaten most of his carrots to have dessert when the decreed standard is that *all* carrots must be eaten first. Standards should be reasonable and promote character or order. Standards must not be arbitrary, so numerous as to be stifling, or require too much of young children. However, once a standard is adopted it should be enforced consistently.

And finally, dishonesty, physical violence, and disobedience must not be tolerated. The weak willed parent must not only rebuke her child, but also inflict enough pain on the child to "drive the folly far from him." I understand that the standards for spanking may be different from family to family and I am sensitive to the fact that some parents use spanking as an excuse to abuse their children. However, it is my observation that weak willed parents allow their children to repeat unacceptable behavior many times before punishment is administered, they are too quick to employ techniques like "counting to three" or "time-out" when a spanking is necessary, and when they do spank they don't cause enough pain to make the punishment effective. A spanking that hurts a child's feelings but doesn't involve physical pain may not be enough to cause a change in behavior.

My heart goes out to the weak willed parent. Her natural tendency is to be gentle and peaceful, but her instincts betray her when it comes to disciplining children. She embraces her role as nurturer, but recoils at her role as disciplinarian. Whether she likes it or not she is God's agent of discipline to drive folly far from the heart of the child. Her tepid acceptance of this role endangers the very soul of the child her heart loves.

I have used the pronoun "she" because I believe wives are especially vulnerable to weakness in this area. However, it must be said that men are also prone to weak willed parenting. Eli, Samuel, and David are biblical examples of men who did not have success restraining their sons. In fact, because a man is the head of the family, a weak willed man may do even more damage than a weak willed woman.

For the sake of their children and as a service to their God who desires godly offspring, weak willed parents must pray for wisdom. They must accept their role as God's agents of discipline to drive folly far from the hearts of their children. They must set reasonable standards – standards they can bring themselves to enforce. They must not tolerate dishonesty, physical violence, or disobedience, and their punishments must be decisive and painful enough to help the children to change their behavior.

The Habit Makers

"Did you brush your teeth this morning?"

I've asked this question many times in my household. (And to some children more than others!) I do this because I believe that one of my functions as a parent is to instill good habits in my children. If my children establish good habits, it will have a positive effect on them the rest of their lives. Good habits will save my children time (they'll know where their car keys are because they always put their things back in the same place), keep them healthy (because they eat healthy even when they don't want to), save them money (because they don't waste things), stay clean and organized (because they have good housekeeping skills), and generally keep their stress down and make them more productive.

When I teach my children good habits, I not only tell them what to do, but also show them how and even more importantly tell them *why*. Older children especially respond better to our training if they understand the reasons behind what we tell them to do. If, for example, we tell them we must eat the older food first so that we can be good stewards of God's gifts and also save money on food, they understand the motives are good and wise – not that we don't care about what they enjoy! They understand that our decisions are based on values and principles and that we aren't just being overly concerned about little things that don't matter.

Obviously, many of the habits we try to instill in our children have to do with physical things – our diet, brushing our teeth, putting our things away, living according to a budget, etc. But I believe that as Christian parents we also need to instill in our children good *spiritual* habits. The Bible exhorts us to *train* our children: "Train up a child in the way he should go, even when he is old he will not depart from it." (Proverbs 22:6) And, "Fathers, do not provoke your children to anger, but bring them up in the discipline and instruction of the Lord." (Ephesians 6:4) We are also to *instruct* them: "Hear, O sons, the instruction of a father, and give attention that you may gain understanding." (Proverbs 4:1) The Bible tells us to *teach* them: "These words, which I am commanding you today, shall be on your heart. You shall teach them diligently to your sons and shall talk of them when you sit in your house and when you walk by the way and when you lie down and when you rise up." (Deut. 6:6-7) There are many ways we can train, instruct, and teach our children. One of those ways is by helping them establish good habits. This isn't legalistic; it's practical. A habit is just something we have come to do routinely. We not only tell our children to brush their teeth, but we show them how and make sure they do it.

The author of Hebrews writes to his readers, "Let us not give up meeting together, as some are in the *habit* of doing..." (Hebrews 10:25, NIV) The writer is defining continually not meeting together as a bad habit that some have established. Wouldn't it then follow that the goal is the habit of meeting together, and that this is a good thing?

He wanted them to meet together and to do it routinely. We can tell our children that our habits, or practices, do not get us into heaven, but they help foster our relationship with God. For example, our family now has a practice, a habit, of spending one day a week together. This builds our relationships with each other. Routinely spending time with God will make our relationship with Him grow and remain strong. These habits would include personal Bible reading, prayer, worship, and fellowship.

How can we help our children establish these good habits? The first way is by talking about it. As I mentioned before, we want them to understand what to do and why to do it. They need to know that these things are not for our salvation, but for the spiritual benefit of our relationship with God. The issue is not how many minutes we pray, how many chapters we read in our Bible each day, or how many church services we attend each week. The issue is that we routinely, habitually, spend time with God. We all know that we are less likely to do things if we don't make a habit of it. Spending time with our family is a good thing and so we set apart a certain time to do that – we make it a habit. Is it any different with God? Spending time with Him is a good thing, so we want to make it a habit so we are sure to do it and are sure to make it the priority that it should be.

Next we need to set an example. Our children should see us reading our Bibles daily. They should notice that we make it a priority to attend church and fellowship with other believers on a routine basis. They need to see that we won't skip church just because we stayed up too late the night before or because we'll miss the pre-game show. They learn that we won't skip our family devotions because somehow it has gotten too late or because we are visiting relatives overnight.

Talking about these things and setting a good example will make these habits a natural part of the daily life of our family. From early on these things will be a regular part of our children's lives. They will see that we value these things and hold them in top priority.

We also need to show our children how to do these things. How do we make them a habit? How can we choose the best time for us to do them? How do we pray? How do we choose a church? How do we prioritize our time? This way our children will not only know that our spiritual habits are important, but they will also learn how to make them habits and how to do them in the most beneficial way.

We can also give our children practice in our family setting. For example, sometimes we have the older boys plan and lead our family devotions. Our children take turns praying at meals and devotions. Jim and I also take turns so our children can hear how to pray. We instruct them on things that can be included in prayers, and remind them of things they can pray for. For example, we may say, "OK, Keenan, it's your turn to pray. Remember to pray for so-and-so because they are sick." If one of our older children has said the same two sentence prayer for the fourth time in a row, we will remind them what else they can pray for and instruct them to do better next time. This is important not only for their own spiritual walk, but also for the walks of those who will follow them – their children whom they will eventually instruct in the ways of the Lord. This isn't about saying certain words, but about keeping meaning in our habits.

There is a degree to which we can hold our children accountable in these matters. We ask our children if they brushed their teeth to hold them accountable to what they need to do. We can do likewise in certain spiritual habits. For example, in our house we have a Bible reading chart on the wall. All of our names (the readers) are on this chart, including me and Jim. Every day we each are to write down the chapters we have read. Everyone can tell in an instant who has read and who hasn't! We may also ask the children to tell us about what they've read – cuts down on the sly ones getting away with something! This helps them establish the good habit of Bible reading and helps them understand how important we view it.

Finally, we can praise our children for their efforts, remind them to continue on, and ask about what they're doing. Another example: our son Michael is going to college this fall and on his own started attending a weekly Bible study there. I told Michael how happy I was that he's been doing this – and that he's done this on his own. I try to remember to ask him about what they're studying – to show my interest. (And, yes, to verify he's in a good group, although I believe Michael has good judgment in these areas.) Again, our children can see how much we value good spiritual habits and that we care about their spiritual walk.

We have been told that this isn't a good approach. We've been told that if we "push" reading the Bible, etc., (let's remember, though, that "push" is a relative term and depends on the individual's response) our children may rebel when they leave the house. Let's return to our physical habit of teeth brushing. It is true that if I keep reminding my child to brush his teeth (because he keeps forgetting) and take him to the dentist (even though he hates it), that he may forego any and all good dental practices when he leaves our house. But that shouldn't deter me from my responsibility to help him get on the right track. I'm not going to stop enforcing good dental habits because they may rebel against them. What's the chance of them brushing their teeth every day if they don't learn it at home as a natural part of their lives? And so it is with good spiritual habits. My child may decide to skip his Bible reading or go to church only occasionally, but that will be his decision. He would be responsible for the decisions he makes. I, however, am responsible for my actions. I must fulfill the responsibilities God has given me towards my children. Yes, they may abandon these habits we have worked so hard to instill, but if we don't try to instill them, the chances are less that they will ever establish good spiritual habits!

I certainly pray that my children will practice good, lifelong spiritual habits – those which are full of meaning and spiritual benefit, habits which they love doing because they love the Lord and love spending every day with Him. Of course, should this all happen, it is only because of the grace of God. Only He can take our meager efforts and produce a rich, bountiful spiritual harvest in our children.

Praise the Permissive Parent?

Previously I have criticized the weak-willed parent, who, like Eli, doesn't have the strength of character to forcefully and consistently discipline his children. This, I believe, is a chronic problem even among Christian families because most of us were raised by parents who didn't forcefully and adequately discipline us. And our culture reinforces the overly permissive parenting style. These days, spanking a child can get you a visit from Social

Services who may consider biblically principled discipline as child abuse. Schools are notoriously lax in discipline as incorrigible children realize that the worst thing that will happen to them is a trip to the office. We even punish murder with an extended form of time out. Overly permissive parenting usually has disastrous results and Eli's sons (and the undisciplined children we know personally) are frightful examples for us all.

That being said, I would like to change gears and caution against the other extreme. We also have to guard against being overly restrictive parents. Many of us have a tendency to reflexively say "no" to our children's requests, micro-manage and over-regiment them, criticize them too frequently, and vent our anger at them when they act their age. Paul wrote to fathers, saying, "Fathers, do not provoke your children to anger, but bring them up in the discipline and instruction of the Lord." (Eph. 6:4) Being overly restrictive and overly critical exasperates and discourages our children. It breaks the spirit and confidence of some and stirs up rebellion in the rest. Either way, the overly harsh parent should not be surprised if his children reject his values and his way of life when they get out from under his tyranny.

Let us take a closer look at the characteristics of the overly restrictive parent:

Reflexively say no: I know I have struggled with this one personally. With eleven children it is impossible for me to cater to every child's individual preferences. For the sake of order and efficiency, even seemingly reasonable requests must sometimes be turned down. However, there is a fine line between necessary order and efficiency (indeed, the needs of the many may outweigh the needs of the one) and parental selfishness. We often say "no" because we have a selfish attitude and don't want to take the time or energy to consider – not to mention fulfill – our child's requests.

We are fortunate that God doesn't have the same attitude towards us. God said to us, "Ask, and it will be given to you; seek, and you will find; knock, and it will be opened to you. For everyone who asks receives, and he who seeks finds, and to him who knocks it will be opened. Or what man is there among you who, when his son asks for a loaf, will give him a stone? Or if he asks for a fish, he will not give him a snake, will he? If you then, being evil, know how to give good gifts to your children, how much more will your Father who is in heaven give what is good to those who ask Him!" (Mat. 7:7-11)

God is not saying here that He will grant us every selfish whim. James writes, "You ask and do not receive, because you ask with wrong motives, so that you may spend it on your pleasures." (Jam. 4:3) But God does have the desire to give us what we ask Him for. Jesus said, "Whatever you ask in My name, that will I do, so that the Father may be glorified in the Son. If you ask Me anything in My name, I will do it." (John 14:13-14) Jesus adds, "In that day you will not question Me about anything. Truly, truly, I say to you, if you ask the Father for anything in My name, He will give it to you. Until now you have asked for nothing in My name; ask and you will receive, so that your joy may be made full." (John 16:23-24)

We should have the same desire to fulfill our children's requests that God has to fulfill our requests. In other words, we should say "yes" to our children unless we have a good reason to say "no." Perhaps we can stop saying "no" to our children before we fully understand what they're asking.

Micro-manage and over-regiment: No one likes to be micro-managed and children are no exception. One of my criticisms of formal education (and specifically of Christian academies) for small children is the obsession with structure. Perhaps large groups of small children require a great deal of structure, but I think this stifles children – especially young boys – and life becomes unnecessarily tedious and frustrating. However, many of us who homeschool treat our children similarly. Some schools make children wear special clothes and make them stay neat and clean. No running is allowed. Everyone must line up in single file and march into the next room without talking. Silence must be maintained 50 minutes of every hour. Naptime is enforced whether the children are tired or not. There is so much structure that freedom, spontaneity and fun are all smothered. I'm reminded of how Captain Von Trapp ran his home in "The Sound of Music." Yet, academies pride themselves on this sort of thing and many parents, although usually not so extreme, have similar tendencies.

Even playtime, when it is allowed, is overly regimented. One of the tendencies of modern culture is to organize games for small children. Soccer, baseball, and football are examples. When we were young, there was no organized baseball until age 9, no organized football until Junior High, and no organized soccer until at least High School. (I think even then there was too much emphasis on organized sports.) These days, however, kids who have barely mastered running are playing organized sports of all kinds. There's more special clothes (although they may be allowed to get these dirty), more waiting in line, and more micro-management.

I hate to say this, but I think our culture's view of raising children is similar in kind and principle – although not yet in degree – to the Communist and Nazi view. To be sure, organization and structure can be positive ideas, but many children are hyper-managed. In the end, I believe many micro-managed, overly regimented youngsters will surprise their parents and throw off all restraint when they get the opportunity to do so.

Over criticize and get angry when they act their age: It is so easy for us parents to be overly critical of our children. As adults we have learned to master many skills, but we have forgotten how difficult they were to learn when we were children. We see many tasks as being simple and assume every child should be able to perform them with ease. Then, when our children mess up, we are critical of them and may insult them – even though we may have messed up just as much when we were children.

Children should certainly and forcefully be disciplined when they do something they know is wrong. We discipline our children when they lie, cheat, hit, bite, disobey, or disrespect authority. However, a child should never be disciplined for doing his best and failing. A child who does what he knows is wrong should be punished, but a child who innocently errs should be taught. A child who makes an honest mistake should be kindly told what he did wrong and shown how to do the job correctly. Too many of us yell, criticize, and insult as a shortcut for teaching.

One specific manifestation of the overly critical parent is the one who disciplines his child for acting his age. It seems some parents expect adult behavior from their children almost from birth. Perhaps the baby who makes noises in church needs a little patience instead of a spanking. Perhaps breakable or precious items should be kept out of an exploring toddler's reach instead of placing these items within his reach and then punishing him for touching them. Perhaps our older child's lapses in judgment should be judged within the context of the child's age and ability. This is a matter of discernment and may differ from child to child, so it's likely that sincere people will disagree about what age children should be expected to do certain things. To one parent a child's error may be innocent and to another the same error may be lazy negligence. However, there should be some grace given for age. Some of us simply have unrealistic expectations as to what kind of behavior should be expected of young children. Our culture is beginning to advocate school for 3 and 4-year-olds, reading for infants, organized baseball for 6-year-olds, and dating for 12-year-olds. Do you think maybe we are expecting adult behavior (in some areas) too soon?

Conclusion: In an age when so many parents are weak-willed and overly permissive and Christian parents are trying to rediscover biblical principles of discipline, an essay advocating less criticism, discipline, and structure may leave the wrong impression. I don't want to be misunderstood. I believe children need constructive criticism, discipline that includes spanking, and structure. However, sometimes we lose our balance and limit, criticize, and discipline our children too much and for the wrong reasons. God's commands seem restrictive to many, but consider how much God permits us to do in comparison with what He has forbidden us. Starting in the Garden of Eden, there was only one forbidden fruit. Everything else was permitted. The Mosaic Law limited and regulated many things, but the list of permitted things would have been infinitely longer than the list of forbidden and regulated things. In fact, the Law of Moses is miniscule compared to the laws and regulations of our "enlightened" American system. We are, indeed, permissive when it comes to sin. If you're a homosexual, an adulterer, or a baby killer, this is a great place to live. But overall, we are severely over-regulated and much more restricted than the Israelites were under God's Law.

And our government reflects our parenting style. We are quite permissive of sin, such as disobedience, disrespect, violence, and dishonesty – we don't have the will to discipline our children for holiness, but we regulate, structure, and criticize many of our children into exasperation. It is my opinion that anyone who sends his young child away for formal schooling is over-regulating his child by delegation. But even in the home, many of us are prone to be overly restrictive. We reflexively say "no" to our children's requests, we micromanage and structure them unnecessarily, and we humiliate them when they do anything that doesn't work out well. It takes love, patience, and self-control (do these sound familiar?) to supervise, train, and protect a child, while maintaining an encouraging, positive environment where most things are permitted. God has been this way with us, so perhaps we can be more God-like and treat our children similarly.

"Now the Lord is the Spirit, and where the Spirit of the Lord is, there is liberty." (2 Cor. 3:17)

War of the Siblings

Having so many children, I tend to get asked a lot of questions. From some of those inquiries I get the feeling that people think that there is a lot of fighting and quarrelling going on in large families. I understand how they get to that conclusion. They probably see the discord in smaller families and just multiply it by two or three or six. Arguing and fighting is part of the sinful human nature, but how do we deal with it between our children?

We all have seen families where absolutely no quarreling is allowed and the parents will intervene at the first notice of a disagreement. On the other hand, there are also those families where just about anything goes and the parents rarely get involved. I am thankful to say that quarreling is not a big problem in our house, but it still happens. We have a few set rules that apply to quarreling and they are:

No physical aggression. No biting, hitting, kicking, pushing, etc. I do know that some people feel that physical aggression is natural and good – especially for boys. It helps them learn how to deal with controversy, gives them confidence, helps them find their place, and gives them a sort of respect in the eyes of others. I don't agree with that. Physical aggression is natural, but it is part of our old sinful nature and no longer are we to live by that. God has called us to peaceful, productive relations with people, and physical aggression doesn't fit in with that.

No name calling or insults. That is disrespectful and not proper for the people of God.

No accusing people of things you have no proof of. No one wants to be treated like that.

The question is left: when do we as parents step in? I think I can safely say that the younger the children, the more we step in. They need to be taught how to deal with these problems rather than allowing their natural tendencies to dominate. Also, the smallest ones are definitely at a major disadvantage and may not even really understand what is going on. We tend to step back and stay out of it when the controversy is between older kids. It is good for them to be able to solve it on their own rather than running to us all the time or having us solve it all the time. We intervene only when we feel it is necessary. A few examples of such situations are:

When the situation continues to escalate. Nothing is being solved and things are only getting worse. We don't want anyone to be bowing to temptation or anyone getting hurt.

When the situation isn't escalating but it's not ending, either. Again, nothing is being solved and it may develop into something worse.

The apparent outcome is unfair or unjust.

Definite unchristian behavior is being exhibited.

A child's behavior requires parental discipline. This discipline is not to be neglected, nor conducted by the sibling, nor should it take the form of revenge between the siblings.

If we get called into the quarrel by one of the children we try to quickly assess what is going on and then decide how much we should involve ourselves. Say two children are playing a game alone and one comes in saying, "The dice said five but he moved six spaces." Meanwhile the accused cheater is vehemently denying it. We can ask them what they think the possible solutions are and what would be fair. If the kids are younger, we can give them options. For the oldest kids we may say, "You guys are old enough to settle this yourselves." Or say one child is yelling because a sibling did something he "didn't like." My responses may include: "Did she know you don't like that? Did you ever tell her? Then tell her now and let me know if she does it again." Our reactions may vary a great deal depending on the children involved, their ages, and the quarrel.

I would like to make a comment about games such as "rough-housing" or "giving people a hard time" or "innocent teasing." We put a stop to those games when they no longer seem innocent or fun but rather mean-spirited and hurtful. I think parents have a good feeling for when the line gets crossed.

Disagreements are going to happen and it may be hard to know what our proper reaction should be. We can use these opportunities not only to teach our children about problem-solving, but more importantly about what a Christian response should be. We can teach them about showing mercy to others and forgiving when they've been wronged. We can even teach them that it's OK to be wronged or to let others have the more advantageous position. We can teach them about sharing, justice, fairness, bearing one another's burdens, and living at peace. We can teach them about being Christ-like in our relations with others. It is to these things that we are called as the people of God.

"If possible, so far as it depends on you, be at peace with all men." (Romans 12:18)

"So then we pursue the things which make for peace and the building up of one another." (Romans 14:19)

Balancing the Rod

Professional experts' opposition to spanking

It is clear that the tradition of spanking children has fallen into disrepute in the eyes of our culture – especially among child care "experts" and psychologists, who consider spanking a form of child abuse. The American Academy of Pediatrics states, "Spanking may relieve a parent's frustration for the moment and extinguish the undesirable behavior for a brief time. But it is the least effective way to discipline. It is harmful emotionally to both parent and child. Not only can it result in physical harm, but it teaches children that violence is an acceptable way to discipline or express anger. While stopping the behavior temporarily, it does not teach alternative behavior. It also interferes with the development of trust, a sense of security, and effective communication. (Spanking often becomes the method of communication.) It also may cause emotional pain and resentment." To ensure there be no misunderstanding of its views, the top of the page containing the previous statement reads, "The American Academy of Pediatrics strongly opposes striking a child."

According to the American Academy of Child & Adolescent Psychiatry, "Corporal punishment signals to the child that a way to settle interpersonal conflicts is to use physical force and inflict pain. Such children may in turn resort to such behavior themselves. They may also fail to develop trusting, secure relationships with adults and fail to evolve the necessary skills to settle disputes or wield authority in less violent ways. Supervising adults who will fully humiliate children and punish by force and pain are often causing more harm than they prevent."

A similar point of view is expressed by the National Association of Social Workers. This organization has written, "It is becoming increasingly clear that physical punishment of children in any setting is not an effective way to encourage desirable behavior; to enhance children's ability to learn expected skills, abilities, and attitudes that are necessary for effective interaction with others; or to develop self-esteem and a sense of morality."

Recently I picked up three books from the public library on the topic of child discipline. The first book described spanking as "risky" and stated we now have more "loving" and "humane" ways to discipline. It also said, "We now know too much about how to raise children in healthy ways to return to methods of the past," and that our society is now changing to one "in which parents use kinder, more thoughtful, and more psychologically appropriate methods of discipline." The second book echoed the same philosophy, saying that "nonviolent" ways of discipline are "higher forms of discipline" and that this "reflects our evolution as thinking human beings." The third book discussed spanking as a recognized type of discipline, but as a concession and not as a recommendation. It stated that spanking has "marginal value" but it is risky and more likely to be harmful than beneficial. What harmful risks do these "experts" say are inherent to spanking? Well, how about these: parental guilt, parental loss of control, damaged relationships, physical injury, psychological damage (including anger and low self-esteem), and violent behavior on the part of the child.

These risks are taken so seriously that nine European nations have made spanking illegal. These countries include: Sweden, Finland, Denmark, Norway, Austria, Cyprus, Croatia, Latvia, and Italy. In the United States, "At least 22 states, including Maryland and the District of Columbia, prohibit corporal punishment of foster children, and specialists say that most states have some restrictions. Child-care experts contend that spanking children who may already have been neglected or abused has the potential to do substantial damage." (*Washington Post*, 3 Sept. 2000) In the schools, too, corporal punishment is being outlawed. The National Education Association writes, "Many child advocates, however, view corporal punishment of students as a form of child abuse, even when corporal punishment has otherwise been legal. In addition to actions by many individual school districts, 23 states have outlawed corporal punishment in schools, most in the last few years. ... NEA's current (1992) resolution on discipline states: 'The Association also believes that corporal punishment should not be used as a means of disciplining students.' " Of course, we are all aware of the true stories of people who have been tried as child abusers simply because they have spanked their children. Social workers have entered private homes without search warrants and terrorized families – to the point of strip-searching children in search of bruises.

It is truly impressive, if you are impressed by worldly credentials, how all the most respected professional organizations representing those considered most knowledgeable about children (pediatricians, child psychiatrists, social workers, and educators) have concluded that spanking is unnecessary, risky, and usually harmful.

The arguments for corporal punishment

How could I support spanking a child in the face of such overwhelming expert opinion against it? I could argue from personal experience that my parents spanked me and I turned out normal. (OK, that isn't such a strong argument.) I could argue that almost everyone I know has been spanked and wouldn't say it harmed them. I could argue that the great majority of parents in our country still spank their children. Recently I read somewhere that 81% of parents still spank their children. (Majority rules, right?) I could argue that there are experts out there who disagree with the findings of their professional organizations. And I could also argue that the experts cannot prove from the evidence that a modest amount of spanking harms children at all. In fact, if you go back two or three generations (when spanking a child wasn't controversial) you may find that people in general were more polite, more honest, and more responsible.

However, none of my arguments and none of their arguments matter in the least because God has left us sufficient testimony through His Word for me to say with confidence that spanking is recommended and offers tremendous benefits. In fact, the Bible's warnings about the dangers of withholding corporal punishment from a child should "put the fear of God," so to speak, into anyone who doubts whether spanking is necessary.

In the Scriptures it is written, "He who withholds his rod hates his son, but he who loves him disciplines him diligently." (Prov. 13:24) "Foolishness is bound up in the heart of a child; the rod of discipline will remove it far from him." (Prov. 22:15) "Do not hold back discipline from the child, although you strike him with the rod, he will not die. You shall strike him with the rod and rescue his soul from

Sheol." (Prov. 23:13-14) And, "The rod and reproof give wisdom, but a child who gets his own way brings shame to his mother." (Prov. 29:15)

Judging the experts

Given the clear biblical statement on the matter, why do you suppose the professional organizations for pediatricians, child psychiatrists, social workers, and teachers all oppose corporal punishment? I can only think of two potential explanations. Either the pediatricians, child psychiatrists, social workers, and teachers who make up these organizations don't know the Scriptures that deal with this issue and have come up with their own ideas, or they do know the Scriptures that deal with this issue and have come up with their own ideas. The first scenario says the so-called experts are foolish because they are ignorant; the second says the so-called experts are foolish because they are wicked.

And it seems much more likely that they are wicked because nearly everyone in our culture knows that the saying, "If you spare the rod, you'll spoil the child," is derived from the teachings of Scripture. Anyone who makes it his business to pose as an expert on raising children and knowingly advises great numbers of people to contradict the clear teachings of God's word is a wicked fool.

Contrary, then, to our learned experts, we should make corporal punishment a normal part of child discipline. And discipline – not anger – should be the reason we strike our children. Notice that three of the four verses we quoted in support of corporal punishment for children also mentioned discipline. The purpose of discipline is to drive the folly bound in the heart of a child far from him (Prov. 22:15), to save his soul from death (Prov. 23:13-14), and to impart wisdom (Prov. 29:15).

Of course, the motivation for corporal discipline is love. It is hard for us to inflict pain on the child we love, but it is far better than allowing Satan to destroy him. This is the same way God deals with His children. It is written, "My son, do not regard lightly the discipline of the Lord, nor faint when you are reproved by Him; for those whom the Lord loves He disciplines, and He scourges every son whom He receives ... He disciplines us for our good, so that we may share His holiness. All discipline for the moment seems not to be joyful, but sorrowful; yet to those who have been trained by it, afterwards it yields the peaceful fruit of righteousness." (Heb. 12:5b-6, 10b-11)

Questions about "the rod":

When should I spank my child? The Scriptures do not tell us exactly when we are to use "the rod." We know from the Scriptures already mentioned that the rod is supposed to rid a child of folly and save his soul from death. It seems clear to me that a child who breaks a plate by accident is not committing folly or endangering his eternal soul. The rod, then, was not meant to punish children for honest mistakes or lack of competency, which are prevalent in children due to their physical limitations and lack of experience. The rod is reserved for correcting behavior that if left unchecked would threaten the child's soul.

What kind of behavior would that be? Certainly, disobedience of God's commands would endanger the child's soul. God said, "Not one of the men who saw my glory and the miraculous signs I performed in Egypt and in the desert but who *disobeyed* me and tested me ten times – not one of them will ever see the land I promised on oath to their forefathers. No one who has treated me with contempt will ever see it." (Num. 14:22-23, NIV) This theme is repeated in the New Testament in the book of Hebrews, which says, "And to whom did God swear that they would never enter his rest if not to those who *disobeyed*?" (Heb. 3:18, NIV)

What has God commanded that a child could disobey? We need look no further than the Ten Commandments, where God said, "You shall not take the name of the LORD your God in vain, for the LORD will not leave him unpunished who takes His name in vain." "Honor your father and your mother." "You shall not murder." "You shall not steal." "You shall not bear false witness against your neighbor."

This is the reason we spank our children for lying, stealing, hitting, and for disobeying or disrespecting their parents.

Is there an age limit to corporal punishment? There is no age limitation mentioned in the Scriptures. In fact, corporal punishment was allowed under the Law of Moses even for adults. God's word says, "Then it shall be if the wicked man deserves to be beaten, the judge shall then make him lie down and be beaten in his presence with the number of stripes according to his guilt. He may beat him forty times but no more, so that he does not beat him with many more stripes than these and your brother is not degraded in your eyes." (Deut. 25:2-3) Of course, the death penalty is the ultimate corporal punishment and it was much more common under the Law than it is in our culture. However, if the parent spanks the child properly when he is young, he probably won't need to be spanked when he is older.

Regarding babies: we don't normally spank a child before he is a year old, but two-year-olds get the most spankings from us. I don't have a Bible verse to support an age at which spankings should begin, but we think the child should clearly understand the rules before he is punished for breaking them.

How hard should I spank? The purpose of spanking is to inflict enough pain on the child to effect a change in behavior. It is common for many parents (and especially mothers) to spank too gently. They do not spank hard enough to inflict any meaningful pain on the child and this may have little effect on the rebellious child. In this case, the severity of the spanking must be increased. On the other hand, there are people who spank too severely. I don't think a spanking should be a risk to the child's physical well-being, but the Social Services standard that there can never be visible signs of a spanking is too strict. It isn't difficult to find a good balance between excessive gentleness and excessive severity.

What should I use to spank my child? The Scriptures do not specify the size, weight, or material of the rod. The important principle is that pain is inflicted on the child to correct disobedient behavior. I don't think it makes a lot of difference what is used to spank a child, so long as it doesn't harm or deface him. We have always used our hands for a couple of reasons. First, my hands are always conveniently with me and second, my hands are more sensitive to how much force I am using. I disagree with those who find psychological reasons for not using your hands. I don't think children are confused as to the source of the pain – whether it is a belt, a rod, or a parent's hand.

Conclusion:

It doesn't matter that educated child-care experts oppose corporal punishment. No matter how many years of school they have attended and no matter how many children they have seen in their professional lives, they oppose the clear teachings of Scripture and shouldn't be heeded. The Scriptures are clear: "He who withholds his rod hates his son." (Prov. 13:24a) We must also remember that the motivation for corporal punishment is love. We care enough for the child's eternal destiny that we attempt to drive rebelliousness out of the child before it becomes an intractable part of his character. And when we experience hardship or pain, we must remember that God inflicts pain on us for our welfare as well. "My son, do not regard lightly the discipline of the Lord, nor faint when you are reproved by Him; for those whom the Lord loves He disciplines, and He scourges every son whom He receives." (Heb. 12:5b-6)

Lost Children (part 1)

One of the saddest things a Christian parent can experience is the realization that his child is lost. I don't mean lost in the sense that the parents don't know where the child is – although that would be frightening – but lost in the sense that the child is living in sin and seems to have rejected the Lord. In other words, he is lost spiritually.

When we see Christian parents with a godless child, how do we react? Some pity the Christian parents for the trial they are going through. Some judge the parents as having been negligent or incompetent in raising their children. If the rebellious child belongs to us, we may become defensive, guilt ridden, or ashamed.

In this essay, we will discuss the reasons a child rejects the Gospel. In the future, we will talk about what – if anything – we can do to raise godly children and what we should do if we have lost or fear we are losing a child.

Why Christian parents have ungodly children:

Reason #1 – God chooses not to save all the children of godly parents (or, it's the child's fault): The first thing we need to understand is that children are saved by God's grace and not by their parents. The Apostle John wrote, "But as many as received Him, to them He gave the right to become children of God, even to those who believe in His name, who were born, not of blood nor of the will of the flesh nor of the will of man, but of God." (John 1:12-13) Paul adds, "For by grace you have been saved through faith; and that not of yourselves, it is the gift of God; not as a result of works, so that no one may boast." (Eph. 2:8-9)

When we teach our children the Gospel and see one child after the other come to faith in Jesus Christ it is tempting to give ourselves some credit for our children's salvation. This is especially true when we see Christians, who we consider poor parents, losing many of their children to the world and – with few exceptions – the children of the ungodly following in their parents' footsteps. We seem to think the children of the ungodly are saved by grace, but that our children are saved by godly parenting. The truth, however, is that we cannot save ourselves, our children, or anyone else. It is by the grace of God that our children are saved.

A biblical example is cited by Paul, who writes, "And not only this, but there was Rebekah also, when she had conceived twins by one man, our father Isaac; for though the twins were not yet born and had not done anything good or bad, so that God's purpose according to His choice would stand, not because of works but because of Him who calls, it was said to her, 'the older will serve the younger.' Just as it is written, 'Jacob I loved, but Esau I hated.' " (Rom. 9:10-13)

We must acknowledge, then, that God takes responsibility for which children will be saved and that having a godly parent – such as Isaac – does not guarantee that our children will be saved. Paul writes, "For He says to Moses, 'I will have mercy on whom I have mercy, and I will have compassion on whom I have compassion.' So then it does not depend on the man who wills or the man who runs, but on God who has mercy." (Rom. 9:15-16)

This is sobering and sad in one respect, but it is liberating in another. It is sobering to think that God might choose not to have compassion on all our children and it is liberating in the sense that a godless child doesn't necessarily mean we are awful parents.

We must be careful, however, not to blame God for our ungodly children. God may take the credit for saving our children, but God will not take the blame for their sins. James writes, "Let no one say when he is tempted, 'I am being tempted by God'; for God cannot be tempted by evil, and He Himself does not tempt anyone. But each one is tempted when he is carried away and enticed by his own lust. Then when lust has conceived, it gives birth to sin; and when sin is accomplished, it brings forth death. Do not be deceived, my beloved brethren. Every good thing given and every perfect gift is from above." (Jam. 1:13-17a)

Therefore, each child must bear the responsibility for his own sins. Ezekiel says, "The person who sins will die. The son will not bear the punishment for the father's iniquity, nor will the father bear the punishment for the son's iniquity; the righteousness of the righteous will be upon himself, and the wickedness of the wicked will be upon himself." (Ez. 18:20) Every ungodly child, then, must be held responsible for his own sins.

Reason #2 – Children are lost through poor parenting: After acknowledging that our children are saved solely by God's grace and lost solely by their own sins, how then can we say that children are saved or lost by good or bad parenting? The answer, of course, is that God saves people through certain means and the witness of parents is one of the most effective means. God's grace comes to us is through faith. Faith comes through the Word of God and the Word of God comes through messengers. Very often, these messengers are our parents.

We know from experience that some messengers of the Gospel are very effective and others are not. When the evangelist speaks God's word with power and conviction, and when the evangelist's life is consistent with his words, he is much more likely to have an effective ministry. On the other hand, a timid evangelist who speaks more human wisdom than God's word, and whose life is a worldly contradiction to his words, will probably not be an effective minister of the Gospel. Granted, it is God's word and not the evangelist that works faith in the listener, but a timid and worldly messenger garbles the message and confuses his hearers.

Since we Christian parents are God's messengers to our children it is the same with us. Parents who speak God's word to their children with conviction and whose lives are consistent with those words will have an effective ministry to their children. Parents who are timid or worldly will be a stumbling block to their children and the consequences may be severe and eternal.

I wish every parent could be consoled with the message that they are not accountable for their ungodly children, but it wouldn't be the truth. God expects us to sound a clear signal to our children to warn them of the consequences of their evil deeds. God appointed us to be watchmen for our households the same way God appointed Ezekiel to be a watchman for the house of Israel. God told Ezekiel, "Now as for you, son of man, I have appointed you a watchman for the house of Israel; so you will hear a message from My mouth and give them warning from Me. When I say to the wicked, 'O wicked man, you will surely die,' and you do not speak to warn the wicked from his way, that wicked man shall die in his iniquity, but his blood I will require from your hand. But if you on your part warn a wicked man to turn from his way and he does not turn from his way, he will die in his iniquity, but you have delivered your life." (Ez. 33:7-9)

So then, the Christian parent who acts as a faithful watchman – clearly warning of God's wrath against evildoers and offering the good news of forgiveness through faith in Jesus Christ – will not be liable for his ungodly child. However, when the Christian parent does not carry a clear message to his children – that parent will be held accountable.

Ways Parents Garble the Message:

#1 – Parents sometimes neglect their obligation as ministers of God's word to their children: Parents should be reading God's word to their children at an early age. As soon as children are able to read, the Scriptures should be placed in their hands and a habit of daily Bible reading should be expected. When we consider the important role God's word has in our salvation and in the process of spiritual maturity, it is hard to understand why some parents make God's word such a low priority in their children's lives. Jesus said, "It is written, 'Man shall not live on bread alone, but on every world that proceeds out of the mouth of God.' " (Mat. 4:4) When we don't make God's word a daily habit for our children we stunt them spiritually and say by example that we don't think God's word is all that important. All Christian parents want their children to be people of faith. Since faith comes through hearing and hearing through the word of God, one would expect that Christian parents would make God's word a priority. Instead, many leave the impression that God's word isn't necessary to live each day, and then they wonder why their children don't have faith.

#2 – Parents are sometimes too lenient with their children: When our children are disobedient, when they lie, or when they are violent they should be punished. That punishment should be consistent, firm, and include corporal punishment. Solomon says, "He who withholds his rod hates his son, but he who loves him disciplines him diligently." (Prov. 13:24) He adds, "Foolishness is bound up in the heart of a child; the rod of discipline will remove it far from him." (Prov. 22:15) The advice of Scripture seems harsh to a culture that has rejected most forms of corporal punishment. Many "experts" consider spanking child abuse and even most murderers get away with an extended form of "time out."

Given our cultural aversion to discipline, it has become commonplace – even in Christian families – to see children challenge the authority of their parents and get away with it. Parents tell their children they can't have something or do something, but relent when their children make a fuss. When we do this we teach them to despise authority – not only our authority but God's authority as well. God says in the Scriptures that children are to obey their parents in everything. Therefore, when parents allow their children to disobey them, they are allowing them to disobey God. Parents who are afraid to discipline their children are really telling them that the negative consequences of sin and rebelliousness are small. Someday our disobedient children may go from snitching cookies and refusing to honor their bedtime to even more destructive sins, such as sexual immorality and drunkenness.

This was the case for Eli the priest in the days of Samuel. Eli did not restrain his sons and God cursed the entire family forever. The Scriptures say, "The LORD said to Samuel, 'Behold, I am about to do a thing in Israel at which both ears of everyone who hears it will tingle. In that day I will carry out against Eli all that I have spoken concerning his house, from beginning to end. For I have told him that I am about to judge his house forever for the iniquity which he knew, because his sons brought a curse on themselves and he did not rebuke them. Therefore I have sworn to the house of Eli that the iniquity of Eli's house shall not be atoned for by sacrifice or offering forever.' " (1 Sam. 3:11-14) Therefore, when we fail to discipline our children we "hate" them (Prov. 13:24) and we threaten to bring a curse down on our entire family.

#3 – Parents are sometimes overly harsh with their children: Although God disciplines us and expects us to discipline the children He gives us, God is not harsh and He commands us not to be harsh with our children. Paul said, "Fathers, do not provoke your children to anger." (Eph. 6:4) And, "Fathers, do not exasperate your children, so that they will not lose heart." (Col. 3:21) The truth is that we do not always treat our children very well. Sometimes we vent our anger about other things on our children, sometimes we treat them badly simply because they irritate us, and sometimes we treat them badly simply because they act their age.

We are also harsh when we are never satisfied with our children's work or fail to praise and encourage them. Many of us have experienced an employer or a parent who could not be pleased and it is an awful experience. Therefore, we need to control our tempers and our tongues, and offer some encouragement to our children or we risk turning our kids against us and against the message of salvation we bring them.

#4 – Parents sometimes contradict each other: The most obvious example would be when one parent is a believer and the other is not. In that case, the children are presented with two views of the world and, sadly, many are led astray by the unbelieving parent. Even when the believing parent is not led astray by the unbelieving spouse – as Solomon was – and the Christian parent speaks and acts in accordance with God's word, that message is garbled by the simultaneous and conflicting message and lifestyle of the unbelieving parent. That is one of the reasons the Bible so clearly prohibits us from knowingly marrying an unbeliever. Clearly, Solomon and his family were heavily influenced by the idol worship of his foreign wives, and Israel, too, was led astray when they intermarried with the heathen around them. Likewise, good king Jehoshaphat's family was decimated by his decision to allow his son to marry the daughter of Ahab and Jezebel. Therefore, Paul warns us against being yoked with unbelievers and counsels widows who remarry to marry "in the Lord."

Even when both parents are Christian, however, the Gospel message can be garbled when there is conflict between the father and the mother. When the parents regularly argue in front of the children, the credibility of both are severely diminished. If the parents don't respect each other, why should the children respect their parents? If the parents are the messengers of the Gospel and they have lost credibility and respect in the eyes of the children, the children are less likely to heed the message.

#5 – Parents don't protect their children from harmful influences: When the Gospel message is consistent inside the home, the message may be garbled by influences from outside the home. Many Christians send their children to public schools, which convey an unchristian world-view and foster close friendships between our children and unbelieving children. Given that children in the public schools spend at least half their day in school and may spend more time doing homework or playing with unbelieving school friends, it is inevitable that Satan will use the opportunity to lead some of our children astray.

Other influences that compete with the Gospel come from the movies, music, and computers that may absorb many hours of our children's time and fill their minds with compelling images of violence, rebellion, and sexual immorality. We spend money on our children for entertainment that is filled with the vain use of God's name, cursing, vulgar language, graphic violence, and graphic immorality. This kind of entertainment also promotes antichristian philosophy and encourages a barrage of subtle evils as well.

Paul says, "Finally, brethren, whatever is true, whatever is honorable, whatever is right, whatever is pure, whatever is lovely, whatever is of good repute, if there is any excellence and if anything worthy of praise, dwell on these things." (Phil. 4:8) "But immorality or any impurity or greed must not even be named among you, as is proper among saints; and there must be no filthiness and silly talk, or coarse jesting, which are not fitting, but rather giving of thanks." (Eph. 5:3-4) "For we are the temple of the living God; just as God said, 'I will dwell in them and walk among them; and I will be their God, and they shall be my people.' 'Therefore, come out from their midst and be separate,' says the Lord, 'and do not touch what is unclean; and I will welcome you.' 'And I will be a father to you, and you shall be sons and daughters to Me,' says the Lord Almighty.' " (2 Cor. 6:16b-18) When parents allow their children to flirt with unholiness they are playing with a fire that may consume their offspring. It isn't worth the risk.

#6 – Parents sometimes don't spend enough time with their children: One reason children don't get a clear Gospel message from their parents is because the parents don't set aside enough time to properly give the message. Sometimes both parents work long hours, run errands, have date night, have social engagements with friends, taxi their children to activities, and attend age-segregated programs at church. Meanwhile, the kids may attend school, do their homework, play with friends, participate in sports or other activities, and also attend age-segregated church programs. In this situation, parents and children have very little time for each other. It is difficult to minister the Gospel to our children when we hardly see each other.

Typically, the little time parents do spend with their children is not spent in spiritually edifying ways. We may watch movies or television shows that leave little or no time for teaching or worship. It is a mistake for us to abdicate our responsibility to raise our children "in the fear and admonition of the Lord" and assume that the Christian school or the church will do it for us. The Bible gives the father the task of teaching his children about God – perhaps because the close and trusting relationship children are supposed to have with their parents make the parents ideal messengers of the Gospel. Parents have a wonderful opportunity to introduce their children to their heavenly Father and to help their children develop a close relationship with Him. However, many Christian parents have made themselves mere acquaintances to their children and, even worse, they have made God a distant relative or historical figure with whom their children have no personal relationship. Therefore, parents should devote enough time to their children to teach them the things of God and to build a relationship that will increase the chances that their kids will listen to what they have to say.

Conclusion: If we have loved our children, been faithful in getting them in the habit of reading God's word, have diligently taught them the meaning of what they have read, have regularly prayed with them and for them, and have lived a life that conforms with our teaching, we can be confident that God will reward our efforts. If, under these circumstances, some of our children should reject God's purpose for their lives, we will surely be grieved but will not be held accountable for their sins. On the other hand, if we have failed to immerse our children in God's word, have not disciplined them properly, have not protected them from worldly influences, or have been worldly ourselves, we must bear some guilt for having a child who rejects the Lord. We have been negligent in our duty as watchmen for our households by allowing our poor witness to muddle the Gospel message.

Thankfully, the grace of our Lord Jesus Christ will reach even to our failings as parents. There were many righteous men in the Bible who had suspect records as parents. Isaac blatantly favored his ungodly son Esau.

Jacob, too, had a record of obvious favoritism that extended to his wives. That favoritism caused his sons to be jealous of Joseph to the extent that they nearly killed him and sold him into slavery. Simeon and Levi killed an entire city for the sins of one man and Judah thought he was sleeping with a shrine prostitute when it was actually his daughter-in-law. Consider David also, who was called a man after God's heart and yet had sons who were guilty of murder, rape, and treason.

There are many other examples, but the lesson here is that poor parenting – even though it has profound eternal consequences – can be covered by the blood of Jesus. Anyone who has received Jesus by faith needs to learn his lesson, change his behavior, and leave his guilt at the foot of the cross. Having a child who is led astray at least in part by our poor parenting should not mean that we live the rest of our days in inconsolable grief, shame, and guilt. After repenting of our sins, we need to accept the peace and joy that are available to us in Christ Jesus. Since there is no such thing as a perfect parent, this should be good advice for us all.

Lost Children (part 2)

We have just discussed how children become spiritually lost. This time, we will talk about what we can do to prevent our children from going astray and what we can do if it seems they have turned away from the faith.

It is an awful, heart wrenching experience to see our children being lost to the world. None of us wants that bitter experience to happen to us, but we know that parents since the beginning have struggled and sometimes lost the spiritual battle for their children. Adam and Eve's son Cain was known as an evil man and the murderer of his brother Abel. Noah was shamed by son Ham, causing Noah to pronounce a prophetic curse on Ham's son Canaan. Our spiritual father Abraham had a son named Ishmael, whom God described in this way: "He will be a wild donkey of a man, his hand will be against everyone, and everyone's hand will be against him; and he will live to the east of all his brothers." (Genesis 16:12) Isaac had a son named Esau, who was singled out in the Scriptures as a godless and sexually immoral man. (Hebrews 12:16) Jacob's sons were guilty of murder, sexual immorality, incest, and selling their brother into slavery. The Lord put to death Er and Onan, the sons of Judah, because they were wicked. God also put to death the oldest two sons of Aaron. We could go on in detail about the wickedness of the sons of Samuel, David, Solomon, Jehoshaphat, and Hezekiah. The lesson here is that it has been painfully common for godly parents to have ungodly children. Some of our wayward children, like the prodigal son, come to their senses and return to us. Others are lost for good.

Things we can do to prevent our children from being lost:

#1 – Make sure they are reading the Scriptures every day: We can teach our children proper manners and morals, but if their hearts aren't changed it will benefit them little. Their unconverted hearts will usually succumb to the temptations of evil once the structural barriers of living in a Christian home are eliminated. We shouldn't be surprised, then, when our "good kids" who have a very shallow knowledge of the Scriptures go crazy when they begin to gain their independence. If we want our kids to have a sincere faith in Jesus Christ we must understand that faith comes by hearing and hearing by the word of God. We must, therefore, immerse them in God's word so we can know we are providing our children with the means God uses to bring them to faith and to mature them spiritually. When we help our children come to faith and nurture that faith, they are not as likely to be swayed by false teaching or led away into serious sin. God's word, then, is crucial to our children's spiritual well-being, but many Christian parents don't get their children into the habit of reading their Bibles on a regular basis. This is probably the greatest failing of Christian parenting today and a major reason we are losing our kids – our kids don't know God's word.

The encouraging thing here is that correcting the problem is so easy. In a land where God's word is accessible to all and very inexpensive, all of our reading children should be reading their Bibles daily. It's just a matter of placing the Scriptures in our children's hands and seeing that they read it. In our family we post a Bible reading chart and every reading family member – including the parents – writes down the Scripture they have read that day. Our new readers read only ten verses a day. As their reading improves we lengthen their reading. By age eight or nine they are reading four chapters a day – two chapters in the morning and two chapters at night. We also read one chapter of Scripture at family devotions. Using this system, each child will have normally read through the entire Bible by 9-years-of-age and then once a year from that point on. This works in most cases, but sometimes we quiz the kids on what they have read because we have caught some of our children writing down readings they never read. Thus, a system of regular Bible reading is necessary, but holding everyone accountable is also important to make sure no one is falling through the cracks. We believe the teaching they get from the Holy Spirit through the Word has done more than anything to keep our kids on the right path. It has helped them survive spiritually in the face of worldly influences and less than perfect parenting.

#2 – Pray for and with your children: This is an area I need to work on as a parent. When we had a small family I would always pray for my infant children whenever I put them in the crib. There were times when I told my wife I wanted to pray together for our children every night before bed, but I never made it a habit. I'm sure there are others like me who have underestimated the importance of prayer. God is certainly sovereign over the affairs of men, but the prayers of men do matter. James said, "You lust and do not have; so you commit murder. You are envious and cannot obtain; so you fight and quarrel. You do not have because you do not ask." (James 4:2) And, "The effective prayer of a righteous man can accomplish much." (James 5:16) James continued, "Elijah was a man with a nature like ours, and he prayed earnestly that it would not rain, and it did not rain on the earth for three years and six months. Then he prayed again, and the sky poured rain and the earth produced its fruit." (James 5:17-18) Joshua prayed that the sun and the moon would stand still in the sky so he could continue to fight against the Canaanites and the Scriptures say, "So the sun stood still, and the moon stopped, until the nation avenged themselves of their enemies. Is it not written in the book of Jashar? And the sun stopped in the middle of the sky and did not hasten to go down for about a whole day." (Josh. 10:13) Jesus said, "Have faith in God. Truly I say to you, whoever says to this mountain, 'Be taken up and cast into the sea,' and does not doubt in his heart, but believes that what he says is going to happen, it will be granted him. Therefore I say to you, all things for which you pray and ask, believe that you have received them, and they will be granted you." (Mark 11:22-24)

Therefore, we should pray. We should pray on behalf of our children that God would make them strong in the faith and protect them from the evil one. We shouldn't wait until a problem has developed, but instead begin praying for them immediately. To make sure our prayers aren't hindered, we need to heed the Scriptures that tell us to treat our wives well, to forgive those who sin against us, and to pray with pure motives. When Jesus walked the earth He answered the prayers of many grieving parents by casting out demons, healing the sick, and even raising the dead. God has shown a willingness to honor the requests of praying parents, so we must remember to pray.

#3 – Get your kids out of the public schools: Usually, no human cares more for the spiritual welfare of a child than his parents. When we send them off to public school in the care of teachers who may or may not be believers, in a classroom environment where Christian beliefs are taboo, among children who may, for the most part, be unbelievers, we are risking our children's eternal future for a "free" education. The public schools are not conducive to a child's spiritual growth. I don't recommend that anyone send his children there. It isn't worth the risk.

I grew up in the public schools and I was led astray by the friends I made along the way. My friends were considered clean-cut, but none of us had a relationship with God that had a noticeable impact on how we lived. The work that was done at home to teach me biblical truths was being undone by the people I spent most of my time with. Thankfully, the Lord chastened and humbled me until I came to my senses, but not every parent will see all their children return like the prodigal son.

Most parents take care to protect their kids from physical predators, but we lack sense when it comes to spiritual predators. In the book of Job, God describes the ostrich mother as a poor example of motherhood. God said of her, "For she abandons her eggs to the earth and warms them in the dust, and she forgets that a foot may crush them, or that a wild beast may trample them. She treats her young cruelly, as if they were not hers; though her labor be in vain, she is unconcerned." (Job 39:14-16)

In a spiritual sense, leaving our kids at a public school all day is like the ostrich that lays her eggs on the ground. It is true that some of her offspring may survive (just as children may survive the public school), but she exposes them to danger by making it easy for a predator to consume them – not seeming to care that all her work may be undone. We are naïve if we think the public school environment doesn't leave our children exposed to evil forces that can make our spiritual nurturing a vain effort. By homeschooling, we protect them from spiritual predators until they are old enough and strong enough to wield the weapons of spiritual warfare well enough to protect themselves. Our 5-year-olds are no more prepared for spiritual warfare than they are for physical warfare.

#4 – Do things as a family: One of the reasons we have so little influence over our children is that their "fun" activities tend to involve friends or acquaintances outside the family. Certainly, there is nothing inherently wrong with having fun with friends, but our ability to minister to our children will be greatly diminished if all their fun takes place outside the home. If we want to influence our children we should seek time with them. We can play baseball, pick fruit, visit a museum, have pizza together, or go to the park. It doesn't matter much what the activity is. When we work and play as a family we are building ties that will make our children more likely to want to please us and to accept our Christian beliefs – and these family ties can bind us long after the children leave home.

#5 – Choose your church wisely: Sadly, a common source of temptation for our kids comes from church youth groups. Sexual immorality, alcohol, and drugs are often common problems with the teenagers who attend church youth groups. In the church we used to attend, a youth group sleepover was held at the home of a family that had a boy in the group. The parents who owned the home were going to rent movies and were suggesting movies we would never consider watching. At the same church our son roomed at a youth group retreat with a boy who took off all his clothes and plopped himself on the bed. Later, this junior high school student suggested the boys call up the girls' rooms. This particular church had solid preaching and wonderful Christian music at its Sunday morning services and its large youth program attracted many parents of school-aged children.

I am more impressed with the quality of the youth than I am with the size of the youth group. It can be a challenge to find churches where the youth group doesn't pander to worldly behavior to help boost attendance. Youth group leaders have to be "hip" (or whatever they call that now) so the teenagers can "relate" to them. Christian teenage girls often attend youth group meetings in immodest attire.

Be careful, then, what youth program – if any – your older children attend. Just because a church sponsors the program doesn't mean that it is in your child's best interest to attend.

#6 – Don't allow your kids to be unequally yoked: While it is true that we should reach out to the lost world with the Gospel, that doesn't mean our closest relationships should be with those outside the faith. Paul says we are not to be unequally yoked with unbelievers. We understand that this means that we are not to choose an unbelieving spouse, but I believe it would apply to friendships, business partnerships, and other alliances as well. It seems to be a fair application of the principle to say that our children's best friends should not be unbelievers. Paul said, "Do not be deceived: Bad company corrupts good morals." (1Cor. 15:33) Christian parents, then, should know who their kids' friends are and compel their children, if necessary, to spend most of their time with believers.

#7 – Disallow corrupting movies, TV shows, music, and web sites: If the stuff we watched on TV or the songs we listened to on the radio were performed live in our house, many of us would be disgusted. We shouldn't allow our kids to fill their minds with violence, immorality, coarse humor, and raunchy lyrics.

Children aren't born with a need for offensive TV shows and music. Someone introduces the kids to this stuff and they develop a taste for it. Unfortunately, the vehicle by which kids are commonly introduced to media garbage is their parents. To protect our children we must first set the example and shield ourselves. Much of what passes for adult programming isn't fit for anyone to watch. We have the ability to ensure that our own home is a place where our kids won't pick up a taste for media filth.

We can also make sure our kids aren't soaking up media filth from their friends. If our kids go to other people's houses, they need to know that they are to maintain the radio and TV standards there or they will not be allowed to return.

#8 – Have a contagious form of Christianity:

Possibly the most important way to prevent our children from being lost is to possess a Christian walk that they can respect and look up to. If our Christian walk is just about going to church, attending a Bible study, and praying before meals and bedtime, our children may think the Christian life is nothing more than jumping through a few hoops and staying out of trouble. Our kids should see that our faith affects every area of our lives. They should see that it's something we're really passionate about. They should know that there is more meaning to life than having a good job, a nice family, good friends, and good health. Our kids need to see the Christian faith as something beautiful and noble and they need to see by our example that the life of a servant of Jesus Christ is a different and better calling than the life of the unbeliever.

What if we're losing them? What if they're lost?

If we see that our kids are headed down the wrong path we need to continue to insist that they read their Bibles daily, attend family devotions, attend church services, and participate in family activities. We should also continue to pray with them and for them – never giving up and never discounting the power of prayer to effect change.

We might also evaluate our own lives in case we have been a stumbling block to our children. Perhaps we've been too lenient or too harsh with them. Perhaps mother and father enforce different and conflicting standards in the home, or perhaps mother and father don't get along with each other very well. Maybe we've not spent enough time with our children or maybe we've set a poor example of Christian behavior for them. If any of these have been problems we need to repent of our sins and correct our own problems.

Finally, we need to disconnect our children, if possible, from the sources of ungodly influence. Sometimes a child may resist, but the parent must be strong and enforce the disconnection no matter how much the child complains. What I mean by disconnection is physical separation. This could involve taking the child out of school, discontinuing a friendship, leaving a youth program, or censoring media choices. As long as the child is living under the authority of his parents at home, these decisions to separate the child from ungodly influences must be enforced.

God willing, these things will steer him in the right direction. As long as the child is outwardly submissive most of the time, we should stay the course and pray that his heart will be changed over time. On the other hand, if the child is insubordinate and beyond correction he is a cancer that should be removed from the family – for his sake as well as for the sake of the other family members. Circumstances such as the age of the child may limit our options, but generally no child who engages in perpetual, willful, and substantial insubordination of parental authority should be allowed to continue in the home. Like the man involved in gross sexual immorality in 1 Corinthians 5, the rebellious child should be separated from the group and handed over to Satan so that his flesh may be punished in the hope of saving his soul. Under no circumstances should the child be allowed to enforce his rebellious will upon his parents, so that he is allowed to listen to offensive music, watch offensive TV shows and movies, attend a school that has proved a negative influence, or run around with an ungodly crowd. I'm sure some children have survived the sins of their youth and credit their longsuffering parents who allowed them to flaunt an ungodly lifestyle while living in the home, but I believe more children are lost that way than are saved.

My own mother was adamant about enforcing a reasonable curfew in our home. When I dropped out of college after my sophomore year, I chose to work 500 miles from home as a dishwasher to avoid having to live under my parents' rules. But I was nearly forced to come home almost immediately because I barely had enough to eat – I was so hungry I would eat what looked like untouched food on the dirty dishes. However, I lied about my previous work experience and landed a job as a manager trainee at a fast food restaurant. Things went well for me at first – I was the general manager of a fast food restaurant at age 20 and had a small salary about double the minimum wage, health insurance, and a little paid vacation. From my perspective, though, the best part of it all was that I was out from under my parents' authority. I was free, or so I thought. However, my character flaws soon got the best of me and a year later I was sitting in Cincinnati, Ohio having lost all my possessions and having to decide between humbling myself and going back home, or living a life of at least temporary homelessness. At that point God changed my heart and I have tried to live my life for Jesus Christ ever since.

I'm convinced that my mother's refusal to allow me to make my own rules at home hastened the end of my youthful folly. That is not to say that I didn't suffer consequences – I did. My career choices were severely limited by the circumstances I created for myself. When I met Cindy, therefore, I was not the provider I could have been or should have been. Except for God's grace, however, my situation would have been much worse. At least I started my new life in Christ in my early twenties. For those who are allowed to go on in their sin for longer the consequences are that much greater. As some of us know, when we turn from our sins when we have kids who are half grown it is sometimes too late for our children – they may already be lost.

I recommend, then, that rebellious children not be accommodated. Even though there is a risk that handing them over now will hasten their destruction, that approach will also generally yield the best results and is more consistent, I believe, with biblical principles. It is also better for the other children in the house who are more likely to respect the parents and obey the rules if they see that the price for rebellion is so high.

Final thoughts: As the proverb goes: An ounce of prevention is worth a pound of cure. It is a lot easier to protect our children from spiritual predators than it is to get them back once the predator has them in his grasp. My heart goes out to those parents who wonder about the salvation of their grown children. God understands how you feel, for God is the Father of the human race and look how many of His children have rejected Him. Therefore, God knows what you are going through and understands your grief.

Nevertheless, we cannot allow the actions of our rebellious children to take away our Christian joy. Even if our blood relatives desert us, we have a spiritual family that will stay with us into eternity. Jesus had brothers who didn't initially believe in Him and when they came to see Him (they wanted to take Him home because they thought He was crazy) He said to his listeners, " 'Who are My mother and My brothers?' Looking about at those who were sitting around Him, He said, 'Behold My mother and My brothers!' " (Mark 3:33-34) So then, when our children go their own way we need to draw strength from our spiritual family.

Jesus knew that not everyone in a family would always agree about Him. In fact, Jesus said, "Do not think that I came to bring peace on the earth; I did not come to bring peace, but a sword. For I came to set a man against his father, and a daughter-in-law against her mother-in-law; and a man's enemies will be the members of his household. He who loves father or mother more than Me is not worthy of Me; and he who loves son or daughter more than Me is not worthy of Me. And he who does not take his cross and follow after Me is not worthy of Me. He who has found his life will lose it, and he who has lost his life for My sake will find it." (Matthew 10:34-39)

A lost child, then, is a cross some of us must bear. We are to love our lost children and some of them will return to us, but others may even become our mortal enemies. We need to trust in Jesus for the strength to overcome such trials and we need the body of Christ to be our comfort when our children go astray.

Keeping the Home

I confess to thee that I am not worthy to rock the little babe or wash its diapers, or to be entrusted with the care of the child and its mother. How is it that I, without any merit, have come to this distinction of being certain that I am serving thy creature and thy most precious will?
(Martin Luther)

Distracted!

Distracted. That word seems to describe me much of the time. I sit down after a long day and I ask myself, "What have I accomplished today?" Sometimes the answer is awhile in coming. Sometimes no answer comes at all! The puzzling thing about all of this is that I have been busy all day. My feet haven't been propped up and I haven't eaten one single bonbon. Yet I know what the problem is: I've been distracted.

You know what I'm talking about. The distractions come in all shapes and sizes. The non-moving ones are easy to deal with. You don't call your friend until your work is done. You turn on the answering machine so you can finish teaching. You decide to check your emails at the end of the day. The TV is off-limits for the whole family until such-and-such a time. With self-discipline and establishing a few good habits, we can eliminate most of the distractions of our technical world. But it's the "old-fashioned" distractions that are trickier to deal with. You know – the children! (Oh, yeah, the husbands, too!) While Jim and I were planning this issue of SALT, we were interrupted at least four times by various children with "just one question" or an earth-shaking dilemma or a horrible injustice that was done to them. Suddenly inspired by real life, Jim said, "How about an article on how to get things done in the midst of distractions?" I told him that after ten children I was an expert on the distractions themselves, but on how to work around them, I wasn't so sure; I'm still figuring it out! I do have some suggestions, though.

Probably the best thing that we can do to deal with our lively distractions is to change our attitude. The things we must deal with – the questions, the hugs, the demands for attention, the conversations, the quarrels – are not really distractions that take us away from our primary work. Those things are our primary work. They are our ministry. Those are the things we should expect to deal with in loving and raising godly children. Each "distraction" is an opportunity to show our children that we love and value them. Each is an opportunity to teach our children about God and about living the Christian life. They're opportunities to touch our children's lives for their good during the few fleeting years they are living in our households. These things require just a moment of our attention – a moment well spent because of its eternal significance to our children. It won't matter if some housework doesn't get done or if the letter gets in the mail a day later. What are our priorities? What are we really trying to accomplish? What are the things that really matter?

Another method in dealing with these "distractions" is to try to anticipate them and meet the needs ahead of time. We can occupy our toddlers with toys before we start our homeschool lesson. We can put our baby in the care of an older child while we make that doctor's appointment over the phone. We can give our children a chance to talk before we finish breakfast and start the day. We can invite our toddler to our lap before we start our next project. We can feed our family on time and avoid those crabby stomachs! The list goes on.

You may be thinking that these ideas are well and good, but you can't anticipate every need and desire, and even with a good attitude, there are still things that we have to get done during the day. I certainly agree with that! So my next suggestion is to set limits. For example:

-Make an announcement that you will be on the phone and are not to be disturbed. Then don't entertain whispered pleas or not-so-silent requests until your call is completed. (Unless, of course, it's an emergency.)

-If you need five minutes to plan the day with your spouse or thirty more seconds to sign the check because the mailman is next door, tell the children they are not to bother you for that amount of time. When your task is done, check with them and ask them what they need. If they know that you certainly will help them when you are finished, they may be more likely to leave you undisturbed to finish your task.

Another thing that can be done is to teach your children manners and expect them to use them. That means not interrupting a person when he is speaking to another, speaking quietly and respectfully, waiting patiently, etc. Any time they do ask for help, then, will seem less of an interruption.

Speaking of manners, we can remember our manners and treat our children politely and respectfully. That means responding kindly to their requests and not interrupting them, if possible, when they are in the middle of something.

Try to instill within your children a sense of respect and love for others. This will cut down on the fights and squabbles. And should one of the children have a problem, another child may willingly, without being asked, tend to his or her needs.

As they say, timing is everything, so attempt to perform tasks that need greater concentration or little interruption when the children are asleep, at a friend's house, well-occupied, or when your spouse is around to intervene. Many times when I have to work on the computer Jim will say to the children, "Mom needs to finish this, so ask me instead of her."

And now I am finished. I've probably written this article with at least five or six interruptions. For my sanity it's probably better not to count! Of course, they weren't really interruptions. Just chances to interact with and help and teach my children. And you can see this article still got finished. Now, isn't that amazing!

A Mother's Work ... (part 1)

"How do you get everything done?" I asked.

"You do what you have to do."

That interaction took place years ago with a patient of mine when I found out she had nine children and lived on a farm. Now, several years and several children later, I receive the same question.

I frequently reply the same way she did. I didn't completely understand her answer at the time, but now I have a special appreciation for it. I believe that setting priorities is at the heart of doing "what you have to do." Sometimes we make these priorities automatically and without much thought. Other times require that we sit down and evaluate where we are and what needs to be done. We can't do everything. It's just not possible. We cannot have a successful career, an immaculate house, solid and loving family relationships and well-behaved and academically excelling children while volunteering in the church and community and still having an active social life and knock-out figure. We don't have the time and energy to say all that – much less do it all! So we need to decide what things are the most important to us and plan around those. For example, we homeschool because we believe that it is the best environment for achieving the goals that we have for our children and family. That requires a commitment of time and energy which has likely affected our personal time, our time as a couple, our careers and income, our social lives and our activities outside of the home. But that is OK to us because we feel the benefits of homeschooling are more important than those other things. Let's say I know someone who has spent countless hours and many dollars decorating her living room. The results are gorgeous. I'd really love to know how to do all that. And then it hits me: I could have that knowledge and those results, too, but I've chosen other matters. These matters are more important and they can't wait until another time. I'll have opportunities for other things later in my life; right now I have things to do that are more important to me. And should, for whatever reason, those opportunities never come, that's OK. Some things really don't matter.

There are many worthwhile things we could be doing, but our priorities need to be balanced. We could spend all of our time with our children but not have any money to buy food because we aren't making an income. We could spend all of our time teaching our children and then make ourselves sick because we aren't giving ourselves the most basic cares of moderate exercise and adequate sleep. We can have a lot of good priorities, and sometimes it's not a question of *which* priorities, but how we are going to balance them and how much time we are going to invest in each one. For example, I can acquire a healthy body by working out two hours a day, but that's not necessary. My muscles don't need to be sculpted quite so much. I can achieve a healthy body in much less time, and then better invest that extra time elsewhere.

Perhaps one of the best determinations for choosing our priorities should be its value in the light of eternity. Which will probably have the most eternal significance: our immaculate house or the time we invest into our children? It could be argued that having a clean home is a good witness to nonbelievers. That is true, but a clean and orderly home is adequate; an immaculate and costly home isn't necessary. Is God pleased with how we spend our time, energy and resources? Will the results of our efforts still be standing at the close of Judgment Day, or will they be burned with those things that are temporal? "For ground that drinks the rain which often falls on it and brings forth vegetation useful to those for whose sake it is also tilled, receives a blessing from God; but if it yields thorns and thistles, it is worthless and close to being cursed, and it ends up being burned." (Hebrews 6:7-8) It is more important to do the lasting things well than spread ourselves thin among things that are, in the light of eternity, stubble.

Concentrating on those matters with eternal significance will make us different than those around us. Hurray! We are supposed to be different than the nonbelievers we live and work next to. Sadly, though, it will also make us different than a lot of Christians around us. But we are not here to please ourselves. We may take fewer vacations and have less free time. Our carpets may not be so thick and soft. People may not understand us. They may look at our relatively small income and think it is a function of our intelligence or drive rather than the priorities we've made. They may look at all the time we spend with our children and think us odd for not going out golfing with our friends every chance we get. They may look at our humble household furnishings and wonder why we don't put the kids in daycare so we can have two incomes. And on it goes.

Maybe you think I've digressed. I started out discussing how mothers can get everything done and ended up on this tangent. But it's really not a tangent. We can't do everything, so we need to set priorities. As Christians, these priorities should have eternal significance and should honor God. That may make us different than a lot of people around us. So be it. I will set my priorities and let the rest fall by the wayside. I will not let it worry or bother or tempt me. I have a limited amount of time to impact the world for God's Kingdom, and it starts in my own home. I desire that the results of my work will stand, for the glory of God, and out of my love and respect for Him.

A Mother's Work ... (Part 2)

"How do you get everything done?" A lot of people ask me that question when they find out that I have eleven children, homeschool, and work outside of the home. As mentioned before, I believe that the most important factor in getting things done is using wisdom in setting priorities. We can't do everything, and we certainly can't do everything well. It would be better for us to concentrate on fewer things and enjoy more favorable results. But there are so many good things that we can spend our time doing. That's the reason we need to evaluate our choices in light of eternity. How does God want us to spend our time? How can we accomplish the most for Him?

I know, though, that once we focus our priorities, we still have limited time. Not only are there many usual and scheduled things we need to do, but as mothers our days fill up with those things that are unplanned and not scheduled – from sick babies to unexpected phone calls to naughty toddlers and discouraged teens. So how do we get everything done that we had planned, plus take care of the things we hadn't planned?

The best tip I have for getting things done is to enlist the help of your children. No, this won't work if you have a house filled with babies and toddlers. At one time, we did too, so we certainly know how that is. When our fifth child was born, our oldest was only five-and-a-half. At that stage, you really have to make use of all the other ideas I mention, because this one won't work for you! But the time will come when the kids will be big enough to help, and their contribution will grow as they do. Even children at five years of age (or younger) can help. In the past we have written articles in SALT about the value of having children help in the home. Their participation not only adds to the efficiency and productivity of the household as a whole, but it also prepares them for running their own households, and helps instill in them the values of hard work, responsibility, family, and community.

We also need to be efficient. We can do this in several ways. For example, if we homeschool we can teach children who are similar in age or in ability as a group rather than individually. We can spend less time with crafts and labs and field trips. We can have our children do more self-study. Maybe this isn't your first choice of how to homeschool, but again, we only have so much time and we need to find ways to achieve the best results in the most efficient manner. Outside of the home classroom we can be efficient by cooking simple meals, paying a couple cents more to avoid a trip to a second store, or writing all of our bills and cards for the month at one sitting.

We will also be more efficient if we accept results that are less than perfect. I don't have time to scrub and polish the outside and bottoms of my pots and pans. I can't get the dirt out of every nook and cranny in the house. A couple of streaks on the mirror will be all right. I don't have to iron to make sure every article of clothing is wrinkle free. A couple of less Christmas decorations or a few less cookies won't ruin the holiday. In most things perfection isn't at all necessary; it really doesn't matter. Maybe it is good for our surgeon to be a perfectionist, but I don't think it's necessary for most of us in our daily lives. It's OK if people don't understand why or what we do. It is by necessity that our standards must be different than theirs. Often I will catch myself saying, "It's not perfect, but it's good enough."

Flexibility is also important! I alluded to this at the beginning of this article. It is quite likely that as parents our days will not go according to plan. There are too many events that we can't control. The children may quarrel. A needy neighbor may call. A child may want your attention. We may not be getting this day's planned work done; yet, this *is* our work. Through these things we are accomplishing our bigger purposes. We are raising godly, loving children. We are taking opportunities to teach them and show them we love them. We are keeping them safe and providing for them. We are reaching out to those outside of our family with the love of Christ. We are being flexible to achieve God's purposes for today.

And there is certainly advantage in working hard! Being focused and efficient alone will not help us to get everything done. Sometimes when people ask me how I get everything done I tell them, "You decide what's important, and then you keep moving!" I'm certainly not advocating working ourselves sick or never having fun, but often we do not work as hard as we could or we should. Often we spend time doing things we don't need to be doing – like watching TV or being on the internet. This may involve some self-sacrifice. People ask me, "Do you have any time for yourself?" I tell them, "Well, I take a shower every day!" Personal time is overrated. There will be another season in my life when I will have more time for hobbies or doing things for "me." I am making sacrifices now in order to achieve a higher goal and purpose. If I work hard until the day I die, it really is OK. Eternity will be pretty awesome.

And surely not the least is prayer and trust. God can give me strength when I feel I have none. God can fill in all of the gaps that I leave behind. God can see the things that I am blind to. God can bring clarity out of the haze. God can bring wisdom out of confusion. God can make it all make sense. God loves my family more than I can possibly know.

And finally, I believe we need to let ourselves fail and get over it – with a renewed determination to do better. Maybe I stayed up too late. Maybe my conversation with my friend on the phone was unnecessarily long. Maybe I puttered around all day without any real focus or plan. I can't change that now. I can ask God's forgiveness and then start over again – and keep going!

We may still feel unable to get everything done. But thank God that He has given us such great and meaningful work to do! By His grace and according to His leading He will accomplish His purposes for and through us.

"Whatever you do, do your work heartily, as for the Lord rather than for men, knowing that from the Lord you will receive the reward of the inheritance. It is the Lord Christ whom you serve." (Colossians 3:23-24)

Before You Start Organizing

When people find out that we have eleven children, they often say, "You must be so organized!" I don't always know how to answer them. I guess we must be organized to some degree. After all, we get to appointments, eat three meals a day, wear clean clothes, do school and errands, and don't lose anyone in the process. But since I'm in the thick of our day-to-day operations, I also see the areas we need improvement in. I know that Jim and I talk a lot about ways to get more organized and what's been working and what hasn't. Even though I still feel like a novice in this area, let me share with you some basic things I've learned about getting organized.

We strive to be organized for the glory of God. It's not just that we want to find our gloves easily before we leave for work in the morning. Being organized will help us to stay focused on the important things. It will keep us from wasting time trying to find things or trying to determine what we should be doing next. We will be more efficient and therefore more productive for God. Being organized will be a good witness in front of others.

We've learned that it is important to start from the beginning and keep on top of it. When we were first married we were fairly organized but didn't give it a lot of effort. All of a sudden, it seemed, we were moving three times in less than two years and were having babies every 16 months or so. Suddenly being organized was really important, and we were getting behind. It is much easier to be organized from the beginning and keep it up than to have to start in the middle. But even if you do fall behind, there's still hope. It will just take more effort.

Organization is a work in progress. This is especially true for households which are changing - such as those that are growing, those that are shrinking, and those whose children are changing in age and abilities. Households also move to larger or smaller quarters. Changes in income can affect the organization of time and activities. Acquiring more stuff also has an effect on organization. Becoming involved in new commitments is another change. These frequent changes require frequent adjustments in organization. What was once adequate may need to be changed again. Just because you need to make changes doesn't mean you never were, or never will be, organized. It's OK to keep fine-tuning the process.

There's more to an organized household than just knowing where everything is. An organized household also has to do with the organization of time, money, and energy. All of these things contribute to a smoothly running family. Knowing where our car keys are won't make up much time if we go to the store four times in a day because we keep forgetting what we need. So, there are many areas we need to work on!

What I have also learned is that it's OK to have people help you. Yes, mothers, this pertains even to you! There have been many times when I've been running around doing this and that when Jim will say to me, "Why do you think you have to do this all by yourself?" Well, for me the answer is quite easy: I'm the mother! Shouldn't I be completely responsible for organizing the house? You may bear some responsibility for it, but that doesn't mean you have to do everything yourself. Enlisting the help of others will help you get organized faster and stay organized. You may get some new ideas. And if your kids are helping you, they will learn a lot about getting organized. You're not a failure if people help you.

Another thing I've learned is to make the best use of my strengths and yield to others in the areas where they are strong and I am not. For example, I'm very detail oriented, but rather slow in the process. I tend to save things (to put it politely) and, according to Jim, can see through piles to know what's underneath. On the other hand, Jim is fast but not detail oriented (to also put it politely). He loves to throw things away because he can't see through piles. How, therefore, can we live so happily, and hopefully neatly, together? We yield to each other's strengths. In some situations, such as going on vacation and having to pack medicine for children with chronic health problems, it is good for the detail oriented one to be doing the job. In other instances, such as cleaning out the storage room, it is better to let the quick one do it. (While I go away, do something else, and not think about what's going on there!) The job is done better or faster and with less stress for each of us in the end. We both can be happy with the results.

So there are some things to think about to get you started organizing when your sweater pile has fallen out of your closet on top of you yet again and you can't find last month's electric bill. There's hope for all of us. Really.

Lessons on Household Organization from a Chronically Disorganized Man

When I was in grade school my father called me the absent-minded professor. With frightening regularity I forgot the assignments my teacher gave me or lost the assignments I had completed. When I was a junior in high school I got a D in trigonometry because I lost an entire semester's worth of homework assignments. But I lost or forgot many other things as well. I forgot to bring my music to one cello recital and forgot to bring my bow to another. I lost a hat and a pair of gloves almost every year, and the life expectancy of the watches I owned was about a month. I also had a reputation as a bit of a slob, which stayed with me into adulthood. After I dropped out of college, I got an apartment and invited my college friends to a party. My ex-roommate was shocked to find the apartment clean, and he kept checking closets to find where I had hidden the mess. He had a hearty "I knew it was too good to be true" laugh when he opened a closet door adjacent to the kitchen and was almost injured by the pile of junk that fell out of the door.

As time progressed I improved tremendously. One of my fantasy goals is to become a truly organized person, but it seems that whenever I begin getting a handle on my mess I add another person to my family. When I add another person to my family, I get behind on things again. Since I have added a wife and ten children since 1985, I have been "getting behind again" a lot.

You probably think a guy like me would be the last person you would like to hear from on the topic of organization. Pardon my saying so, but your thinking is all wrong. You see, there are two kinds of people you don't want to hear from on the topic of organization. The first is the kind of person who has never had anything to organize – like a guy who has always lived by himself, worked by himself, lived in a condominium, and rarely cooked at home. The second is the kind of person who has been organized since he was a toddler. This guy has never struggled to be organized and can't understand why other people make such a simple thing so complicated. He's the kind that gives you hints on organization that you read and say, "I could never be that organized." It's the same principle that says the best athletes are the worst coaches. They do by nature what others have to learn by the sweat of their brow. Since I have struggled with the issue for a very long time, I – the man who has never managed to get organized – will share with you the wisdom I have obtained through my misadventures. What follows is a list of organization tips and pitfalls. As you would expect from a disorganized man, the items listed are in no particular order.

Pack rats are enemies in the war to be organized: People who can't bear to throw things away give themselves so much more to organize, and their accumulations of useless junk cause all kinds of organizational problems. There is a law of nature that states that without intervention, useless piles of junk always grow. Piles of useless junk become tremendous hiding places for things you really need and they also attract more messes. These living, growing junk piles can cause real damage when they overflow their holding containers. If you've never seen the fronts of dresser drawers fall off, or the destruction of closet and cabinet doors, you've never seen the real power of a growing junk pile.

Solution: If you want to be organized, only keep the stuff you really need. The important word here is need. Need is defined as something you can't do without, not something you may use in a highly unlikely hypothetical future scenario.

Messy people of all ages need to put their stuff away when they're done: Anyone with toddlers in the house knows they are like walking tornadoes. Their natural tendency is to pick up anything of interest to them, play with it for a couple minutes, put it on the ground, and then move on to the next item. Although a toddler would never admit it, I think his purpose in life is to make messes for others. Unfortunately, people like me had a problem growing out of the toddler stage. I can get out of bed – without making it, of course, use the bathroom and leave my shaving stuff out, go into the shower and leave my dirty clothes on the floor, and come back into the bedroom and leave the dirty towel on the floor. That way I can make a mess of the shower, the bathroom, and the bedroom within 15 minutes of the moment I leave the bed. Of course, the whole day can be more of the same. The car trash stays in the car, the mail goes into a pile that only gets reduced when I can't find the bills, the book is left in whatever room I happen to read it, and I come back from the grocery store and stuff everything into the cupboards and the refrigerator in such a way that the next person who cooks needs to trash the place in order to find the ingredients she needs.

The problem with people like me is that we are too busy to put our stuff away when we're done. Since our time is so scarce, we naturally get frustrated when we are late because we can't find our clothes, or we spend one entire day trying to find everything we need to fill out our tax forms. We know we could get a lot more done if we didn't have to look around for stuff all the time, but we are like senseless toddlers who go from one mess to the next without picking up after themselves.

Solution: Put your stuff away and clean up your mess before you do something else. Make the bed as soon as you get up, put your dirty clothes in the hamper as soon as you take them off, sort and file the mail as soon as it comes in, and take the trash out of the car the first time you stop.

Putting your stuff away presumes you have a place to put it: To be organized, everything should have a place. That doesn't mean a general place, like in the house or even in the cupboard. We had a cupboard that was reserved for things like spices, food coloring, measuring cups, coffee, and baking powder. Eventually, the cupboard got so full it was a nightmare finding anything. When I went through the cupboard the other day, I found 3 bottles of Italian spice, 2 open instant coffee containers, 2 open chili powder bottles, and 3 open bottles of dill weed. This dill weed is something we can probably plan to pass on to our children as an inheritance.

Thus, every thing must have a very specific place or every drawer, closet, and cabinet becomes a specialized junkpile container. The closets and dressers become clothes junkpiles, and the drawers become school supply, office supply, and hardware junkpiles. Although dividing messes by category may qualify as some form of order, it is not to be confused with organization.

Solution: Assign everything a specific place. That place should be accessible if it is used a lot. For example, if I assign my dill weed the place at the front of the spice cabinet and put the salt and pepper in the back, I will probably keep knocking over the dill weed bottles at every meal. If I don't pick the bottles up, it becomes a junk pile, which will attract more stuff. And before you know it, the spice cabinet door will fall off. Therefore, I should assign dill weed to the back of the spice cabinet and salt to the front.

The place of everything must be strictly enforced. Most disorganized people are not very good at enforcing a thing's place. Once a place has been assigned, every time someone uses the thing it must be put back. Disorganized people like me tend to be too lenient with things that stray from their places. For example, if I take a pen away from its assigned place and take it into another room to write a list, when I'm done with my list I notice that the pen has no desire to go back to his assigned place. My tendency is to allow the pen to stay there as long as he wants. I've noticed, however, that pens are sneaky and like to hide under the cushions of couches, behind dressers, and even in the glove compartment of the car. Once I bought a case of 144 pens and it didn't last a year. Pens and all other things need strict discipline. If the place is assigned, the place must be enforced.

To organize a household of, say, eleven children, the children must also be taught to enforce the place of pens and other things. The parent gets the honor of holding her children accountable to enforce the assigned place of things. This calls for the patient endurance of the saints, but in the long run it is worth the effort.

Don't be lazy. Put the traveling thing back in its assigned spot every time, and force your children to do the same.

How these principles of organization are specifically applied can be a matter of tedious and time-consuming discussions. For example, we may debate where the car keys should go at the end of the night. Some people have a hook on the wall, some put them in a container, and others put them on or in the dresser. Even then, we would have to decide which wall, what kind of container, and which dresser. My guess is, however, that if you get rid of the junk you don't need, assign everything an appropriate place, and strictly enforce that place, you will go a long way toward winning the organization war against things.

Confessions of a Pack Rat

For those of you who know us well, or have been curious enough to put the pieces together, I am the pack rat so affectionately referred to in Jim's articles. I have the solace, however, of knowing that I am not alone. Some of my good friends are also pack rats. (Not that we travel in packs.) We know from experience that having the characteristics of a pack rat is like bearing a double-edged sword.

Let's begin, though, by using a different term than "pack rats." That label isn't very affectionate, is it? It has all sorts of bad connotations attached to it. Those of us in that category are often misunderstood and the target of all sorts of jokes. Are we really deserving of such treatment? On the other hand, those people who would throw their own mothers away, without even noticing they did it, maintain a higher, more respected place in our society. Just remember this: they're the throwers, but we're the ones who recycle. Now that's an interesting perspective, don't you think? So I prefer to think of myself as a saver. That's more affectionate, and we really are a likable bunch.

And let's get another thing straight: we savers aren't savers necessarily because we like having a lot of stuff around. It's just that a lot of stuff doesn't bother us as much as it does the throwers. That's because our stuff serves a higher purpose.

Our stuff is necessary and important because it's going to come in handy some day. Some day I'm going to be glad I saved all those buttons because someone will be missing one as he's racing out of the door. All of those pipe cleaners will come in handy for art one day. Later I will have time to read that free magazine; it looks like it has some really good articles in it. That sales receipt will be important when the appliance breaks. Those papers will be proof of this or that just when we need it. And I have to save that info on Pennsylvania because you don't know when we'll vacation there next.

Don't laugh because it really does work out like that sometimes. My girls have enjoyed making doll clothes out of the material scraps I have saved. Jim has managed to keep his pants up because there were buttons handy. Last week the phone cord came in contact with the stove and began melting. I had thrown the extra cord in the toolbox, so we weren't found phoneless. It also saved us some time and money. There have been other times, too, when my "'saving" mentality has come in handy. Stick a feather in Mom's cap!

Now comes the confession part. I realize that not all of my stuff comes to such useful purposes. I also admit that sometimes I have trouble finding what I am looking for amid my things. And sometimes things become part of my piles because I think I'll have time to deal with them more fully later. That's the other side of the double-edged sword. How can we savers soften that side?

I know I can start by thinking more objectively about the likelihood of needing my stuff in the future. Do I really think it will be needed? Can it be replaced if needed? Do I need *every* cute picture the kids have drawn? If I decide it's a keepsake or that it has a good possibility of being used, I need to have a workable system for organizing and keeping it. Saving has to be balanced with the ease of storing it. If you have limited space, either because of the size of your family or the size of your house (or both, like us!), you may need to make a greater effort to resist saving a lot of things.

If you find yourself with lots of piles and boxes already, be patient with yourself, but begin to make the concentrated effort of going through them. It's going to take time. If some of it is old, you'll find that it'll be easy to throw a bunch of it away! File or box and label the items you want to save. If you have the desire for a neater, more organized environment but you don't have the stomach to do it, allow your thrower spouse to do it. If you're not sure he knows what you really want or need, let him know. Make a clear plan for the both of you. Then get out of the way and go someplace else so you don't hear or see what's going on. (If you feel you need to, arrange with him to peruse the garbage quickly. We know how those throwers are! But then be true to your word and do it fast. He's there to help you.) Be brave! Gotta get rid of those haphazard boxes and leaning piles! And you'll probably be happy when it's done!

The other thing to do is to be more objective about our time. When I place things to the side, I really do think I will have more time to deal with them later. But later rarely comes unless I make an effort for it to come. So I'm left with a few options. First, I can face up to it and just get rid of the stuff right away – like those magazines. I may have an interest in them, but not the time. If I develop the time later, I should be able to find the information again at the library or through the internet. Another option is to just deal with it right away. Sit down and read the article today. File the papers right away. Just a couple of minutes may save the frustration of misplaced items or having too much junk around. The final option, which is sometimes necessary, is to put it aside but be committed to carving out the time for it later – but soon. Even set aside a specific day and time on your calendar. Let's be realistic, and disciplined, about it!

Now, in case you throwers are putting too many feathers in *your* caps right about now, remember that things generally thrive best on balance. Be gentle with us and we'll return the favor. Please keep your mother. And we'll be happy to throw away last week's grocery receipt.

Stockpiling

I just took you into the psyche of the packrat. (Although I believe the preferred word is "saver.") I'm probably quite qualified to do so, as I have been accused at one time or another of being a saver. I talked about the good and the bad of it all and how we savers can temper our natural instincts to stockpile. But I feel that there are some more spiritual principles to take into account. You see, to me, everything is spiritual. Our Christian beliefs and principles can – and should – impact everything we are involved in. Those stockpiles scattered around our house are no different.

You know what I'm talking about. Just about anything can fall into a stockpile – and you don't necessarily have to be a packrat. It can be clothes, nails and screws, foods in the freezer, etc. and etc. The most recent stockpile discovered in our house is tuna. I think it's such a good deal to be able to get brand name tuna on sale for 33 cents a can. Since it takes at least six cans for one meal for us, I take advantage of the sales when I can. When our pantry gave up all its hidden tuna cans, we had 40-something of them. (You can stop laughing at any time.) Needless to say, we've been eating some tuna lately.

Generally, the underlying motive for stockpiling is a biblical one. We want to be good with our resources. This is important whether you have much or you have little. If saving clothes will save me money down the road, that is a good thing. The money saved can then be prudently directed elsewhere. It can also save time – the time needed to leave the house and buy more clothes.

At the same time, we should be good with our resources of space. We only have so much to work with. When we begin to have more stuff than space, it may be harder to perform our family duties efficiently. It is harder for us to keep our houses clean and organized. Having a lot of stuff can also wear on family members emotionally – like being dragged down by weights. I don't think God wants us to live like that.

Another very important biblical principle is that of sharing. Hebrews 13:16 says, "And do not neglect doing good and sharing, for with such sacrifices God is pleased." If we have bags and bags of clothes in our attics which we don't use, it is a waste. There are people who could use them and we are being selfish for hanging on to them. It is better to share them with someone who has a need for them. As God has freely given us many things, so we can freely share those things with others. If we are piling our house with more gadgets and knick-knacks than we can really enjoy or use, that, too, is a waste. That money can be better used to share with others – whether it be with those inside or outside of our houses. "Do not merely look out for your own personal interests, but also for the interests of others." (Philipians 2:4)

Why are we really hanging on to all of our things? Is it that we have the willingness to lighten our houses, but haven't set aside the time to do that? Or is there another reason? Are we ever afraid that when we do need something, we won't have it? Is that trust? Let me share with you a personal example. After seventeen years and ten children, we have actually spent comparatively little money on clothes. Most of our clothes have come from hand-medowns, hand-me-overs, or thrift stores. For years I saved too much – forgetting what I had and not making the best use of what I saved. Gradually I have worked on reducing what we have. We will bag it and send it off to charity. I especially do this with boys' clothes. Our last boy was born nearly eleven years ago and we've had five daughters since. It's a waste for a bunch of boys' clothes to sit around here unused. I don't know if I will ever have a boy again. But saving all those clothes "just in case" is wasteful and selfish when there are people who can use them now. God has provided for us all of these years. I know God will provide for all our future needs. We may not have tuxedos and ball gowns and we may not have designer labels, but those aren't needs. Will we have clothes? Most certainly, yes. God promised that.

So a final principle to consider is trust. If I trust God to provide for our needs as He has in the past and as He has promised He will do in the future, I don't need to stockpile and hoard over worry or concern about not having enough. Do I trust God or don't I?

I think that God wants us to be balanced – balanced in our saving, disposing, sharing, and spending. I really do think it's a spiritual issue. "Whether, then, you eat or drink or whatever you do, do all to the glory of God." (1 Corinthians 10:31)

We've been eating our tuna supply lately. I ignored the first sale that came around. Then a couple weeks ago they had another great sale. I controlled myself and only bought enough for one meal. Well, I'm getting better. God's working on me. I know it's OK if we eat all of the tuna. If we need it, we'll have more. You know, I even bet God could have one of those good sales come around again. He's pretty awesome.

99's the Limit!

I have found that there were a lot of things I didn't know when I started a family and later began homeschooling. I was unprepared for some of the things I was to encounter. Not all of those things were necessarily major things. For instance, I didn't know the volume of library books I would have to tend and track.

Our family uses an incredible amount of library books during the year. First, we have books for homeschooling. Because we create most of the curriculum for the younger children, we get a lot of text books and books for unit studies from the library. If the children have special projects or reports to do, those are borrowed as well. Our school-aged children also have literature reading everyday, so most of those books come from the library. Next we have pleasure books – times twelve people! I am happy to say that all my children (though some more than others) like to get materials from the library. It is interesting to see what each individual likes to spend his time reading. We come home with quite an assortment of materials – from Curious George, to animals, to football, to political books and on and on. Lastly, we borrow books that help us with projects, business, and other such "practical" things. So you can see that can add up to quite a large number of books.

You would think it would be better in the summer, but it really isn't. The library has special programs each week that my children like to attend, and then they always ask, "Can we get just a couple of books?" So summer or winter we must rank with the library's best customers. I remember standing in line once while our books were being checked out. In mid-pile the librarian stopped and said, "I'm sorry. You can't check out any more books. Ninety-nine books is the limit and that's what you have." Needless to say, I was a bit surprised. First of all, I didn't know there was a limit. Second of all, I never dreamed we had reached it. I was almost embarrassed. Had the woman behind me in line heard this? Was she laughing? Was she, like me, a little surprised? On the way home I said to Jim, "Do we really have that many books at home?" Still puzzled when I got in the house, I glanced around and said, "Do we really have that many books in this house?" Since that same scenario has happened more than once, I still find myself asking, "Can we really have that many books?"

Despite the limit, I've figured out how to check out as many books as we need. If my card gets maxed out, I borrow my son's or my husband's card, even in mid-pile. The librarians don't care. The library system recently started a "family card" – many cards (one for each family member) but one account number. My son thought it was a cool idea. Not me. Everyone who has a card in this family ensures ninety-nine more books we can check out. You can't fool me.

I'm also learning how to make the most of our library system – as if we really needed any more books to check out! I just love accessing the library catalog through their website on my home computer. I search for books or create unit studies and then have the books held for me or sent from other libraries to my local branch. Two of my children have caught on and also frequently request books. I also love the "ask a librarian" feature. If there's something I can't find I'm not afraid to write and ask. They must think, "Oh, no, not those McDermotts again!"

I guess there are one or two advantages in being frequent customers. The librarian knows us by name now and will start taking our reserved items off the shelf just as we're getting to the front of the line. They'll let my son get my reserved stuff with his card and vice versa. Yes, we do get the most out of our library tax dollars.

Keeping track of all those books can be quite the challenge. We've gone through a couple of different systems, trying to find the most effective one. Our first one was putting all the library books on the shelf above the wood-burning stove. When that shelf proved too small, we began putting them on top of the stove itself. (Note: remove books before starting fire!) That didn't work very well. It was kind of sloppy looking. Next we had the kids keep their books in a box in their rooms. That was OK for the older kids, but not for the younger ones. I don't know why or where the books went, but we spent a lot of time trying to find them. Our most recent and most effective system has been putting the homeschooling books on a certain shelf and the rest of the library books in a big tub I got from the Dollar Store. Without being too restrictive, we also have limits as to where they can take the books inside the house.

We've discovered some materials tend to get lost more than others. The worst books by far are those little board books. I have a soft heart so I can't bear to say no to my little ones who want to take those home. But they're just a disaster waiting to happen. They're way too small and can get lost easily. When I feel their interest in the book has waned, I snatch it and put it up and away until I can get it back to the library. I know the way those books are, and they're not going to get away from me! Another problem is magazines. I'm sure that at least once a library magazine has ended up in the garbage because someone thought it was one of those free samples you get in the mail. (I won't mention the name of the dark haired adult who lives in this house who did that.) The kids also have subscriptions to magazines so I suspect sometimes the library magazines end up in those piles, too. The last class of dangerous library materials is audiotapes. Not only do you have to worry about the tape, but about the insert and case as well. It should be easy, but I'm still working on a system for those. "Systems," it seems, are always complicated by many children and many *small* children.

Every once in awhile we do lose a book. My kids know it drives me crazy, and they better be quick about finding it. It seems like we find them eventually, sometimes later rather than sooner. We have found stray books in all sorts of places – the attic (now, why didn't I think to look there?), stuck inside a larger book, in couches or between board games, just to name a few places. When a book is found it becomes a type of delinquent in my eyes. The book gets placed high on "my" shelf, sort of in solitary confinement until it gets taken back to the library. It doesn't get mixed back in with the other books because it can't be trusted and will try to escape again. When you check books out it's hard to know which ones are the derelict type. They all have their hidden natures.

It seems like the three weeks we can have the books go by quickly. I try to limit the number of things we renew. The longer you have the items, the more you accumulate and the easier it is to misplace (i.e., LOSE) something. The younger kids must return everything before they get more. But I'm more lenient with the older kids because their books are longer. Plus, a lot of the homeschool items are needed for a longer period of time. Renewing items used to be a nightmare. I used to renew them on the automatic phone system. It would really drive me crazy. The numbers you have to punch in on the phone are umpteen digits long, and if you make a mistake – look out! The system is quite unforgiving and you have to start over again. Then there's that computer voice you have to listen to. He's quite repetitive with a distinct monotone and has no personality whatsoever. So sometimes I would have a librarian renew the books. I felt kind of bad about doing that. When you have to renew ten or whatever number of items, it takes awhile, and there's always some poor person waiting in the line behind you. That's why I was excited when I discovered

I could renew books online. That way the only person I bore is myself and the only time I waste is my own.

That reminds me. We have books due tomorrow. I hope we don't have any thugs in this batch. I detest the day, should it ever come, when we move and have to return all ninety-nine (or so) books at once. Wow. Just the thought. Better start looking underneath those couches now.

"But beyond this, my son, be warned: the writing of many books is endless, and excessive devotion to books is wearying to the body." (Ecc. 12:12)

Land of the Misfit Socks

One of the most challenging things about mothering, I think, is making sure everyone has socks. One late night I figured out that we use about 84 pairs of socks every week. That's 168 individual socks! I wish I could use that high number as my excuse for how hard it all is, but deep down I know that if we used just a fraction of that amount, I would still have troubles. You see, I have spent some time in the study of the problem, and have determined that there are several obstacles a pair of socks must encounter as it moves through the cycle from being a dirty sock on your foot to being a clean sock on your foot. Let me show you what I mean.

The first step is safely making it into the laundry bin. This is especially difficult if you have toddlers. For instance, our Bridget is 2 ½ years old. She may begin the day with her shoes and socks on, but all of a sudden I will look down and discover she is wearing neither. They're not in sight, either. You can ask everyone if they saw her taking them off, and everyone will say no, because she is the stealth sock-remover. If she slipped up and someone had seen her, you can bet that the evidence is no longer at the scene of the crime. Of course, this step in the sock cycle is not fool proof for the older ones, either, but let's just concentrate on Bridget's little socks.

Somehow, though, we manage to find (or discover - there's a difference, you know) her socks and get them into the laundry bin. This is not a safe place for socks. They can't get out, but as I separate the laundry into lights, darks, etc., it is easy for them to filter through the pile.

Socks soon and easily become separated from their partners. But I'm bigger than they are, so usually I can manage to get them into the washer.

Now, you would think that the trip between the washer and the dryer would be pretty straight and easy, but let me tell you that it's not. How often have I found socks that have fallen down the space between the two machines! That problem should be easily solved: just push the machines close together. I've done this, but my machines must shake, rattle, roll and do the Irish jig (must be the Irish Rovers music we listen to) when I'm not looking, because that space keeps reappearing.

For the sake of this article, though, let's say that Bridget's socks have safely crossed the chasm between the machines and are now dried and ready to get into the laundry basket. How hard can that be, since I put the basket right in front of the dryer? This wouldn't be hard if socks couldn't defy gravity, but they do so herein lies another obstacle. I know they defy gravity because often I will open the dryer to put a new load in, only to find one lonely dry sock on the bottom of the dryer. I figure that it clung to the top of the dryer while I was emptying its load, then it let go and fell to the bottom after I shut the door - you know, when it was dark again and the danger was gone. But I finally caught it, so off it goes to be folded.

Two of my daughters fold the laundry, and they like to do it in the living room. Sometimes they like to dump the basket out, usually on the couch. Here is our next obstacle. There are all sorts of places a sock can hide – behind the couch, under it, between the cushions. But I'm on to them now, so I can quickly find Bridget's socks and add them to the clean laundry pile again.

That's not the only danger in the folding step, however. The next potential problem lies, I will admit, with my children who do the folding. Sometimes I think they need a refresher course in distinguishing between sizes and colors. One of Bridget's bright pink socks may end up in her pile, and the other in her 15-year-old brother's (he has no pink socks). I haven't figured out the solution to this problem yet, but I'm a college graduate so I just might.

Let's say I was just passing through the room while this little oversight was occurring and I managed to get both Bridget's socks into her pile. Next a different child will come along and put the piles into the appropriate rooms or drawers. Little Bridget's socks are now safely tucked away. Ah!, you might think. All is well! You just go on thinking that until it's time to get those socks out of the drawer. Socks have this amazing ability to migrate through the drawer, ending up away from their partners, on the other side of the drawer or on the very bottom. But truly amazing are those socks which can climb over the back of the drawer and end up in the drawer underneath! The most horrible scenario, though, occurs when these last two problems occur *at the same time.* One of Bridget's pink socks may be at the bottom of her drawer, and the other may be in her brother's shirt drawer! (Because it climbed over the back of his sock drawer.) But then again, how do you know it's not lurking in her sister's drawer?! So you see, this step is the most dangerous one of all. But remember, Bridget does wear socks, so these problems can be overcome!

All of this is complicated by the fact that our society expects everyone to wear matching socks. What do you think when you see a guy with mismatching socks? Are you impressed? No! You wonder if he's color blind or why his wife doesn't dress him. I just don't get it. I see lots of "in-style" outfits that don't seem to me to match very well. So why is our culture so obsessed with matching socks? If my family was considered a trend-setter (I wish), I would make sure my kids never wore matching socks. If their shirts were blue and their pants red, I'd have them wear one blue sock and one red. No, wait a minute. I'd have them wear a green one and a yellow one. That way everyone could be sure that there was no color coordinating going on at all. Then my pile of matchless socks would come in handy. (Do you have a pile like that, too?)

Motherhood certainly is a challenge, but I'm up to it. I showed you how I can get one pair of Bridget's socks safely to her feet. Whew! What a relief! Only 83 more pairs to go this week!

That Silly Sock Saga

I just spent some time telling you about the hazardous trip that socks make through the laundry. So what can this article possibly be about? I guess that years of trying to keep all the feet in this house warm and dry have finally gotten to me. I just can't let the topic go. I have become quite the expert on the nature of socks and it's pretty troublesome. If it wasn't enough that you have to chase them through the laundry and hope you have an even number of socks in the end (preferably of the same color), they have to go and make things really complicated. They have to get *holes.*

Of course, there is a solution to this. It's called darning. It's an art and my mom is the master. My mother always did her art form quickly and seemingly effortlessly. The socks always came out perfect. Not long ago, in the recesses of my drawer, I found a finely darned pair of socks. I could tell this wasn't my handiwork. It had to be the master's. Now, with me having ten children, you can pretty well guess that it's been quite awhile since my mother darned any of my socks. Yet here they were, as good as new. We kids didn't know we were living in the midst of greatness.

Unfortunately, my children can't say the same. How often has a child come to me, holding out a pitiful sock of holes, saying, "Mom, can you sew this?" When I was a fairly new mom, and having been raised by the master, I'd say with confidence, "Certainly!" I'd then get out my needles and darning thread and get to the task. I soon realized that I wasn't very good at it. It's not just sewing two pieces of material together. It is weaving cloth and suspending it in midair. Too loose and your toe will still stick out. Too tight and it becomes a wad of material rubbing your foot in your shoe. It calls for a delicate but firm touch. And I just didn't seem born with the talent.

After awhile I found my own solution to this problem. It's called the thrift store. Some people do not like to readily admit that they shop in such establishments, but I'll tell you that they're a fine place to get socks. I figure I can spend a lot of time and frustration trying to keep our socks mended (and I remind you that we wear 80+ a week), or I can go to the thrift store and painlessly and effortlessly toss them into my cart for a mere 30 cents a pair. (They're only 15 cents on Mondays.) I did my own private cost/benefit analysis and the thrift store won hands down. (Especially on Mondays.) I still have all of my charts and graphs to prove it.

So I'm pretty pumped when I step into that thrift store. I must be a sight to behold. I head straight to the sock section and start throwing them into the cart right and left, socks flying like dirt from a puppy digging a hole. It doesn't matter too much what size the socks are, because the feet in my house come in all the sizes.

The skeptics among you are probably thinking that pre-owned socks don't last long, minimizing the cost benefit. Unfortunately, there have been times when I've had to break down and buy socks new. I'm amazed by how much they cost. And then I'm disappointed that my added investment doesn't amount to much. Those new socks just don't seem to last any longer than our pre-owned socks. That's on my charts and graphs, too.

Yes, indeed, it is discouraging when I can't find all the socks I need at the thrift store. This happens especially with socks for ten-year-old boys. If my mother is the master sock darner, my ten-year-old son is the master hole maker. He puts incredibly big holes into his socks incredibly fast. I used to think that maybe he had extra pointy toes or he ran extra fast and wore out the heels, but now I don't think that's true. Since there are so few socks for him at the thrift store, it must mean that most ten-year-old boys destroy their socks beyond recovery. Sock manufacturers must produce extra socks for that age group just to keep up with the demand. Now I know where to invest my money.

All in all, I am quite happy with the way I have dealt with this problem in our family. The only thing I regret is not being able to teach my children the ancient practice of darning. I'm sorry, Mom, for not passing on the greatest art form known to man. Maybe I should send all the kids to your house with a couple dozen holey socks so you can teach them how to darn. Where else to learn, but from the master? Yes, that's a fine idea, I think. I'd hate to think that I was the demise of such an important craft. Besides, thirty cents saved is thirty cents earned. How about next Saturday?

Chores for All

One of my patients at work loves to have her visitors guess how many children I have. Of course, they never can guess, and when one woman found out, her first reply was, "How do you keep up with all their clothes?" I proceeded to tell her that all of our children have jobs to do around the house. That seemed kind of like an intriguing idea to her. She told me that when she lived with her parents, she was busy with this and that and all she had to do was "maybe make my bed." She told me that when people like her have one or two children, they don't really think of giving them jobs to do; they pamper them. Needless to say, *her* idea seemed rather intriguing to *me.*

Jim and I have always felt very strongly about giving the children jobs to do, even from the very beginning. At this point, with eleven children, there is no physical way that Jim and I can do all the work plus homeschool plus make a living plus raise children, etc., etc. But there are other reasons we feel so strongly about it, too.

First off, we feel it is important that our children learn how to maintain a household. When they leave home, they will be able to cook simple meals, clean a bathroom, wash clothes, and do all the other things that must be done to care for oneself and a house. They will also have some knowledge about painting, fixing things, and taking care of a yard. Usually the best way to learn is by doing, not just by watching someone else do it. Their transition away from home will hopefully be a little smoother for them, and for their spouses if they have them. What girl wouldn't want a guy who can change a diaper? What guy wouldn't be thrilled to have a girl who can cook?

We also believe that having chores builds a sense of community and family. Together we take care of the home that we share. Together we can make it more clean and comfortable. It is a team effort. It is now *our* home and *our* house and we can take pride in it.

I do not want my children to become spoiled. They must help care for themselves and our home. But it's not just about doing the work; it's also about appreciating the work that is done for them. It is easy to desire and to demand a seven-course meal, but once you've prepared one you realize all the planning and work involved. It's then easier to appreciate the hamburgers that Dad makes or the one-pot meals Mom likes to put together. If you hate cleaning the bathroom, because you've done it a few times, you'll enjoy the clean bathroom that someone else has scoured, and you'll be grateful to the person who did it.

After a few hit-and-misses and trial-and-errors, we've found some things that work and others that don't work so well. For instance, at the beginning we had all the kids go with us into first one room and then the next, cleaning as we went. It didn't take long for us to learn that if humans aren't compelled to do unpleasant things, they most often won't. Saying, "Let's all clean this room together" didn't exactly motivate people to clean. The kids were often lax in their work, waiting for the other ones to carry the burden. Maybe you can chastise a child for being slow or looking lazy, but without a set standard it's harder. So we learned that it is better to assign different areas to different kids. That way the work is more likely to get done, and quicker. Children can be told what standards are expected and then can easily be held accountable for their area.

Giving children certain areas to clean also has resulted in a nice side effect: the kids become proud of the work they do. They can see the "before and after" pictures and realize that it's clean because of them. They also become protective of their areas, asking others to clean up after themselves, and even cleaning their areas when not asked.

It's good to have children do different jobs, but the jobs should be within their ability. That sounds pretty self-evident, but it's a good reminder. Once we assigned one of our younger children to maintain the hallway closet, not really realizing that she was too short to hang up a coat! Well, that arrangement didn't work too well so we had to change it. That's the reason why five-year-olds don't take out the garbage; the bags are almost as big as they are. Soon enough they'll get to do it. Short people should have short people's jobs.

We change the jobs our kids are assigned every few months. This way everyone can "share the joy" of cleaning the bathroom; but more importantly, everyone can learn how to do it. As said, I want my children to learn every job before they leave the house, and we take each one down a mental checklist when assigning jobs.

We incorporate into their assigned jobs not only the tasks which are done daily, but also those which are done less frequently, such as weekly or monthly. For example, right now Meghan and Keenan are responsible for the dining area. Each day the floor needs to be picked up and swept. But in addition to this they must clean the chairs weekly, as well as the walls. The patio door is cleaned less frequently. The floor must be washed more often. All of this is their responsibility. This way we can be sure that these jobs are getting done regularly, contributing to a cleaner and more organized house.

I usually post all the jobs on a large paper on the wall. That way there is no question as to who does what, especially when we're just changing jobs. I like to headline the list with, "It is the Lord Christ whom you serve." (Colossians 3:24) That's what it really comes down to. We take care of ourselves and our things as a service to Christ, to be good witnesses and good stewards. This is an important lesson for the kids. Our purpose is not to fill our children's time with busy work, nor is it to be obsessive about the appearance of our house. Our ultimate purpose, as always, is to glorify God.

The day is winding down, now, and I need to check on the house. Who is supposed to be cleaning my room? It's looking a little sloppy. Oh yeah - that one's on my list. I'd better get to work.

Kid Work

Jim and I have long been proponents of having children participate in housework. It helps to build a sense of responsibility and community within the family. It makes one appreciate the clean bathroom because you know how disgusting that job really is. It allows everyone to spend a little time on work and more time on the things that are truly important. And, it prepares the children for maintaining a household of their own. We have a sort of changing system on how to train our children in housework, but basically it's teaching the children how to do it, and then having them do it. Sounds rather straightforward and fool-proof, but it has been anything but that. I don't know if it's "us" or "them," but here are some of the problems we've run into.

Distributing the work. We've had lots of variations on this theme. For awhile we were pairing a younger child with an older with the purpose of having the older teach the younger how to do the job. Sometimes the older children would just delegate jobs to the younger children without providing much oversight or training. That defeated the whole purpose of this set-up. At another time we designated an older child to check everyone's work for quality and completion. This not only freed us up a little, but also taught the children to respect other authority (doubly hard when it's your sibling!). The problem was that our designated checker was not always consistent. Sometimes things were not checked, were not checked well, or the checkees did not respond in an appropriate manner. We've learned that no matter how the work is delegated, we must set the standard and make sure that it is upheld. We are the final teacher and authority. The buck stops here.

Sometimes we have children of similar age pair up on a job. Generally this hasn't been good because one ends up doing more than the other or they have to wait on each other before starting the job. But sometimes this pairing up is very practical, especially on big jobs. Like folding laundry. Once we had a certain pair of children folding and stacking the laundry together. It was a mess. Clothes were constantly missing. We knew they had been washed because the washer person had seen them. So they were clean *and* lost. There is no surer way to get a parent cranky than when she can't find her clothes. Worse yet is when she finds them under or behind the couch. Similar in result is when she finds her clothes in the baby's drawer. ("Now, why didn't I think of looking there in the first place!!!") We instructed and exhorted our little folding team, but it was no use. We couldn't stand it anymore and ousted this pair. We're not giving them a break and accepting shoddy work. They will both revisit folding clothes. But they won't be doing it together! Sometimes the needs of the many become an important factor in how the work is distributed!

The fairness issue. Children keep wonderful tabs on the fairness of any situation. One area in which we've heard those infamous words: "It's not fair!" is the question of fairness between the sexes. It seems to me that, generally speaking, God has created men better able to do certain jobs and women to do others. Boys are better at moving furniture because of their strength. Girls tend to be better with babies and small children because of their temperament. And so on. So I might ask the girls to help me watch the little ones while the boys go to the dump with their father. Would my daughters rather throw heavy bags into a smelly landfill while being nose-dived by gulls? OK. Some would. But that would not be maximizing their strengths.

We also try to keep in mind that our children need to be prepared to fill their future roles. Boys may need more practice in household repair and girls more practice in sewing and entertaining. It's not unfair if we call our girls to help us set the table for company when we ask the boys to plunge the toilet. It's not a matter of fun vs. boring jobs or dirty vs. clean. It's a matter of preparing our children for their future roles.

At the same time, each child should have a basic understanding of and ability to perform each job. Everybody should experience each job – at least once. So it's a thin line we walk. We need to balance the fairness issue with the bigger picture.

Teaching quality and setting expectations. Setting expectations is tricky because setting them too low can be just as dangerous as setting them too high. Setting expectations is a function of the child's age and physical capabilities. It wouldn't be right to expect my four-year-old to put away heavy china on the top shelf or expect my child with a broken arm to shovel snow. I don't think I would have any critics on that one. But it gets more difficult when the expectations are a function of the child's personal ability. Some kids just do better work at certain jobs than other children. I have a child who is just not detail oriented and does not possess fine motor skills. I would set a certain standard of cleanliness and neatness in the jobs assigned to this child, but this child just wouldn't achieve those standards. Wouldn't? Couldn't? Should we have made him do it over and over again until he did it right? Those were the questions we faced. As the child grew older we began to see that the problem really wasn't his attitude. It wasn't a problem with rebellion. We noticed that he just didn't excel in fine motor activities of any kind. He wasn't good with detail. What he liked to do and what he was good at didn't require perfection. Making him do his chore over and over again until he "got it right" came to the point of absurdity. He just wasn't going to "get it right!" I became satisfied that he knew how to clean a kitchen, even if the results weren't what I wanted. Since he knew how and had some practice, we could now give him a different job. I don't think we were copping out on this. We set a standard in line with his abilities – not his attitude, but abilities. Again, it's a thin line, because you have to somehow evaluate his motives and heart and abilities. You have to evaluate not just his work, but his whole personality and "lifestyle" in general. That takes some time to make sure you come up with the right result!

Who would have known that delegating and supervising children's work could be so much work? I guess it will always be that way since humans aren't naturally a disciplined and righteous lot. But hopefully my children will leave my home knowledgeable and responsible. And hopefully my house will get cleaned in the meantime.

Our Family Vacation

I'm sure many of you are staying up at night wondering what it is like to take a week's vacation with nine children and no money. Since I hate seeing people lose sleep and since by coincidence we recently took our nine children on a week long vacation with no money, I will tell you all about it.

Planning these vacations is fairly simple. Since we can't afford to stay in hotels (it takes us two rooms now) we look for places we can stay for free. We have found that this conveniently limits our choices to relatives' houses. Although our relatives generally do not have houses designed for eleven overnight guests, we gladly volunteer our children to sleep on the floor. We soothe the concerns of our hosts by telling them that our house wasn't designed for nine children either and that our smaller children sometimes sleep three in our upstairs linen closet at home. This always makes our hosts feel better.

This vacation began from our home in Maryland and our first destination was my sister's house in the middle of a cornfield somewhere in the middle of Illinois. We left home in our 15-passenger Chevy van, (doesn't everyone need one?) which has almost enough room to carry our family of eleven and our luggage, and our cooler, and our food, and our portable playpen (crib), and our toys, and our diapers, and our diaper bags, and our strollers, and our office and art supplies, and our books, and our baby seat, etc. Thankfully, my brother gave me and installed a luggage carrier on the top. The van is three-tone (original blue, primer gray, and orange rust) and has no radio, but boasts an environmentally friendly open-the-windows-when-the-van-is-moving air conditioning system.

Our first stop was a McDonald's bathroom, just a short forty-minute drive from our house. When you travel across this great country with nine small children, one of the advantages is the incredible number of bathrooms you get to see.

After getting back on the road we decided to have breakfast. When our family was smaller we used to enjoy the convenience of boxed cereal on our vacations, but this time we brought bagels. Boxed cereal eventually became a logistical nightmare because everyone would be calling for more milk and more cereal and everything had to be passed between five rows of seats. Inevitably the milk would be spilled as well as a bowl or two. So now we have bagels.

Shortly after breakfast we got on the Pennsylvania turnpike. You may think turnpikes are expensive, but we just love them. They have those super convenient rest stops right off the highway with buildings that have lots and lots of toilets. When you have a wife and six daughters, the number of toilets is crucial.

We had lunch in the car somewhere in Ohio. What's nice about not being able to afford eating out is that it eliminates the stress and divisiveness that trying to agree on a restaurant can cause. We had subs and trail mix. We had learned on a previous trip that chocolate melts rather quickly in a car without air conditioning in the summer. Fortunately, the trail mix only had M&Ms. The melted chocolate did make the trail mix a messy finger food, but we had never had trail mix before where everything tasted like chocolate. We love trying new foods.

The trip had gone faster and smoother than we expected, until we hit road construction in Indiana. It amazed me how the entire interstate across Indiana was under construction. Their efficiency in tearing up 150 miles of road at the same time was a marvel, but it made for inefficient travel.

Anyhow, it gave me a chance to get my first break from behind the wheel. My wife Cindy graciously took over the driving while we were stopped in traffic on the interstate. After having driven 500 miles on half a night's sleep, I was exhausted and fell asleep immediately. The ten-minute break I got was invigorating. I woke up to the soothing, natural sound of a screaming baby who suddenly decided that mother's milk was needed immediately.

The Indiana delay, however, was all for the best because we still got to the appointed Illinois cornfield two hours before the designated time. You see, my sister and brother-in-law both work second shift and were due home at midnight. We arrived at 10:00 p.m. Some may think that spending two hours on the front porch of a locked relative's house in the dark with nine children surrounded by cornfields would be a challenge. First of all, it wasn't completely dark. They had a lamp on in their front yard, which was actually very interesting because it attracted swarms of June bugs. Unfortunately for the bugs, quite a few died next to the lamp on the walk leading up to the house. This gave the children a topic for much interesting conversation. There was much speculation on the cause of so many bugs' demise. There were also so many fireflies in the cornfield that one of my kids thought people were shooting off fireworks. (It was July 3.) We did our usual family devotions and then my children started running around on the lawn. As we sat on the porch wondering whether the police would come by, whether we were at the right house, and whether my sister had forgotten we were coming and went on vacation herself, the time drew near for our hosts' arrival. At this time, we began wondering whether the cars that traveled down the country road were our hosts. Quickly, we turned it into a thrilling game, as everyone guessed which car would be them.

Of course, since my sister got out late from work the game became intense and dramatic as cars became visible on the horizon and then at the last minute passed us by. Finally the fun ended and my sister and her husband came home. (Nobody did win the game.) After talking to my sister for three hours, we went to bed. The next morning we ate and talked. The afternoon and evening were similar as we ate and talked until three in the morning. The next morning, we ate and talked and then went to Wisconsin. I'm sure my brother-in-law wonders how people can eat and talk for 36 hours straight. Actually, it's very easy because talk is cheap compared with going places that charge admission, and besides, our family has so many interesting (crazy) people in it that we can talk about each other for days. Our kids were treated to water gun fights, bubble blowing, basketball, and a huge color TV. In this way they survived the eating and talking quite well.

We then went to Wisconsin and stayed with Cindy's parents, where we visited with lots more relatives. The kids really enjoyed the fireworks (free), the pool table, the cards, and the piano. I think Cindy's parents would have liked the piano part better if someone actually knew how to play, but everyone was so busy enjoying themselves talking and eating that no one seemed to notice.

Our trip home was smooth and uneventful, but isn't it amazing how those red light cameras work even in the dark?

The Unvacation

As you know, overnight travel requires suitcases and suitcases are a major inconvenience in a car when you have ten children. As you can imagine, we were thrilled when my brother gave us a luggage rack for our van. Unfortunately, we didn't lock it up correctly on our first long trip and the top flew off (without us realizing it) into a cornfield near my sister's house. At this point we bought bungee cords and a tarp and we were still able to use our beloved luggage rack. So last year we headed off to my mom's house in Florida. After we fixed it so the eye of the tarp stopped beating on the top of the van, it worked pretty well, but we had a problem on our way home when we ran into a terrible thunderstorm in South Carolina. We could hardly see in front of us, so we pulled off at the first exit (a gas station - not a rest area), and I got on the roof of the van and threw all the luggage into the van. All of the suitcases, not to mention all the clothes inside them, were soaked. To be efficient we used the bathrooms there and it took half an hour and everyone got saturated with water while running from the car to the bathroom and back (the restroom was on the side of the building). After another incident when we lost a suitcase with two children's vacation clothes in Ohio, we decided we'd have to save up for another luggage carrier.

Considering all we've learned about luggage carriers and vacationing with 10 kids and no money, we thought we would be able to apply it to this year's vacation and write you a glowing report. (You would have been so proud of us!) Unfortunately, through circumstances beyond our control, our vacation (that is, our trip to visit relatives) fell through. Since we already had vacation days approved, we decided to take an unvacation. For the benefit of you who don't know the meaning of "unvacation," it means we stayed home.

On our first unvacation day we went to the park and had a family baseball game. I had been feeling tired all week, and I was wondering if that is what it was like to be old. (When I wrote this article I had no idea I had Lymes Disease!) I had my seven-year-old daughter run the bases for me when I batted. I caught every ground ball I didn't have to bend over for. I'm sure my energy and exuberance made a memorable day for my kids. Some of my older girls are starting to lose interest in baseball anyway. One of my daughters sits in the outfield and stares at the sky while the game progresses. This isn't a big deal until a ball is hit toward her. Usually she realizes where the ball is when it is past her by about thirty feet. This endears her to her competitive brothers.

The next day, I took my wife out to hear an Irish folk singer at a nearby eating establishment. When we got there, the only table available was so close to the singer he could have hit me over the head with his guitar without taking a step. Cindy decided she would save her eardrums and her hearing for her old age, so we went to another town and another establishment that had also advertised an Irish folk singer. We parked two blocks away and walked to the restaurant. The host stood outside on the sidewalk encouraging people to go inside. They had a bar in front and a restaurant in the back. The host on the sidewalk had been so successful that it was nearly impossible to get to the restaurant because the little bar was packed with people like a can of sardines. We walked outside – taking care not to look at the host on the sidewalk – and walked down the street in order to find another restaurant. We couldn't find anything in our price range that appealed to us. So, hungry, frustrated, and tired, we went back to the Irish restaurant and fought our way through the enthusiastic bar crowd and got a seat in the dining room. The food was excellent, the service fair, and the customers interesting to look at. We never knew there were so many varieties of tattoos and hair color.

The next day I was going to make it up to my wife and children. My wife had read about a sand sculpturing competition at the Inner Harbor in Baltimore, so we headed for the big city for some free big city entertainment. I got a reasonably priced parking spot a few blocks away and we walked to our destination. It's amazing how long it takes us to get our ten children to walk a few blocks, but finally we arrived at the grand sand sculpture competition. Unfortunately, there weren't many sand sculptures and the ones they had weren't very big and weren't very good. Some people have more sand in their backyard sandboxes. We studied each sculpture very carefully and stretched the joyous event as long as we could – that is, about five minutes.

Now, we were stuck in Baltimore hot, tired, and frustrated, with nothing to do and nowhere to go. At this point I came up with a wonderful idea. I would splurge and we would all eat at the food court at the Inner Harbor. When we got there, my wife reminded me that we had a meal in the crock-pot and suggested that we have a drink or an ice cream cone instead of a meal. I sat everyone down and I walked through the food court and realized that ice cream cones cost almost as much as a meal. Since I didn't want to spend fifty dollars on ice cream, we got up and went home. I carried the toddler the whole way back. I was able to see all the empty parking spaces I could have had that would have considerably shortened the walk. I guess the grand sand sculpture competition wasn't a big draw.

The trip to Baltimore was added to the list of trips that have made my wife legendary in our house. We have our yearly trips to Washington, D.C. to see the cherry buds and cherry leaves (we see blossoms once every ten years). We also went to the FBI twice and weren't able to get in. We visited a national museum that had just been closed for renovation for about three years. And finally, we had the trip to the pick-your-own farm where the prices were significantly higher than they were in the grocery store.

That was OK with me at this point, because the next day was Father's Day. We were going to visit a wonderful church in Virginia and come home to a steamed crab dinner. This day was bound to be good. Father's Day is terrific when you have ten kids at home. As Saturday night was approaching its conclusion, my wife noticed that my neck was red. I took off my shirt and she noticed that the redness went halfway down my back as well. My wife, who is a registered nurse, advised me to go to the emergency room. When I got there they gave me a yellow bracelet and told me to sit down and wait. We noticed that some people had red tags, some white, and others yellow like myself. I had a lot of time to think about the meaning of the tags since the wait was so long.

Well, it turned out I had an infection on my skin. (This was a misdiagnosis.) The reason I had been tired was because my body was fighting the infection all week. They gave me intravenous antibiotics and sent me home with a prescription. As I was walking out to the car it was starting to get light outside. It was then that it occurred to me that the yellow band they gave me probably stood for people who weren't going to get out until it was daylight.

I slept most of Father's Day, but the next day was our final day of vacation and in the summer heat we decided to do something really exciting. We went to the mall.

You may think that the mall is the last place you would want to take ten children on your vacation, but it has one very big attraction: air conditioning. You see, our air conditioner expired and the cool air is a real treat for us this year. The mall lost money on us because a substantial amount of cool air escaped when all twelve of us entered and exited the mall. We would have bought drinks there, but they must have the same management as the Inner Harbor food court - $30 for sodas.

Now you have heard of our vacation and unvacation experiences. We have decided we like vacations better than unvacations. Long, hot drives with a bunch of sweaty kids are adventurous, while unvacations are too similar to everyday life. We haven't decided yet what relatives we will impose on next year. I don't think there are any weddings next year, but you never know. Hopefully our van will survive another winter. Maybe we'll have another baby to cart around – and maybe not. It really doesn't matter where we go next year or whether we go – as long as we're going there together. It's all in God's hands and as long as we have a lot of children and no money, vacations will always be an adventure.

It's His Time

Whether we are managing time, money, possessions, or people, the goal should be the same: To make the most of the time, resources, and talents God has given us in order to advance God's kingdom in the world. Jesus said, "Seek first his kingdom and his righteousness." Our motivation for doing our King's work should be our love and gratitude to Jesus Christ for taking our sins upon Himself and paying for them on the cross. We are also mindful that the work we do for our King will be judged. The writer of Hebrews wrote, "The Lord will judge his people," (Heb. 10:30) and Paul said our work "will become evident; for the day will show it because it is to be revealed with fire, and the fire itself will test the quality of each man's work. If any man's work which he has built on it remains, he will receive a reward. If any man's work is burned up, he will suffer loss; but he himself will be saved, yet so as through fire." (1 Cor. 3:13-15)

The work available for us to do for the kingdom is great. Jesus said, "The harvest is plentiful and the workers are few." However, we have only an unspecified and very limited amount of time to do this great work. James warns, "Yet you do not know what your life will be like tomorrow. You are just a vapor that appears for a little while and then vanishes away." (James 4:14) Solomon adds, "If no one knows what will happen, who can tell him when it will happen? No man has authority to restrain the wind with the wind, or authority over the day of death." (Eccl. 8:7-8a)

Since the work is so great and our time so short, we need to effectively manage the time God gives us. In this article we will discuss three biblical principles of time management.

Principle #1 – Give God the first, the best, and the rest of your time: God asked the Israelites for their firstborn, their firstfruits, and the first ten percent of their increase. Giving God our first and our best honors Him and expresses tangibly our faith in His provision. We should consider, then, beginning our day with Scripture reading and prayer. If our time in God's word is the first thing we do every day, we can be sure we will never miss reading our Bibles. If we wait until lunch or until after our work day is completed we are likely to have situations that push our Bible reading and prayer time out of the day altogether. It might be a surprise meeting at lunchtime, a longer than expected work day, unexpected duties at home, or we may be so tired that we cannot keep our eyes open to read. When we miss our time with God we are saying that everything in our life that day is more important than Him and that we don't need Him to get through the day. We dishonor God with the leftovers of our day – if there are any – and then we want Him to honor us with His blessings. Therefore, we ought to give God the first and the best of our time.

That being said, I don't want to leave the impression that the first few minutes of the day are all God deserves. God told Joshua, "This book of the law shall not depart from your mouth, but you shall meditate on it day and night, so that you may be careful to do according to all that is written in it; for then you will make your way prosperous, and then you will have success." (Josh. 1:8) We should also consider the example of godly Daniel, of whom it is written, "he continued kneeling on his knees three times a day, praying and giving thanks before his God." (Dan. 6:10) Joshua and Daniel were men who had demanding and responsible jobs, so we can't use our busy schedule or our job as an excuse. If we are to make proper use of our time we need to be in constant communion with our God. Indeed, Paul goes so far as to say, "With all prayer and petition pray at all times in the Spirit." (Eph. 6:18)

In addition to making sure our own souls are nourished through meditation on God's word and through prayer, we parents must make sure our children's spirits are nourished as well. We need to make sure our children, too, are giving God the first and the best of their time, that they are meditating day and night on God's word, and that they are learning to pray in the Spirit on all occasions. We can see to it that they begin every day in God's word, and that they set aside time every day – as Daniel did – to pray. We should also have daily family devotions where we teach our children to worship, to sing, and to pray to our God – even as we read and explain God's word to them. We have been poor stewards of God's time if we don't make time in our day to feed our children spiritually. Jesus said, "Man shall not live on bread alone, but on every word that proceeds out of the mouth of God." (Mat. 4:4) We generally feed our children's bodies at least three times a day and would consider it child abuse to feed them only on Sundays or whenever we could fit it into our day. We need to give the souls of our children the same importance we give their bodies. We know that the souls of men will last into eternity but everything else we see around us will not. We should, therefore, use our time to have the greatest impact we can on the souls of men. We should start by feeding our own souls and the souls of our children.

Principle #2 – Work as unto the Lord: God commands us to work, so we should work diligently. Paul wrote, "Whatever you do, do your work heartily, as for the Lord rather than for men, knowing that from the Lord you will receive the reward of the inheritance. It is the Lord Christ whom you serve." (Col. 3:23-24) If we truly believed that our job, our housework, and our work in the church were being overseen directly by the Lord and that He would reward us for our efforts, most of us would make better use of our work time. Many of us apply a standard of mediocrity to ourselves regarding our work. As long as we are working as hard as the next guy we are not very hard on ourselves. Instead, we should be trying to be the most productive workers we can possibly be. No matter what others are doing, if we are not working "with all our heart" we are not meeting God's standard.

However, the fact that God wants us to work hard doesn't tell us how much hard work He wants us to do. What biblical guidelines can help us determine how long our work day or our work week should be? The first guideline is that we are to work six days a week. God said, "Six days you shall labor and do all your work, but the seventh day is a sabbath of the LORD your God; in it you shall not do any work, you or your son or your daughter, your male or your female servant or your cattle or your sojourner who stays with you. For in six days the LORD made the heavens and the earth, the sea and all that is in them, and rested on the seventh day; therefore the LORD blessed the sabbath day and made it holy." (Ex. 20:9-11) Therefore, if we, our children, or our employees are working seven days a week, we are working ourselves and them too hard, and if we work less than six days a week perhaps we should consider picking up the pace.

Biblical guidance for how long the work day should be is sparse. We have no direct command from the Lord, but my best guess is that God made the day about twelve hours long and intended us to work during the day. I realize the context of this verse is different, but Jesus did say, “We must work the works of Him who sent Me as long as it is day; night is coming when no one can work.” (John 9:4) If we work as long as it is day we will work about 12 hours per day. Since God gave us a need for about 8 hours of sleep per night, that gives us 4 hours to eat, groom, commune with God, relax, and enjoy each other’s company.

People who are working more than 12 hours a day 6 days a week are in danger of cutting out parts of their life that are necessary for their physical and spiritual health. If we don’t get any physical exercise or an adequate amount of sleep, we may weaken our resistance to disease, shorten our lifespan, and work less efficiently because we are tired. Or perhaps we take care of our bodies, but don’t make time to feed our souls or the souls of our children.

Another biblical principle related to work is that we should work first and rest later. When God made the universe He worked six days and then He rested. Our lives, too, are filled with hard labor, but afterward we will enjoy our eternal rest. God didn’t rest until His work was finished and we won’t get our eternal rest until our work is finished. For this reason, I am constantly reminding my children to work first and play later. We want them to understand that rest is the reward we get for our hard work.

Principle #3 – Do not eat the bread of idleness (Prov. 31:27): The sin of idleness is so serious that Paul said, “Now we command you, brethren, in the name of our Lord Jesus Christ, that you keep away from every brother who leads an unruly life and not according to the tradition which you received from us. For you yourselves know how you ought to follow our example, because we did not act in an undisciplined manner among you, nor did we eat anyone's bread without paying for it, but with labor and hardship we kept working night and day so that we would not be a burden to any of you; not because we do not have the right to this, but in order to offer ourselves as a model for you, so that you would follow our example. For even when we were with you, we used to give you this order: if anyone is not willing to work, then he is not to eat, either." (2 Thess. 3:6-10)

Most of us, however, are not guilty of full-time idleness. We waste our time on a part time basis. Many of us are easily distracted by the emails, the TV shows, the computer games, the telephone calls, the news shows, the crossword puzzles, the novels, the internet, and perhaps even by magazines – all the things that pull us away from our work before the work is done. If we added up and made public the amount of time these things take from our day, I believe many of us would be embarrassed. We ought to work when it is time for work and save our extracurricular activities for a time after the work is done.

Conclusion: I have read a few books on time management and most of them leave out the most important thing. Apart from the will of God it doesn't matter whether we make a lot of money, advance in our careers, or run a tight ship at home. Our purpose should be to honor God with the time He gives us by working to advance His kingdom on earth.

God deserves the first and the best of our time, but He deserves more than that. Our entire life should be devoted to God as a willing sacrifice of praise and love for what He has done for us. God has given us great and eternally significant work to do and we should work at the tasks He assigned to us with all our heart. This work might seem insignificant or burdensome. Our work might include changing diapers or we might be laboring for a demanding and thankless boss. Even so, we are to do everything as unto the Lord. That baby who needs a diaper change needs help now, but someday he will be the head of a godly home and a witness of the Gospel wherever he goes. Therefore, we shouldn't despise the humble work God has assigned to us.

We must also keep our time in perspective. First, we must keep a proper balance between work and rest. God did not intend for us to be workaholics or to be lazy. I believe a 12 hours a day, 6 days a week work schedule is consistent with biblical principles. Second, we should remember that the souls of men are the only things around us that will survive into eternity. We must, therefore, keep an eternal perspective on time.

Finally, we should avoid excessive idleness – allowing ourselves to be distracted so that we are much less productive than we could be and should be. The work is too important to leave undone and time is too precious to waste.

Managing the Home: Time

The longest part of the day is the part occupied with work. Unfortunately, most of us experience some degree of stress and fatigue just struggling – often times unsuccessfully – to do the things that have to be done. The job, the homeschooling, the errands, the activities, the housecleaning, the Bible studies, the meal preparations, the child raising, and all the other things that have to be taken care of can overwhelm us. This anxiety is unnecessary and sinful. God did require hard work from us as part of the curse, but that doesn't justify our anxiety. When we do our work we need to have faith that God will take care of our families with the limited time and energy our mortal bodies have to work with. In fact, God doesn't need our work, and our survival doesn't depend on it. To be sure, God expects us to "work at everything as unto the Lord," but He is the one who takes responsibility for providing for our needs. We are to seek first His kingdom and His righteousness. If we do that, God has promised "all these things shall be added unto" us. When we stress ourselves over the fact that our best efforts at work don't seem adequate to meet our obligations, we are saying to God that we don't trust him. How foolish we are to take God's worries upon ourselves. God is perfectly trustworthy and able to keep all His promises, yet we worry about things God has promised to take care of. Instead of casting all of our cares upon Him, we cast all His cares upon ourselves. We need to work hard, but we need to relax.

Most of us accept the fact that we need to budget our money, but it doesn't occur to some that time needs to be budgeted as well. We have a finite income and unlimited possibilities for spending money, so we need to budget our spending so that we stay within the limits of our income.

Likewise, we have a finite amount of time and unlimited possibilities for spending our time. Therefore, we need to budget our day so that we don't obligate ourselves to more than we have time for.

In a budget for money we are told to first write down our income. Through our own efforts and sometimes through events beyond our control our income will go up or down. Time is easier because everyone has 24 hours to spend every day. Our time "income," therefore, never changes. Our next step is to list our *necessary* time expenses. We must first budget all necessary items and then we can see how much time is left over for luxuries.

Budget Step #1 – Giving God His due: Our first time "expense" should be the time we *must* set aside for the Lord. I would include personal Scripture reading and prayer, our church's weekly meeting, and family devotions as necessary. Bible studies, youth group activities, and other church activities are important, but I wouldn't consider every church activity a necessity. If we wanted to, we could spend so much time at church we wouldn't be able to take care of our households properly.

Budget step #2 – Identifying the necessary stuff: The next item we can budget is the work that is *necessary* to earn a living. If the household can survive on one income, budget that job in the schedule. If two jobs are necessary – as it is in our household at this time – then budget the second job in the schedule as well. The time budget for work should include commute time, work that must be done at home, and preparations that must be made before leaving.

Once that is accomplished, the necessary housework should be added to the budget. Meals, laundry, homeschooling, and cleaning are items that must be done daily and can be a normal part of the daily routine. There are other necessary jobs that may not need to be done every day but still have to be done. Shopping, medical and dental appointments, haircuts, and house and car maintenance are examples. The biggest challenge is to be honest about distinguishing between needs and wants.

Budget step #3 – Doing the necessary stuff more efficiently: Once we have identified those things that absolutely must get done, we should look at each task individually and see if there is a better, more efficient way to get it done. We should also look at how we can order our work in the most efficient way. This requires planning. Let's use the task of grocery shopping as an example of how we can increase our speed and efficiency in completing necessary tasks. Perhaps right now you're going to the store nearly every day to buy food. I've had days when I went to the grocery store three times. However, if we plan out our food purchases and write an accurate list of what we need, we might be able to go to the store once or twice a week. This could save us a considerable amount of time each week. Of course, planning our food purchases presumes that we know what we are going to eat. Many people write detailed meal plans so they know exactly what they need when they go to the store. This may be the best way, but it requires planning time and the ability to make adjustments when the grocery store doesn't have the needed items. At our house we have tried to keep a small stock of ground beef, chicken, and other meats we find on sale, an assortment of large cans of vegetables, and potatoes, rice, noodles, flour, and other staples. Our kids make most of the meals, so they can surprise us with different combinations of meat, vegetable, starch, and flavoring. When we buy fresh fruits and vegetables on sale, we try to incorporate those into our meals as soon as possible so they don't spoil. For us, this system requires less planning and adjusting, and more flexibility than planning every meal. I'm not saying our way is the best for everyone, but it is time efficient. The point is not that others need to buy into our system for food purchases, but that everyone should have some system for knowing in advance what they need at the store so they aren't wasting a lot of time continually going to the store.

Another issue involving the time it takes to go grocery shopping might be what time and day we do our shopping. We might consider planning trips to the store when the lines tend to be the shortest. Once inside the store there may still be ways to save precious time. We might walk faster as we push our carts through the isles, skip isles we don't need anything from, or we might start bringing a pen to cross off the items on our list once we have them in our carts. We might also write our list in the order we would find the items at the store so we won't keep backtracking for things we didn't see when we passed them the first time. When we bring our groceries home, if we have already decided on a place for each item, we may be able to save time putting the food away. This also makes it easier to make a list the next time we go.

Finally, we might consider what else needs to be done outside the house on the days we go grocery shopping. Depending on the circumstances, it might be more efficient to do all our errands at once. If the barber, the doctor, the department store, the home improvement store, or the job is in the same direction as the store, it might be more efficient to do our errands in a way that saves driving time.

You see, then, that this one job – buying groceries – offers many opportunities for doing the job faster and for doing it more efficiently in conjunction with the other jobs that need to be done. This is difficult to teach and to learn because every person's situation is different and changes continually. Some people have to drive a long way to get to the store, while others may live close by. Some people live near multiple grocery stores and may take advantage of various sales in different stores, while another person has more limited choices. Some people have large families and some have small families. Some people might have to bring children with them to the grocery store and others might go by themselves on the way home from work. Some people have a large freezer and an extra refrigerator, while others have limited space. This doesn't even account for the fact that some people prefer to work in different ways. One person wants to plan everything in detail and stick to the plan, while others will only follow general guidelines and demand room for spontaneity. Consequently, when someone advocates a "system" that works well for him, it will have to be changed to fit your situation if it works for you at all.

The bottom line, however, is to make every necessary job take as little time as possible given your situation, your resources, and your temperament. The same principles that are used to make grocery shopping more efficient can be applied to any job around the house. If you want housecleaning to take less time, take the time to analyze each task, when possible implement ways that will make the job take less time, and see if the work can be done in a more efficient order – taking into consideration the other jobs that must be done. This will work for laundry, housecleaning, homeschooling, or any other task at home or at work.

So far we have been discussing each job as if we were doing each one by ourselves. Part of our job as parents is to train our children to be productive adults. When our kids get married it would benefit them to know how to take care of babies and small children, how to do laundry, how to make meals, how to do dishes, and how to maintain a house and a car. Children, therefore, should be included at appropriate ages in the work of the household. My wife has had people at her job ask her how she goes about assigning jobs to her children because they have never given their kids meaningful jobs around the house. In a house with ten children, we wouldn't be able to make it if we had to do all the work ourselves.

Children, then, need to be taught to share in the work and to do their work as quickly and as efficiently as possible. This requires an extra investment of time because training children to do a job quickly and efficiently requires that someone show them what to do, give them feedback as they learn the job, and hold them accountable even after they are able to do the job on their own. In the end, however, this investment is well worth it because as our children become more productive they will save us much more work than we expended to train them.

Including our children in the work of the household also gives us the opportunity to share our lives with our kids. Some jobs, such as folding laundry or working in the kitchen, can be done in pairs. When we work with our kids it gives us an opportunity to build a special relationship with them and to teach them the things of God.

As toddlers, children can begin to pick up after themselves. At about age 7 we have our kids start doing dishes and folding laundry. Our kids start making breakfast about age 10, lunch around age 11, and dinner around age 12. At age 12 we also start allowing our kids to cut the grass and run the washer and dryer. For cleaning tasks we sometimes pair our younger children with older ones, so the kids learn how to do the job right and to give the older children some help. Older children are assigned rooms and are responsible for keeping them clean. Someone must still check the work, however, because standards tend to slip quickly when the children are not held accountable for the quality of their work. I'm sure we all use our kids in slightly different ways, but too many of us underutilize them in the work of the household. Not only will this make our work needlessly difficult and time consuming, but it will also spoil the kids and make them less able to manage a household when they come of age. If we feel like we need a hand with the work, we should count the hands of our school age kids and get a hand from them.

At this stage in our lives, our kids do more work around the house than we do. They prepare most of the meals, do most of the laundry, and clean most of the house. We are working at making a living (which due to the mistakes of my youth takes the efforts of two people), homeschooling, supervising the household, raising the children, and running errands.

Time traps: Before we leave this topic, I would like to share some time wasting traps I've fallen into. First, I haven't been focused enough to give the necessary tasks the highest priority and I allow myself to be interrupted by the computer, the telephone, or the kids. I end up doing things I haven't planned on – some of which are not very important and others that are totally unnecessary. I'm not saying our kids' needs should be ignored. Infants and toddlers, especially, have needs that cannot be deferred. However, many phone calls, emails, and many requests from children can and should be dealt with at a later time. If the work is done efficiently there should be time to enjoy our children later – when the work is done and we are free from other distractions.

Second, I am often too lazy to do two things at the same time. For example, I might be able to write the bills when the washing machine is finishing and lunch is on the stove. I might be able to clean off the desk while I'm talking on the phone.

Third, I am too lazy to efficiently use small gaps of time between jobs. For example, if I finish this article 15 minutes before mealtime, I might waste that time when what I really should do is clean off my desk. You would be surprised how much time a person can waste in this manner. For some expert time wasters like myself, it could be an hour or two every day. As parents, we also have the obligation to train our children not to waste time either. We need to do the best we can to set a good example and to watch our children's progress, so we can let them know if they are wasting time.

The goal, which will never be fully accomplished, is to get our necessary work done as quickly and as efficiently as possible in a way that utilizes all the members of the household and trains our children to manage their own households as adults. As we do this we should strive to accomplish a much more lofty goal, which is the mentoring of our children in the faith, in the Word of God, and in living the Christian life.

All this requires forethought and planning. We should probably write down all the work that needs to be done and assign each person his tasks. We also need to make sure that each person is held accountable for the work assigned to him. We also need to plan the day so that the members of the family are working together as efficiently as possible. Managing a household, then – especially a large household – will need order, discipline, love, and faith. Order and discipline are required to keep everything running efficiently. Love is necessary to keep us working and living together in Christian unity. And faith is required to make God's vision and purpose for our family our vision and purpose.

Budget step #4 – Budgeting rest and exercise:

Now that we've eliminated the fat from the necessary tasks of our day, we are ready to make formal changes to our time budget. Our budget should now have our necessary time with God, our duties involved in making a living, and the work we must do at home. At this point we can add another necessary item: rest. I think one of the mistakes we make is not allowing ourselves enough time for sleep and for breaks during the workday. Studies have shown that factory workers who get breaks produce more and do better work than workers who must work without a break. It is natural for us to slow down the pace if it is a long time until we can rest. Work becomes a marathon or, even worse, a bad dream that never ends and we slow down the pace to help ourselves survive. Try to give yourself at least a chance to get a good night's sleep and a short break after every couple hours of hard work. Treat the work as a few short sprints. You'll probably find you accomplish more – even though you are giving yourself more time for sleep and for work-breaks.

I realize, as a father of ten children, that new babies make sleep and rest a challenge and that sometimes it is necessary to work tired. Newborns may be up every night for weeks, people get sick, or our jobs may demand we work extended hours. All these things could be happening at the same time. The fact that life gives us days when we are forced to work tired does not mean it is wise to permanently schedule inadequate rest and sleep deprivation. Many of us need to turn off the TV and go to bed earlier.

Most of us also neglect the exercise of our bodies. Unless we have a job that allows us to get our exercise there, we should schedule times of regular exercise. It is recommended that we get at least 20 minutes of aerobic exercise four times a week for a healthy heart. We should also do exercises at least three times a week that tone the other muscles. This does not necessarily require a health club membership. I run and do pushups and situps – just as I did when I was in the military. My wife uses an exercise video. These are inexpensive and time efficient ways of exercising our bodies. We don't have to get ourselves publicly presentable and then drive to the gym before we begin exercising.

Generally, proper rest and exercise will make us stronger and more energetic for the work God has assigned to us and increase our lifespan. We should also be mindful that our bodies are temples of the Holy Spirit. Therefore rest and exercise should be budgeted into our day as necessary tasks.

Budget step #5 – Budgeting what's not necessary: At this point our time budget should have everything in it that must be done. If we have any time left, we can fill our schedule with the time luxuries. Our first priority should be our immediate families. We should make sure we are spending some non-work time with our kids. Our kids need to know we enjoy them and appreciate their company – that we don't think of the older ones as work-savers and the younger ones as time-wasters.

After we have scheduled all necessary items and some extra time with our immediate families we can evaluate our time budget and see how much time we have left – if any – for individual activities, such as hobbies and sports, and for activities that expand our influence in the world, such as extra church and political involvement.

When we have a budget that realistically estimates the amount of time different activities take, we are forced to realistically set priorities and ration our time. We won't over-commit ourselves because before we pledge ourselves to a time consuming activity we will have to make sure we have the time available to us in our budget.

One of the problems many people have is saying no to demands for time from worthy causes. We should not feel pressured to commit ourselves to organizations that help us expand our influence outside of our home when we are unable to adequately meet our responsibilities inside the home. Some of us need to understand that the typical two-child family that sends the kids to school all day will have less work at home than families with disabled or chronically ill children, many children, homeschooled children, no spouse, or disabled or chronically ill elderly relatives. We may be at a stage in our lives that is not conducive to heavy church involvement, community activities, or hobbies. Let the singles be the itinerants who turn the world upside-down for Jesus Christ. Let the childless couples, the couples whose children are grown, and the couples whose household burden is relatively light bear the lion's share of the work in the church and in other worthy organizations. The work you do at home to raise a family should be considered your ministry of first importance. If God has given you a ministry at home that even with diligent work and efficient management takes all your spare time, you shouldn't feel obligated to take on other responsibilities. You need to be satisfied with the stage of life you are in, thank God that He has given you a household that requires so much meaningful work, and wait for a time when responsibilities diminish before you expand your horizons outside the home.

Conclusion: Getting it all together: I have always been known as a disorganized person, but I have struggled for years to overcome my natural weakness. I'm not as organized or time efficient as I want to be, but I know that the sincere struggle has yielded some positive results. If we feel like our lives and our homes are a disorganized mess we tend to get overly discouraged about the problem. Instead of giving up, we should start with one task and try to implement a better, more efficient way of doing it. Then we should move to another task and then another – one task at a time. We should also develop a routine – a plan for doing our work in a set order that maximizes efficiency. If we are patient, we will probably notice that we are accomplishing more work in less time. Whether we become the super-organized, super-efficient people we want to be is not the issue. The important thing is whether we are doing our best to improve as fast as we can. We need to strike a balance, then, between complacency and anxiety. We don't want to condone our poor stewardship of time, but we don't want to depress and worry ourselves either because we are not as time efficient as we could be. We are all works in progress until the day God takes us home.

God's Economy

There is no excuse for being dirty and disorganized. As God's ambassadors in the world and as stewards of the resources He gives us, we are obligated to have a clean and organized household and to manage our time and money as efficiently as we can.

For those of you who don't know, I am eminently unqualified to write this article. I got behind when I was 8 years old (33 years ago) and I still haven't caught up. Household organization, money management, and time management have always been a tremendous struggle for me – and every time I begin making progress it seems God laughs and gives us another baby.

Books on these subjects have always been a source of frustration to me. God gifted some people with an incredible gift of organization. Some of these people develop intricate systems of organizing things that only a person with the gift could possibly maintain. They are perceptually challenged – not comprehending what it is like for the poor slob who can't seem to keep his desk organized or his room cleaned. Similarly frustrating have been books that advised me how to get out of debt and get my wife home from her job. Apparently, all I needed to do was stop eating at restaurants, stop getting pizza delivered, drive a used

Honda instead of a BMW, shop for our family's wardrobe at Wal-Mart instead of Macy's, and forget about buying that trophy home. I'm sure this was helpful advice for some, but for Cindy and I, a three-year-old Honda and new clothes at Wal-Mart would have been luxuries we simply couldn't afford. This article, then, is my attempt to share a perspective that isn't normally communicated, and to share the wisdom I have gained from years of struggling with these issues.

Money and Faith: Prosperity is better than the alternative, but one of the ill-effects of long-term prosperity is our tendency to forget that we are wholly dependent upon God for everything we have. The wealthy man is no less dependent on God to sustain him than the man who can't tell you where the next house payment is coming from. God says in His word, "When you have eaten and are satisfied, you shall bless the LORD your God for the good land which He has given you. Beware that you do not forget the LORD your God by not keeping His commandments and His ordinances and His statutes which I am commanding you today; otherwise, when you have eaten and are satisfied, and have built good houses and lived in them, and when your herds and your flocks multiply, and your silver and gold multiply, and all that you have multiplies, then your heart will become proud and you will forget the LORD your God who brought you out from the land of Egypt, out of the house of slavery. He led you through the great and terrible wilderness, with its fiery serpents and scorpions and thirsty ground where there was no water; He brought water for you out of the rock of flint. In the wilderness He fed you manna which your fathers did not know, that He might humble you and that He might test you, to do good for you in the end. Otherwise, you may say in your heart, 'My power and the strength of my hand made me this wealth.' But you shall remember the LORD your God, for it is He who is giving you power to make wealth, that He may confirm His covenant which He swore to your fathers, as it is this day." (Deut. 8:10-18) Good money management begins, therefore, with the acknowledgement that the power to get money comes from God.

Our next step is to remember that God has promised to meet our needs. Jesus said, "I say to you, do not be worried about your life, as to what you will eat or what you will drink; nor for your body, as to what you will put on ... For the Gentiles eagerly seek all these things; for your heavenly Father knows that you need all these things. But seek first His kingdom and His righteousness, and all these things will be added to you. So do not worry about tomorrow; for tomorrow will care for itself." (Matt. 6:25, 32-34a) When we consider that we are dependent on God to sustain us, we should be comforted by God's promises to provide for us, for God is immortal, all-powerful, and always keeps His word. We should not be concerned, then, about whether we can make it or not. God will see that we have everything we need.

Yet, many of us worry far too much about money. People who are experiencing financial difficulties are often consumed with worry, and others who take good care of their money are often motivated by an unhealthy fear. Fear and worry are opposed to faith, and without faith it is impossible to please God. This anxiety causes us to make poor decisions about what to do with our money. It causes many to give God a small offering based on what is left over at the end of the pay period rather than giving God the first cut. It causes others to be selfish and stingy with the people around them. Some become bitter or discouraged and take their frustration out on the people around them. Still others internalize their anxiety, which may negatively affect their health. At the very least, anxiety about money will cause us to focus our minds needlessly on our finances when we could be communing with God in prayer or noticing the needs of those around us.

Fear about money may also cause us to run from our calling like Jonah. Perhaps God has called us to preach the Gospel, start a business, get married, or adopt a child, but we are afraid that the God who called us may not also provide for us. We are like the fair weather disciples who cried, "Lord, save us! We're going to drown!" when they saw the wind and the waves. Jesus rightly said of them, "You of little faith." Our faith in God, then, should give us a peace and a confidence about money that should distinguish us from the unbelievers around us.

But our faith should do more than that. We should grasp from the Scriptures that God's economic principles are different than the principles they teach in school. The world relies on a finite earth for its sustenance. That is why some worldly people are so obsessed with the environment. This world is all they have, so they need it to last forever. According to the world, the more generous I am and the more children I have – the less I have for myself. That is why many worldly people limit the size of their families and wish everyone else would do likewise. The world may respect a generous or principled man, but the worldly man believes that being too generous or too principled can be detrimental to his financial well-being. The world is engrossed in striking a balance between enjoying the finer things of life now and accumulating enough for a comfortable and work-free retirement. A man who can retire early and spend the rest of his life traveling, eating out, and playing golf is considered to have made it. Jesus told a story about such a man who said to himself, " 'Soul, you have many goods laid up for many years to come; take your ease, eat, drink and be merry.' But God said to him, 'You fool! This very night your soul is required of you; and now who will own what you have prepared?' So is the man who stores up treasure for himself, and is not rich toward God." (Luke 12:19-21)

God's economic principles are so different from the world's. God wants us to rely on Him for our sustenance, and His supply is infinite. In God's economy, manna can rain down from heaven, water can come out of rocks, and five loaves and two fish can feed more than 5,000 people. In God's economy, those who are generous will get more for themselves. Jesus said, "Give, and it will be given to you. They will pour into your lap a good measure--pressed down, shaken together, and running over. For by your standard of measure it will be measured to you in return." (Luke 6:38) In God's economy, large families aren't synonymous with poverty. God promised the Israelites, "If you walk in My statutes and keep My commandments so as to carry them out ... I will turn toward you and make you fruitful and multiply you, and I will confirm My covenant with you. You will eat the old supply and clear out the old because of the new." (Lev. 26:3b, 9-10) In God's economy, no matter how poor our earthly existence becomes, we can be assured of an everlasting retirement with perfect health and unfathomable prosperity. Not even the country club paves its streets with pure gold.

This should cause the believer to prioritize his finances very differently from the worldly man. We understand that the wealth we enjoy in this world is temporary. If we work merely to indulge ourselves in this life, we are foolish indeed, for God will reward us according to how our work impacts eternity. Paul writes, "Each man's work will become evident; for the day will show it because it is to be revealed with fire, and the fire itself will test the quality of each man's work. If any man's work which he has built on it remains, he will receive a reward. If any man's work is burned up, he will suffer loss; but he himself will be saved, yet so as through fire." (1 Cor. 3:13-15) Therefore, we must understand that the car we drive, the house we live in, the clothes we wear, our positions at work, and the money we accumulate will not survive into eternity. However, the souls of our spouses and children, our friends and family, and our co-workers and acquaintances will all survive into eternity. The impact we have on the souls of people, then, is much more important than the lifestyle we enjoy. God has also promised to reward us for our generosity, good works, and the sacrifices we make for the sake of the Gospel.

Money and Planning: However, our faith that God will provide for us should not cause us to spend our money foolishly. We are still God's servants and we will all give an account to God for our stewardship of the resources He has given us. Jesus said, "For it is just like a man about to go on a journey, who called his own slaves and entrusted his possessions to them. To one he gave five talents, to another, two, and to another, one, each according to his own ability; and he went on his journey. ... Now after a long time the master of those slaves came and settled accounts with them." (Matt 25:14-15,19)

Some people of faith do not manage God's resources very well. A good manager reduces expenditures while maximizing income. Sometimes people of faith use their knowledge that God will provide for them as an excuse for undisciplined spending. They squander God's resources on things they don't need or can't afford. For a poor person this can be disastrous, but many wealthy people are also guilty of wasting their resources on an expensive lifestyle that does little to advance the kingdom of God. There is nothing wrong with eating convenience foods, eating at restaurants, driving a nice car, or living in a beautiful home, but we should keep in mind that none of these things have any eternal significance.

On the other hand, there are people of faith who don't maximize their income potential. They have learned to be content and have used it as a cover for laziness. The man who gave his servant five talents of money expected his servant to increase the value of his investment. If we can, we should be looking for opportunities to increase our income. Some of us could upgrade our skills or pursue a business opportunity. Some could pursue a position in management, while others could get more education. Women should not be exempt. The woman in Proverbs 31 "considers a field and buys it; from her earnings she plants a vineyard ... She sees that her trading is profitable, and her lamp does not go out at night" (Prov. 31:16,18 NIV), "She makes linen garments and sells them, and supplies belts to the tradesmen," and "She looks well to the ways of her household, and does not eat the bread of idleness." (Prov. 31:24,27)

That does not mean, of course, that the Christian's greatest motivation to work is for money. We commend the man who gives up a potentially lucrative career to preach the Gospel or to teach. We admire the woman who gives up a promising career to raise her children. We must understand, however, that the men who make their living from the Gospel are dependent for their income upon those who do not. We must understand that the woman who gives up a career away from the home may still – like the Proverbs 31 woman – develop home based businesses. We must understand that a man, too, may be able to manage his family more effectively if he is able to make money more efficiently or from home.

Conclusion: We Christians, then, should work hard at improving ourselves, but our motivation should be much different than that of the unbelievers who surround us. We condemn selfish ambition, greed, and "self-fulfillment." Instead, we work hard to provide for our families as efficiently as possible, to have the means to help those in need, and to support the work of the Gospel. Therefore, we try to obey God's command to be good stewards and managers of the resources He entrusts to us. Even so, we understand that we are weak and unable to sustain ourselves apart from the grace of God. Our knowledge of God's promises to provide for us gives us a peace about finances that should make us the envy of the unbelieving world.

Managing the Home: Money

Now we'll get practical – applying the principles of good money stewardship to our daily lives.

Practical principle #1 – Pay God's portion first: When the bills are being paid, the checks for the Lord's work should be written first. I had not thought much about this until a situation a few years ago when I was struggling simply to survive financially. When we ran into trouble our giving to the church was postponed and then reduced to a trickle. It was then that I realized that all those years of – what I thought was – generous giving were not so generous in the sight of God. It was not until I was tested that I realized that I was giving God the leftovers and not the first cut. This principle – that God should get the first portion of our income – is hard for us to accept. When hardship comes we tend to think of our own survival first. In a crisis, too, many of us would pay the mortgage, the car payment, and the electricity bill and cut our offering to the Lord. It's as if we think our survival depends on ourselves and not on the Lord. Where is our faith?

We ought to remember the lesson of Cain and Abel. Abel brought the fat portions from some of his firstborn. Cain brought an offering too, but God was not pleased with Cain's offering. What distinguished the two offerings was that Abel brought God the best (the fat portions) and the first (the firstborn). The tithe, too, was not contingent upon the Israelites being able to meet their necessary financial obligations. It applied to rich and poor alike. In fact, at one point God said they were poor because they had neglected their tithes. How were the poor Israelites to prosper? By waiting for their income to increase first, or by giving God His share first? Even the poor widow of Zarephath, who was collecting firewood for the last meal she and her son would have before they died, was told by Elijah to prepare something for him first. Thus, even in our poverty, we are to put God first.

Of course, those who have the faith to put God first are guaranteed all that they need. Jesus said, "But seek first His kingdom and His righteousness, and all these things will be added to you." In Malachi God said to the Israelites, " 'Bring the whole tithe into the storehouse, so that there may be food in My house, and test Me now in this,' says the LORD of hosts, 'if I will not open for you the windows of heaven and pour out for you a blessing until it overflows.' " We can write a budget and plan for God to get His portion, but are we sure God is getting His first? The best way to prove that God is getting the first and best of our money is to write the Lord's check first.

Practical principle #2 – Prayerfully make family and career choices: What is God calling you to do with your life? It would be silly to write a budget before deciding what God wants you to do. That would be akin to planning your vacation without knowing where you're going. You may buy new bathing suits and a car-top luggage carrier and later decide you're going to fly to the mountains to ski. It's a waste. We need to pray for God to reveal to us the direction He wants our lives to go before we start planning or doing things. One of the biggest mistakes I made as a youth was not thinking through what it was that God wanted me to do. I made all kinds of preparations for my future – I took the college entrance exams, obtained student loans, bought new clothes, and made other preparations to move out of state so I could go to college. But I hadn't really considered how God could use my abilities, experience, and resources to advance His kingdom. When I became disillusioned with college I dropped out and did something else, and then something else, and then something else. Many young people are like I was – they do not pray adequately for God to show them a direction for their lives. They get a little information about something that sounds good to them and the next thing you know they've made plans and have moved across the country. Then, a few months later they find that things haven't gone the way they expected and the process continues until time and circumstances eventually trap them into greater stability. Once the hard lessons are learned, the potential choices are severely diminished.

Of course, the other extreme is the person who is so satisfied in his present situation that he isn't open to God's leading. He is like a fine-tuned automobile with no steering. The solution to both extremes is a heart that communes regularly with God and is open to His leading. God can stabilize the impetuous – as He did with Simon Peter, and He can get the inflexible moving in the right direction – as He did with Paul.

What does all this have to do with money? Our direction in life shouldn't be determined by our budget. Our budget should be determined by the direction God wants us to go, which we can only discern through reading His word and through prayer.

Practical principle #3 – Make a flexible plan to fulfill your calling (a budget): Unless you have no income and don't spend anything, you need to plan what to do with your money. The more complicated your financial situation, the more complicated and formal managing your money becomes. When I was 13 my income was $6/week from a paper route. I gave 10% of my money to church, put half in the bank (for college), and spent the rest on whatever I wanted. That was my plan. I didn't need to keep records or have a written budget. Now that I have a wife and ten children, a little more planning and record keeping are required.

A budget, whether it is for a large business or a small family, is simply a plan of income and expenditures. If the list is detailed, comprehensive, and accurate it can be very useful. The first step in developing a good budget is to record every expense and every income. The longer this is done, the more useful it will be. Eventually, an accurate picture of your family's finances will develop. You'll know how much you spend on housing, how much on transportation, and even how much on coffee and donuts. Each category of expenses should be evaluated. Some expenses – like the cable TV or the daily trip to the cafeteria – are unnecessary and may be considered as prospects for elimination. Some expenses – like the food budget – are candidates for reduction. Perhaps convenience foods can be reduced, or you could buy in bulk. Other expenses aren't easily changed – like your 30-year mortgage. And still others should be increased –

perhaps the amount you're setting aside to buy your next car, the amount you're spending on hospitality, or the amount you're giving to the Lord's work. Likewise, the incomes should be evaluated. Are you working in the occupation God has called you to? Can you do anything to increase your earning potential? Can you supplement your income in some way? All these questions are personal and will differ with each person's unique circumstances and calling from God. The bottom line is that we are called to be good stewards of the financial resources God has given us. Our budget should show that we are managing our resources efficiently and, more importantly, that we are doing what God wants us to do and heading in the direction God wants us to go.

I would like to offer a word of warning about budgeting. Budgets must be flexible. Incomes and expenses can go up or down suddenly and without warning. A serious illness, a premature death, a fire, a car accident, or a million other things can make our budget worthless. Sometimes a good steward can get so engrossed in the details of the budget that he stresses himself out over all the little things that inevitably break it. He can lose all spontaneity and joy as he counts his pennies. He may also become tightfisted – not wanting to help others if the opportunity is immediate and unexpected. Budgets should be nothing more than a tool for good stewardship. They must never become our masters and they should always be subject to change – not only because change is inevitable, but also because we always want to be open to the Lord leading us in a different direction. We are here on earth as soldiers in God's army and we must be prepared to do whatever He tells us to do wherever He tells us to do it – even if we didn't plan it in our budget.

Practical Principle #4 – Avoid debt: Boy, have I learned this lesson the hard way. I was debt free when I bought my house in 1990 and two new cars in 1991. I have yet to recover. Even after over 11 years, the house is worth less than what we owe on it and we have gone through some "interesting" times. Our culture, our economy, and our government are debt driven – it's a house of cards that will certainly come crashing down if it isn't dealt with. It does come crashing down on thousands every year as 1,452,030 filed for bankruptcy in the U.S. in 2001. As wonderful as our economy and as strong as our government may appear, a day of reckoning will be a certainty unless the cycle of debt is broken.

The Scriptures warn us about debt. Proverbs 22:7 says, "The borrower becomes the lender's slave." Paul advises us in Romans 13, "Owe nothing to anyone." Moses told the Israelites that if they kept God's covenant, "You shall lend to many nations, but you shall not borrow." If the Israelites did not obey the covenant, foreigners would do the lending and the Israelites would do the borrowing. Debt, then, was considered a curse – not a blessing. In our culture we've got it all wrong. Our government makes it easy for us to borrow money. It subsidizes loans to students, veterans, farmers, and businessmen. When our government wants to encourage the economy it helps lower interest rates so that people will borrow more money. That may indeed stimulate the economy in the short-run, but eventually the money must be repaid. It creates a potential long-term disaster for a mild short-term benefit. It works the same for us on a personal level. Borrowing for the education, the house, the car, and then maintaining credit card balances will certainly allow us to live well for awhile, but eventually all the loans must be repaid.

I have learned my lesson the hard way, and I won't let my children forget it. I'm tempted to tell them they should resolve to never borrow a penny for anything – not a college education, not a house, and not a car. But I don't want to go beyond what is written in the Scriptures. The Bible doesn't condemn all debt as sin, but it warns us of debt's consequences and includes debt as part of the curse for disobedience. In our culture, however, we are proud and excited when we get our first credit card, when we buy a house with almost no money down, and when we drive out of the car dealership with a new car and a five-year loan. This is not of God and young people should be sternly warned to avoid debt if at all possible.

To those who, like me, have already buried themselves in debt, I say this: Repent if it is necessary, change your ways as much as your situation will allow, and receive the joy and forgiveness that are available in Christ Jesus. We ought to be like Paul, who forgetting what was behind, strained forward to win the prize for which Christ was calling him heavenward. Paul also said he had learned to have joy in poverty and in plenty. Our joy shouldn't depend on our income or the amount of money we have in the bank. Even if you feel jailed by your circumstances, God can use you in a mighty way. When Paul was in jail he witnessed to governors and kings about Jesus Christ, wrote many books of the Bible, and evangelized the city of Rome.

And no matter how hopeless your financial situation may appear to you, it is never hopeless if you are in Christ Jesus. God said in Joel 2:25: "Then I will make up to you for the years that the swarming locust has eaten." We must never forget that the owner of the universe is our Father. Our debt is nothing to Him. And even if we should go to the grave in debt, that debt will be forgiven like our so many sins. We will certainly enjoy eternity in a place of eternal prosperity where the streets are paved with pure gold. Paul said, "No eye has seen, no ear has heard, no mind has conceived what God has prepared for those who love him." (1 Cor. 2:9, NIV) So lift up your head, debt laden Christian, your situation is temporary. Keep trying to change your circumstances for the better, pray for God's blessings, and never give up. Sooner or later God will come to your aid. And finally, be thankful for your present situation. God has blessed you in many ways and given you many excellent promises for the future.

Conclusion: There are many specific topics of application this essay did not address that will have to be left for a later time. More specific information would be helpful concerning cutting expenses, increasing income, record keeping, and choosing a career – and the specifics are important. What we are eating for breakfast, where we buy it, and how much we buy at one time should be important to us because we are stewards of God's resources. A good steward or manager should maximize his master's profit. We must understand, however, that the profit God is looking for is not measured in dollars. For us, the money God entrusts to us is simply one of the means we have at our disposal to serve our Master and advance His kingdom. The profit God is looking for is the kind that will last into eternity. None of our money or the possessions we can buy with it will last. When we leave this earth we cannot take our money with us and eventually it will be destroyed in the fire that will mark the end of this age. So then, the details are important because the money we make and spend and the possessions we buy and sell can have an eternal impact on the souls of men. The danger in dwelling too much on the details, however, is our tendency to lose sight of the big picture.

One last thought: I don't want to be misunderstood to be saying that every expense on non-essentials is sinful. Such a position would be biblically unsupported. I am also not saying that it is sinful to have a nice house or an investment portfolio. A Christian woman I met has a beautiful home on the Delaware River that she has spent a lot of effort restoring to its present condition. The home was even featured in a magazine that showcases lovely homes. She doesn't need all the room she has for herself, but she has opened her home to complete strangers and uses it as a base of operations for the Christian Coalition and for the Gospel. Likewise, the man who uses a portion of his income as seed money to grow his business and his income may in the long run have more to give than the man who gives all his extra money away today. So then, it is not wrong to be wealthy, but it is wrong to live a life of ease and luxury while the rest of the world literally goes to hell. The rich man must be just as zealous to advance God's kingdom as the poor man.

So whether we are rich or poor we are to give God our first and our best. We are to be generous and practice hospitality. We are to put away our selfish ambition and live to advance God's kingdom. God has promised to give us everything we need and told us not to worry about our sustenance like the heathen. And even though God has promised to take care of us, He still calls us to be good stewards of what He gives us. That requires us to evaluate our income and our expenses – to make sure we are getting the biggest eternal bang for our buck.

Frustrated over Money?

While I was driving the car recently, I heard a few minutes of a Christian radio broadcast that focused on money. The host said something to the effect that anyone who followed biblical principles would have money to invest. This reminded me of something I heard at a business meeting a few years back, where the speaker said that a person's financial situation is a reflection of his faith. Some Christian financial counselors will tell you how necessary it is to fully fund your children's college and your own retirement through regular contributions to your savings accounts. I've read somewhere that a boy isn't prepared for marriage until he has trained for his occupation, is debt free, has paid for his house, and has a nest egg equivalent to a few months' income. Woe is me! Woe is my son!

If you've ever struggled financially, as I have, these kinds of statements can be very frustrating. If I calculated how much money I would need to pay off my house, have an emergency fund that represents 6 months' income, put my 11 children through college, and retire comfortably, I think my entire family would have to stop living inside, eating food, or drinking water. In fact, even then I don't think I would have enough. Does anyone else out there get a knot in his stomach when he hears how much money the prudent Christian should have socked away in the bank, or invested in growth stocks, mutual funds, IRAs, tax sheltered annuities, short term bonds, CDs, etc., etc., etc.?

Please don't misunderstand me. I'm not saying that families shouldn't have a financial cushion for emergencies. I'm not saying that families shouldn't set aside money for college and retirement, and I'm not saying that money is unimportant. But I do think many of us think too much about finances, worry too much about the future, hold our money too tightly, and preoccupy ourselves with our own situation and our own comfort. We also have a tendency to judge others who do not use their money the way we would. I admit that I struggle with these things as well.

That being said, I would like to deal first with the issue of what our financial condition says about our spiritual condition. And the simplest answer I can give is that it says nothing at all. On the one hand, it is undeniable that God blesses His people with wealth. Abraham, Isaac, Jacob, Job, David, Solomon, and Hezekiah were just some of God's people who prospered financially. God said to the Israelites, "But you shall remember the LORD your God, for it is He who is giving you power to make wealth, that He may confirm His covenant which He swore to your fathers, as it is this day." (Deut. 8:18) He also said, "All these blessings will come upon you and overtake you if you obey the LORD your God: Blessed shall you be in the city, and blessed shall you be in the country. Blessed shall be the offspring of your body and the produce of your ground and the offspring of your beasts, the increase of your herd and the young of your flock. Blessed shall be your basket and your kneading bowl. Blessed shall you be when you come in, and blessed shall you be when you go out." (Deut. 28:2-6) In the New Testament there are similar verses. Jesus said, "Truly I say to you, there is no one who has left house or brothers or sisters or mother or father or children or farms, for My sake and for the gospel's sake, but that he will receive a hundred times as much now in the present age, houses and brothers and sisters and mothers and children and farms, along with persecutions; and in the age to come, eternal life. But many who are first will be last, and the last, first." (Mark 10:29-31) Jesus also said this: "Give, and it will be given to you. They will pour into your lap a good measure – pressed down, shaken together, and running over." (Luke 6:38a)

However, it is also undeniable the many godly people have been poor or suffered financial loss. The Lord said of Job: "There is no one like him on the earth, a blameless and upright man, fearing God and turning away from evil." Yet God allowed Satan to take away all his wealth, his health and the lives of all ten of his children. Some of us, I fear, are like Job's foolish friends and accuse a man who suffers financial loss of sin. What about the Christians in North Korea or Sudan? How do you think their college and retirement funds are coming along? The writer to the Hebrews says, "Others experienced mockings and scourgings, yes, also chains and imprisonment. They were stoned, they were sawn in two, they were tempted, they were put to death with the sword; they went about in sheepskins, in goatskins, being destitute, afflicted, ill-treated (men of whom the world was not worthy), wandering in deserts and mountains and caves and holes in the ground. And all these, having gained approval through their faith, did not receive what was promised." (Heb. 11:35b-39)

In the end, God promises that the wicked will come to ruin and the righteous will inherit the land (so we know these things will come to pass), but these promises are often delayed. And because they are delayed, we can say with certainty that God's obedient, faithful servants can have great wealth or be destitute. We know, too, that some evil men live long, successful and luxurious lives, while others suffer constant deprivation. The point I am making is that you can't look at a person's financial condition and know where he is at spiritually. Some of us need to stop judging ourselves by assuming that financial hardship is caused by sin or is a sure sign that God is displeased with us.

Most of us would admit, however, that stress, anxiety, guilt, or an unhealthy preoccupation with money aren't reserved for people who are experiencing financial problems. Some people stress themselves over money when there is nothing to be stressed about, and some prosperous people get entirely too much joy out of reviewing financial documents, projecting the balance of investment accounts, or estimating net worth in the future (which never turns out the way we plan). Sometimes I think this is the modern, dignified way of wallowing in our money. (Before money was transferred electronically, we could throw our money on the bed, count it, and roll around in it for awhile.)

Why does money tend to get more attention than it deserves and why are so many Christians stressed over finances?

1. We lack faith in the promises of God: As we have already seen, God has determined and promised to prosper us. The only stipulation is that this promise may not be fulfilled immediately. Should this give us cause for alarm? Absolutely not! God has promised to provide us with everything we need. Jesus said, "For this reason I say to you, do not be worried about your life, as to what you will eat or what you will drink; nor for your body, as to what you will put on. Is not life more than food, and the body more than clothing? Look at the birds of the air, that they do not sow, nor reap nor gather into barns, and yet your heavenly Father feeds them. Are you not worth much more than they? And who of you by being worried can add a single hour to his life? And why are you worried about clothing? Observe how the lilies of the field grow; they do not toil nor do they spin, yet I say to you that not even Solomon in all his glory clothed himself like one of these. But if God so clothes the grass of the field, which is alive today and tomorrow is thrown into the furnace, will He not much more clothe you? You of little faith! Do not worry then, saying, 'What will we eat?' or 'What will we drink?' or 'What will we wear for clothing?' For the Gentiles eagerly seek all these things; for your heavenly Father knows that you need all these things. But seek first His kingdom and His righteousness, and all these things will be added to you. So do not worry about tomorrow; for tomorrow will care for itself. Each day has enough trouble of its own." (Mat. 6:25-34)

Most of us know this passage of Scripture and would acknowledge that it is true, but most of us do not live like we believe it. We are like the Israelites, who, after experiencing God's favor and His awesome power, grumbled about having been taken out in the desert to die of thirst, grumbled about the food He so graciously provided, and then forgot about God in their prosperity.

The reason we live like we do is because our faith is so small. We are like Peter, who turned his attention away from God incarnate and focused instead on the ominous wind and waves. We are like the disciples who, when told to give the throng something to eat, reacted by calculating how much it would cost instead of asking Jesus how He was planning to use them to feed all these people. We live by sight and not by faith.

How do we get the faith to stop worrying about money? "Faith comes from hearing, and hearing by the word of Christ." (Rom. 10:17) We need to read God's word daily and hear His promises continually. Based on the promises we read, then, we must determine to ignore the wind and the waves and continue to focus on the sure promises of God.

2. We are selfish: When we are overly concerned with our own circumstances we are much more likely to be anxious – or at least preoccupied – about money. We were all turned off as youngsters by the kid who always pushed his way to the front of the line, took the biggest piece of cake, and always struggled to get the first and the best. All he cared about was himself. When the selfish kid grows up, he needs a lot of money to provide himself with the first and the best. If he can't get what he wants, the selfish kid will experience stress.

Most of us wouldn't identify ourselves as the selfish kid, but if we were honest we would have to admit that we have a tendency to give our self-absorbed souls the most important place at the center of the universe. From there, the rest of creation revolves around us. We may not even be aware of the fact that our hopes, our dreams, and the subject of way too much of our thought life is about how we can succeed, how we can prosper, and how we can be happy. We think about our careers, our homes, our cars, our clothes, our appearances, our vacations, our TV shows, our social lives, our hobbies, and our food (perhaps chocolate). Everything we want almost always costs more money than what we have, so we are constantly confronted with the issue of scarcity.

If my hopes and dreams are tied to the things of the world (which require money) and not to the things of God, I will be anxious when my money isn't sufficient to meet my cravings for pleasure, comfort, and success. We need to crucify our flesh, take our minds off ourselves, and see how we can serve God and be a blessing to those around us. Perhaps then we won't have the time to be preoccupied with how much money we have (or don't have) in the bank.

3. We are irresponsible: Some of us are stressed about money because we lack self-control. Just as surely as eating more calories than we burn will make us fat, spending more money than we earn will eventually lead to disaster. I remember hearing a guy on a talk show who was single and had an income of $60,000/year and couldn't make ends meet. Apparently, he didn't like cooking for himself and his eating habits got him deep in credit card debt. This man has no self-control. He is no different than the drunk who keeps drinking – knowing full well that it isn't worth the hangover. Sometimes irresponsible people can be quite generous, but their witness is compromised by their lack of control. This may be easier said than done, but the solution to irresponsibility is quite simple. Don't spend more than you make. If you do, money will give you stress.

Ultimately, irresponsibility and lack of control are spiritual problems that often have financial symptoms. As believers in Christ the Spirit will help us overcome any weaknesses we may have, but we need to repent and believe that it is God's will that we be molded day by day into the image of Christ. Self-control is a fruit of the Spirit that is available by faith to all.

4. We are alone: Sometimes bad things happen to us and it causes a financial hardship. Death, job loss, sickness, accident, famine, war, crime, or persecution can put us in financial hardship in an instant. The Christian should be able to count on his brothers and sisters in the faith to help him in his time of need, but frankly this is not always the case. The body of Christ is divided and the relationships we have with fellow believers are often superficial. When hardship comes, no one may know but the struggling family because no one knows the family well enough to understand there is something wrong.

I'm sure Jerusalem of 2000 years ago was far less prosperous than we are, but the Scriptures say, "There was not a needy person among them." (Acts 4:34) Could we say that today? The church today reflects the impersonal culture we live in and this should not be. Part of the fault is our own. We prefer the music and preaching a large church can provide and we don't mind the fact that most people go there anonymously. We went to a large church in Maryland three times and then went somewhere else. As far as I know, no one missed us and no one called. Small churches are more conducive to building personal relationships, but it is harder to get a good band together. Which do you think is more important?

On the other hand, the church leaders are also to blame. An elder or pastor who is doing his job should know the people under his care "as one who must give an account." Paul wrote, "And if one member suffers, all the members suffer with it; if one member is honored, all the members rejoice with it." (1 Cor. 12:26) If this is the case, it should be difficult for a person to visit a church meeting anonymously and it should be impossible for a believer to go through a financial crisis alone. This requires a personal intimacy and a personal accountability not found in most churches. If the body of Christ started acting like a body, we would soon find out who the needy persons among us were, and help sustain them as long as it was necessary.

Conclusion: Why are we stressed about money? Well, if we don't accept the promises of God that He will provide for us, if we are selfish, if we lack self-control, or if we are alone in the midst of hardship we are likely to be anxious about our finances. We live in what may well be the most prosperous culture in the history of mankind, yet money problems are still a major cause of anxiety. For Christians, anxiety over finances is unnecessary. "I have been young and now I am old, yet I have not seen the righteous forsaken or his descendants begging bread. All day long he is gracious and lends, and his descendants are a blessing." (Psalm 37:25-26)

Bankruptcy, Anyone?

According to the American Bankruptcy Institute, over the past 5 years there have been more than 6,000,000 bankruptcies in the United States. New legislation has recently passed the House and the Senate attempting to limit the number of persons qualifying for Chapter 7 bankruptcy. Specifically, the bill seeks to completely revamp the system by barring people, who have the ability to pay $10,000 or 25 percent of their debts (whichever is less) in the three to five years following their request for debt relief, from filing for Chapter 7 bankruptcy, which allows consumers to erase all of their bills. Instead of having these debts dissolved, it would force them into Chapter 13 bankruptcy, which requires significant repayment under a court-approved reorganization plan. (Source: About.com.) Public opinion is mixed. Some condemn the irresponsible behavior that leads many to bankruptcy and sense that the system is being abused, while others condemn the irresponsible lending practices and excessively high interest rates charged by many credit card companies.

Meanwhile, Christians are divided over the issue. Some say bankruptcy is wrong – a failure to keep one's promises – and others counter that forgiving debt is consistent with biblical principles. What guidance can we get from Scripture on this issue?

Biblical Analysis:
The Borrower's Responsibility:

The first principle that applies to the borrower is his responsibility to keep his word. Oral and written agreements to pay back debt should be honored if at all possible. Paul writes, "Render to all what is due them: tax to whom tax is due; custom to whom custom; fear to whom fear; honor to whom honor. Owe nothing to anyone except to love one another." (Rom. 13:7-8a) Borrowing money without considering one's ability to satisfy the debt is tantamount to thievery. Likewise, those who max their credit cards in anticipation of bankruptcy are deceiving the creditor - agreeing dishonestly to take responsibility for debt they know they will never pay. Jesus said, "Treat others the same way you want them to treat you." How many of us would want to lend someone $5,000 who never took seriously his obligation to pay us back? Because we take seriously our obligations - and so do our creditors - we ought to heed the biblical warning: "The borrower becomes the lender's slave." (Prov. 22:7)

This brings us to our second principle: we should exercise prudence in our financial dealings. Prudence is being cautious, foresighted, and sensible. Prudence helps us not to presume too much about the future. We often borrow money on the assumption that our health will be good, our jobs are secure, and our plans will succeed.

James writes, "Come now, you who say, 'Today or tomorrow we will go to such and such a city, and spend a year there and engage in business and make a profit.' Yet you do not know what your life will be like tomorrow. You are just a vapor that appears for a little while and then vanishes away." (James 4: 13-14) When we sign the 30-year mortgage, two five-year car notes, and carry credit card balances, we may be presuming too much about an uncertain future. We would do better to be like the ants Solomon commended as wise for storing up for the future. War, famine, and plague - whether general or personal - are a part of life. We ought not borrow on the assumption that those things will never happen to us.

The Lender's Responsibility: Lenders are supposed to have qualities you probably won't find in your mortgage company, GMAC, or the bank that sponsors your Visa card. "If there is a poor man with you, one of your brothers, in any of your towns in your land which the LORD your God is giving you, you shall not harden your heart, nor close your hand from your poor brother; but you shall freely open your hand to him, and shall generously lend him sufficient for his need in whatever he lacks. Beware that there is no base thought in your heart, saying, 'The seventh year, the year of remission, is near,' and your eye is hostile toward your poor brother, and you give him nothing; then he may cry to the LORD against you, and it will be a sin in you. You shall generously give to him, and your heart shall not be grieved when you give to him, because for this thing the LORD your God will bless you in all your work and in all your undertakings." (Deut. 15: 7-10) "If you lend to those from whom you expect to receive, what credit is that to you? Even sinners lend to sinners in order to receive back the same amount. But love your enemies, and do good, and lend, expecting nothing in return; and your reward will be great, and you will be sons of the Most High; for He Himself is kind to ungrateful and evil men. Be merciful, just as your Father is merciful." (Luke 6: 34-36) "There were others who said, 'We are mortgaging our fields, our vineyards and our houses that we might get grain because of the famine.' Also there were those who said, 'We have borrowed money for the king's tax on our fields and our vineyards. Now our flesh is like the flesh of our brothers, our children like their children. Yet behold, we are forcing our sons and our daughters to be slaves, and some of our daughters are forced into bondage already, and we are helpless because our fields and vineyards belong to others.' Then I was very angry when I had heard their outcry and these words. I consulted with myself and contended with the nobles and the rulers and said to them, 'You are exacting usury, each from his brother!' Therefore, I held a great assembly against them. I said to them, 'We according to our ability have redeemed our Jewish brothers who were sold to the nations; now would you even sell your brothers that they may be sold to us?' Then they were silent and could not find a word to say. Again I said, 'The thing which you are doing is not good; should you not walk in the fear of our God because of the reproach of the nations, our enemies? And likewise I, my brothers and my servants are lending them money and grain. Please, let us leave off this usury. Please, give back to them this very day their fields, their vineyards, their olive groves and their houses, also the hundredth part of the money and of the grain, the new wine and the oil that you are exacting from them.' " (Neh. 5:3-11)

The Bible and Bankruptcy: What if I'm already buried in debt? Can I declare bankruptcy? I would say the answer is yes. Declaring bankruptcy is a legal means of eliminating debt and bankruptcy laws are consistent in principle to the Mosaic Law that canceled debt every seven years. It was assumed that some needy people would be unable to meet their obligations to repay and were given a fresh start every seven years. The Mosaic Law was much more generous to the borrower who couldn't repay his debts than our bankruptcy laws are today.

Lenders today may charge high interest rates, court costs, and attorney fees to win a court judgment against the borrower. Afterward he may place a lien on the borrower's house or business, garnish up to 25% of his wages, and continue to charge post judgment interest. This process may continue unless the borrower declares bankruptcy. Sometimes the lenders make it impossible for the borrower to survive unless a bankruptcy is declared. Since bankruptcy is legal, consistent with biblical principle, and sometimes necessary to survive, a Christian may declare bankruptcy.

However, that doesn't mean bankruptcy is always best. As Paul says, "All things are lawful, but not all things are profitable. All things are lawful, but not all things edify." (1 Cor 10: 23) Bankruptcy still carries a stigma that may hurt our witness for Christ. Although Paul had the right to receive money from the Corinthian believers, he set aside his rights so that no one could accuse him of spreading the Gospel in Corinth as a means of getting their money. Likewise, we have the right to declare bankruptcy, but it is a right we may choose not to exercise. It becomes, then, a matter of conscience and every situation is different. Since most bankruptcies represent the breaking of a written agreement to repay a loan, however, no Christian should enter into it lightly. Most bankruptcies (but not all) in our culture and in these times are caused by reckless borrowing and other forms of irresponsibility. The Christian who is forgiven his debt should be grateful, but do everything within his power to avoid letting the same thing happen again. We should be mindful that our bankruptcy deprives others of money they had a right to expect for services rendered. It is true that many credit card companies extend easy credit to people who have no credit history or are known credit risks. For the credit card companies, the high interest rates more than compensate for the write-offs – or credit would not be made so accessible.

It is easy, then, to blame our insolvency on our nation's banks. Nevertheless, the Christian should focus on his own shortcomings before blaming others for his problems. The banks may tempt us to borrow more money than is prudent, but we are not required to take the bait. We must take responsibility for our own misdeeds. As Jesus said, "Why do you look at the speck that is in your brother's eye, but do not notice the log that is in your own eye?" (Mat. 7:3)

Conclusion: I do not support the new law because it seems to go farther from the biblical principles that condemn exacting usury from the poor and that allow debtors to get a fresh start. Because the best people are flawed and the worst are worse, people will abuse the law whatever it is. Some lenders will crush the poor to exact every possible penny, while some borrowers will knowingly run up large debts because they have no intention of paying them. We Christians are too easily entangled in the sins of our culture. We ought to try much harder to live debt free lives and provide for our own needy without relying on the high interest or long-term loans of unbelievers. This would require more than just a change in heart and mind concerning money. It would necessitate a closer, more connected Christian community.

A Tip from a Cheerful Giver

A couple months ago I got a job waiting tables. I would recommend this job highly to anyone who wants to learn patience or the negative side of human nature. The wait staff is at the mercy of nearly every other restaurant employee. Bad cooking, bad drink making and bad bus help can make the customers upset, which isn't good when you're paid mostly on how happy the customers are. Of course, bad management can do even more damage. Poor staffing, poor ordering, and poor organization can make any shift a nightmare, especially if too many customers walk through the front door. When my customers are not happy with my service, there are often circumstances completely beyond my control.

There are times, however, when poor service *is* my fault. When I'm keeping track of 20 people's dinners at the same time I sometimes forget something or make a mistake. Overall, I would say this business is very harsh in that you usually pay immediately for your own mistakes, but you generally pay immediately for everyone else's mistakes as well. Not surprisingly, tips decrease quickly when the appetizer shows up with the main course. So we waiters and waitresses pay for shortcomings of every worker in the restaurant.

Usually the greatest source of disappointment, however, is not with our fellow workers or with our own mistakes, but with the people we lovingly call guests. There are three kinds of people that I euphemistically call character builders. The first kind I would call time wasters. Time wasters ask you to take their order when they aren't ready and you wait while the guest looks at the menu and goes through the decision process out loud. Time wasters may also share with me their life stories, or come in a large group and ask for separate checks that each require separate credit card authorization. Time wasters also may ask for many different special items - one at a time. A table of time wasters can make it nearly impossible to give other customers good service.

The second kind of character builder is the difficult guest. The difficult guest is best described as picky and hard to please. Difficult guests may start by demanding a booth or a table by the window. Once seated, they may point out that the table wobbles and the silverware isn't clean enough. When they order, difficult guests ask for substitutions and exceptions to the menu and when the food arrives it is either too cold or too spicy. The steak is never cooked properly and the drink is never made right the first time. Difficult guests are nearly impossible to please because they have exceptionally strong opinions about how things should be and they seem to have extra-sensitive fault antennae. Of course, the tip from the difficult guest is usually small, because they are almost always disappointed.

The third kind of character builder is the low tipper. Difficult guests are usually low tippers, but some of the nicest customers are lousy tippers. A 15%-20% tip is average, but many people tip less. Some people probably think that waiters make good money, but that isn't true. How many wealthy waiters and waitresses do you know? The wait staff makes $2-$3/hour and relies primarily on tips for income. Besides waiting tables there are other duties that require us to be at the restaurant long before the guests show up or long after they leave.

Some who are unfamiliar with restaurant work may be surprised to know that the waitress may not keep all her money. At my restaurant, tips must be shared with the bar, the host, the bus boy, and sometimes a person who takes food to the tables. These workers are tipped a percentage of sales and do not get less if a customer tips poorly or not at all. Low tippers give 10% or even less for average service or better. Low tippers seem to lower their tip percentage as the bill increases. They may tip $2 on a $20 bill (10.0%), but tip $4 on a $60 bill (6.7%). Similarly, many customers seem to believe that waitresses make too much on large groups and deserve a smaller tip percentage. Actually, larger groups tend to take more time to eat and they tend to linger in conversation long after the food is served. The waitresses' tables are tied up so long that they may make much less on a large group than on a series of small tables. That's why some of the wait staff do everything they can to avoid taking large groups of people – even though tables of 8 or more may have a 15% gratuity added onto the bill. There are enough time wasters, difficult guests, and low tippers to build lots of character. Not surprisingly, the turnover for wait staff is high. I work at a popular moderately priced restaurant. Two months ago I started a week long training class for new servers. We had eleven people in the class, but today only three are still working at the restaurant.

Why is all this relevant to the Christian? When Christians do not tip well they leave a bad impression on the waitress, who feels unrewarded and unappreciated for the service rendered. This is multiplied if the group is known to be a Christian group. Twenty years ago I managed a Pizza Hut where waitresses would argue over who would wait on a church group that came in regularly after church. The group spent a long time in conversation and had many coffee drinkers who spent little money, but required refill after refill. They spent two hours at the restaurant and took most of a waitress' section. They tipped 15% on their bill, which amounted to very little because many ordered coffee only. So Christianity was given a bad report by the wait staff, who told other restaurant workers, and probably their friends and relatives as well. As the Scriptures say, "The name of God is blasphemed among the Gentiles because of you." (Romans 2:24) When Christians are stingy in public we mess with God's reputation.

Yes, Christians ought to be known as generous tippers, but not primarily because they feel obligated to tip well. We should be generous tippers because we want to be generous. God gives us more than we deserve every day and we have promises for a future that will be more wonderful than we can imagine. God does all this for us, even though the best of us sin against Him with awful regularity. Shouldn't this cause us to be generous to others? We love others because God first loved us. To love the waitress is to think of the tip as more than an annoying added expense that will leave us with less money in our wallets at the end of the meal. When we leave a generous tip, we are helping a person who works hard for modest wages to have a little bit extra. We are also bringing a small amount of joy to the life of a person who will regularly deal with difficult and stingy people and who serves as a lightning rod for every mistake made in the restaurant that affects her customers.

That is not to say that lazy and incompetent service should be rewarded as well as excellent service. Though He is gracious, God also is just. We encourage good service and promote fairness when better service is rewarded with a bigger tip. We can be more generous generally and still reward good service more than bad.

So, the next time you eat out, see how generous you can be. Your waitress will appreciate the tip from a cheerful giver. "God loves a cheerful giver."

Why Home Based Businesses Fail!

My whole life I have wanted to be in business for myself. I can remember developing a letterhead for McDermott Enterprises with my father when I was about 18 years old. I was inspired to get into the restaurant business after working a couple months at Watson's Burger Hut (closed long ago) and after reading a book called "Grinding It Out" by Ray Kroc – the man who started McDonald's. I worked in restaurants for about 6 years, but never made enough money to start my own. I tried selling sandwiches at college, but that only lasted one night. I eventually tried door-to-door cutlery sales, insurance,

Amway, a Christian newspaper, a political party, and now SALT. You might say I have a lifetime of experience failing at business enterprises. Therefore, I am eminently qualified to write about how to fail in a business of your own.

This issue is dear to my heart not only because it has been a personal thorn in my side for a very long time, but also because home-based businesses have been encouraged by a number of Christians who have motivated many to strike out on their own. Many of my Christian brothers and sisters have boldly started home-based businesses with the hope of bringing the mother home, having more time and more money to disciple their children, and to be free from a tedious, purposeless, heathen-led job.

Unfortunately, the vast majority of people I know who tried to start their own businesses have failed. In fact, bankruptcy is a more common outcome than success. I'm reminded of a comment that was posted on the Patriarch Magazine website after an article encouraging home-based businesses. The writer of the critique noted that the only successful Christian home-based businesses he knew about were in the business of promoting Christian home-based businesses.

Despite the failure rate, I am not critical of those who encourage Christians to start their own businesses. I'd rather be the owner than the employee and I'd rather work from home than work somewhere else. I'd rather keep the fruit of my own labor than take whatever the heathen owner has left for me. It would be easier for my wife to fulfill her biblical calling as a wife and mother from home than from the hospital she now works at. It would be easier to homeschool and to show my children how to live the Christian faith from home than it is from my job. I would rather take Sundays off to rest and commune with believers than to hold down the fort while my unbelieving boss plays golf. Succeeding at a home-based business, then, sounds like a great idea except for the minor problem that it doesn't work for most people. Is a home-based business a good idea for you? Could you succeed in a home-based business? Or, is it something you should avoid?

Ingredients for Business Success

Before deciding whether a home-based business is right for you, you might be interested in hearing from an experienced failure why it is that people do not succeed. Perhaps you can learn from my mistakes and the mistakes of others and avoid the pitfalls that doom so many home-based businesses.

There are four areas of the business that if mastered will make the chances of success very high. Most people who fail have serious problems in at least one of these. Many people go into business naively, with serious issues in all four.

#1. Providing Value: Have you ever noticed that Christian home-based businesses often charge much more than stores do for similar merchandise? It's hard to succeed in a business that charges $7.50 for something that costs $2.09 at Wal-Mart and $1.00 at the Dollar Tree. The truth is that Christian home-based businesses usually charge way too much for their products and services. Most consumers – even Christian consumers – don't care very much what it costs the Christian businessman to provide his product. If I break even selling widgets at $7.50 each and Wal-Mart makes a profit at $2.09, most people – even most Christians – are going to get their widgets at Wal-Mart. Unfortunately for the Christian businessman, Christians are not committed to buying from their own. Many Christians have made the mistake of believing that other Christians would overlook high prices and buy from them simply because they are Christians. If others are offering a similar product at significantly lower prices, you are not providing your customers with value.

The first component in value is price. The second component is the desire people have for the product itself. Have you ever noticed that many Christian home-based businesses sell products people don't need very much? Many Christians who want to start a business cannot compete with those who provide products with mass appeal. This normally requires a huge capital investment to take advantage of economies of scale. Therefore, the Christian home-based business competes in the marketplace with products that few people want or need. Have you ever noticed that a lot of women do not like being asked to product parties because they often feel compelled to buy something they would never buy as an anonymous shopper in a store? You may have initial success, then, with a dubious product line if the people you know are willing to support you in spite of your product. However, it's hard to succeed in business long-term with a product or service people don't want.

Another form of the value problem is the business that provides a product many people buy, but in a high quality/high priced form that most people don't consider a value. The problem again is that the small-scale business cannot compete in a market that normally requires mass production or a large capital investment. Therefore, they peddle common use low-ticket items – such as cosmetics, cleaning products, vitamins, and cookware – that are touted as high quality alternatives to what people buy in the stores. Of course, the price of such quality is often many times higher than the brands people most commonly purchase in stores. Although there is certainly a market for high quality/high priced common use products like cosmetics, cleaning supplies, vitamins, and cookware (some sincerely appreciate the quality difference and have the money to pay for it), it is still very difficult to convince most people to spend multiple times the money for a product when the quality of the cheaper product is sufficient for them.

The bottom line on value is this: If you want to go into business for yourself, provide a product or a service that is a value to your customers. If you are able to provide a product people want or need at a price similar to what they would pay if they didn't know you, you have a good chance of success.

#2. Business Competence: Many successful business owners decide to go into business after having gained experience working for someone else. At some point they realize they can do the owner's job better than the owner and eventually they go into business for themselves. This is a normal progression of events and one more conducive to business success: competence precedes business ownership.

However, for many Christians the decision to pursue a home-based business precedes competence. They are looking for a business – any business – they can do from home. Unfortunately, it is difficult to be optimistic about the chances for a home-based enterprise to succeed when the prospective owner has little or no previous experience in the business. We know, in fact, that prospective owners tend to be overly optimistic about the businesses they are looking into, as the high business failure rate proves.

This lack of competence can take different forms. The first is the lack of experience or talent in making the product or performing the service. If I go into the business of beauty consulting and have never felt comfortable wearing make-up, if I never felt the need to get my hair done, if I am not familiar with skin treatments, and I was never particularly talented at choosing the right clothes, my lack of experience and talent may show when I see my first client. Likewise, if I get into the computer repair business and am not particularly successful at solving the computer problems people bring me, I won't last long in the computer repair business.

This may seem like common sense, but *every* business requires a certain degree of talent and experience to be successful. Whenever anyone chooses to go into a business in which he has no previous experience he is betting that he has the talent and can get the experience he needs fast enough to get his new venture off the ground. Most people lose that bet.

In addition to the competence required to make the product or perform the service, there are other skills that may be just as necessary for a business to succeed. One is the ability to sell. Most people getting into home-based businesses do not have a reputation and a clientele already established. The product or service, no matter how skillfully done, must still be sold. Many disappointed home-based business owners believed that telling their friends and putting up a website was all that was necessary to produce a steady stream of customers.

The hard truth is that many home-based businesses require the owner to make sales. If the business is selling a niche or a high quality/high priced product, sales ability may very well make the difference between success and failure. Some people are natural salesmen, but selling skills can also be learned. However, in a culture dominated by an employee mentality like ours, salespeople are often feared. Although this is not the salesman's fault, selling makes people who are generally insulated from the sales process uncomfortable. Thus, Christians who are sensitive to the feelings of others may struggle making sales. But our culture's aversion to the selling process is unfair. An honest business owner who asks for a sale isn't hurting anybody – just as the potential customer isn't wronging anyone by turning down the seller. The home-based business owner, then, may have to develop the skills and the courage to sell his product.

The final aspect of competence is reliability. The problem with many businesses – and especially with part-time home-based businesses – is reliability. I know this well from personal experience: it is easy for the part-time business owner to let the rest of his life negatively affect his part-time endeavor. Most people – including most Christians – will not put up with poor service because you, the business owner, had other things that required your attention. Potential customers may feel badly for you if your child is ill or your boss is making you work late, but they'll stop buying your product or service if you prove unreliable. People don't want to hear that you forgot, or you ran out, or you misplaced something. Orders must be filled, correspondence answered, stock purchased, inventory maintained – all in a timely manner.

The bottom line on competence is this: Make your product and deliver your service well, sell your business with courage and skill, and be organized and reliable.

#3. Time & Money: There is some truth to the old saying that it takes money to make money. Many home-based businesses do not have the money to buy the best tools and equipment, to advertise, to mass-produce, to carry an inventory, to accept credit and debit cards, or to hire professional help. They may not even be able to work full-time themselves. Although not impossible, it is very difficult to get a business off the ground with little time and almost no money. Many of us go into businesses without realistically thinking through the challenges that an ill-funded, undermanned enterprise will face. In other words, a wrench, a tire iron, a screwdriver, five dollars, and 10 hours/week may not be sufficient to make it big in the car repair business.

Many business owners realize the need for capital, so they borrow money to get the business going. Despite the fact that many successful businesses have been started with borrowed money, I would use extreme caution when borrowing money. To be sure, you are more likely to be ruined financially than to succeed when starting a business with borrowed money, but more important are the sobering Scriptural warnings. Granted, some businesses are much safer investments than others, but generally debt should be avoided.

How, then, can the poor man succeed in a home-based business? The first option is that he save the money necessary to get the business started ahead of time. This may slow the process down, but the extra time can be used productively. The entire enterprise can be considered more thoroughly and careful planning can be done. The second option is to go ahead and start the business ill-funded and undermanned. Perhaps the new owner is capable of business success, but is not capable of saving enough money to invest significantly in the business. Depending on the circumstances and on God's blessing, there is always the chance that the business can start small and see sales gradually increase until the business is able to fund itself. In some cases, this may be the only way the business can succeed. To be sure, sober judgment and discernment are required.

The bottom line is this: Every business requires an investment of time and money. Make sure you have enough to give yourself a realistic chance to succeed – and avoid debt if possible.

#4. Power From Above: It has always amazed me how little support most Christians get from friends, family, and church when they decide to start their own businesses. When I was in Amway, some of the youngest and most unlikely distributors were extremely successful because family and friends got into the business just to support them. It didn't matter that the business was not one they would have chosen. It didn't matter that it was multi-level marketing, and it didn't matter that the prices were not cheap. The fact that a relative was in the business made it worthy of support – and the business was very good to families like that. If Christians treated their brothers and sisters in Christ in this manner, many more home-based businesses would succeed. Seek, then, the support of those you know, but don't be overly surprised or discouraged if you don't get a lot of enthusiastic support.

It also amazes me how little faith people have in God's ability or desire to help them succeed. If faith can move mountains, uproot trees, raise the dead, heal the sick, and allow one man to rout a hundred in battle, it seems reasonable that God can help you succeed in your business. Why, then, do so many Christians fail? One reason is that Christians often pursue a home-based business in their own power. In some instances they rush ahead presumptuously and make all sorts of foolish mistakes. In other instances, they encounter a difficulty or two and are convinced they cannot succeed and quit. Many home-based business owners combine the two – they start out on presumption, make a few stupid mistakes, and then quit when they realize the job will be more difficult than they expected.

Thankfully, these kinds of scenarios are unnecessary. Avoiding presumption and discouragement requires wisdom and wisdom from God is a birthright of every believer. James writes, "But if any of you lacks wisdom, let him ask of God, who gives to all generously and without reproach, and it will be given to him." (James 1:5) Wisdom, then, requires a prayer of faith to a God who never breaks His promises. If wisdom is so easy to obtain, why do so many people lack wisdom when they choose a home-based business? James continues, "But he must ask in faith without any doubting, for the one who doubts is like the surf of the sea, driven and tossed by the wind. For that man ought not to expect that he will receive anything from the Lord." (James 1:6-7) James also writes, "You ask and do not receive, because you ask with wrong motives, so that you may spend it on your pleasures." (James 4:3) Other Scriptures say that an unforgiving spirit and treating your wife harshly will hinder your prayers. Therefore, treat others graciously, sincerely seek to please God, and believe that God will do as He promised and you will have all the wisdom you need to make good business decisions.

God has confirmed His covenant with His people by prospering them. Moses wrote, "All these blessings will come upon you and overtake you if you obey the LORD your God: Blessed shall you be in the city, and blessed shall you be in the country. Blessed shall be the offspring of your body and the produce of your ground and the offspring of your beasts, the increase of your herd and the young of your flock. Blessed shall be your basket and your kneading bowl. Blessed shall you be when you come in, and blessed shall you be when you go out. The LORD shall cause your enemies who rise up against you to be defeated before you; they will come out against you one way and will flee before you seven ways. The LORD will command the blessing upon you in your barns and in all that you put your hand to, and He will bless you in the land which the LORD your God gives you. The LORD will establish you as a holy people to Himself, as He swore to you, if you keep the commandments of the LORD your God and walk in His ways. So all the peoples of the earth will see that you are called by the name of the LORD, and they will be afraid of you. The LORD will make you abound in prosperity, in the offspring of your body and in the offspring of your beast and in the produce of your ground, in the land which the LORD swore to your fathers to give you. The LORD will open for you His good storehouse, the heavens, to give rain to your land in its season and to bless all the work of your hand." (Deut. 28:2-12a)

God says elsewhere of the godly man, "He will be like a tree firmly planted by streams of water, which yields its fruit in its season and its leaf does not wither; and in whatever he does, he prospers." (Ps. 1:3) "How blessed is everyone who fears the LORD, who walks in His ways. When you shall eat of the fruit of your hands, you will be happy and it will be well with you. Your wife shall be like a fruitful vine within your house, your children like olive plants around your table. Behold, for thus shall the man be blessed who fears the LORD." (Ps. 128:1-4) "But you shall remember the LORD your God, for it is He who is giving you power to make wealth, that He may confirm His covenant which He swore to your fathers, as it is this day." (Deut. 8:18)

If we are not prospering, we need to be patient and continue to believe in God's promises. Whether we begin achieving financial prosperity in this life or the next, we can be assured that eventually God will do for us all He promised. Therefore, if we pursue a home business with godly wisdom and faith, we should not be disappointed with the results. If we succeed with God's help, we will be joyful and give the glory to God. If we struggle, we know that God is molding us into the people He wants us to be. In that case, we will be joyful and give the glory to God. If, through God's wisdom, we do not pursue a home business, we will also be joyful and give the glory to God.

The bottom line on power from above is this: The wisdom to know whether we should pursue a home-based business or not is available from God if we ask Him in faith. Our family, friends, and church may help us or disappoint us, but God will never let us down. If God wants us to pursue a home-based business we will be joyful and give God the glory whether we struggle or succeed. All things are working together for our good if we love God and are called according to His purpose. (Rom. 8)

Conclusion: If anyone wants to begin a home-based business to benefit his family spiritually and financially, he desires a noble thing. First, he must seek God's wisdom as to whether a home-based business is God's will for his family. If it is, he must seek God's wisdom regarding which business he should pursue. He should research this business diligently and work quickly to become competent in all aspects of his new enterprise – including the art of selling – if that is required. He should make sure he has enough time and money to get started. He must be patient and prayerful before beginning so he doesn't do anything rash or presumptuous. Once in business, he should work hard to provide his customers good value and reliable service. Finally, he should have faith in his God – that God loves him, intends to prosper him, and will make all things work together for his good. And whether his success comes sooner, later, or not until heaven, he should be happy and give the glory to God.

13 to 2 (People to Rooms)

We arrived in Springfield, Missouri, just short of midnight and got two rooms at a motel. We stayed there a couple of days and soon had arrangements for a closing date for the purchase of our new home. The difficulty was that the date was about two and a half weeks away. We decided to stay at the motel during that time, since who would rent to us for less than three weeks? Jim got a deal as far as the cost. Expensive when compared to a mortgage, but quite the deal as far as motels go. Then again, you do get pretty much what you pay for. But we could be thankful for a roof over our heads, running water, locks on the doors, and air conditioning. (Something our last house didn't have!) So the rooms served their purpose.

But as you can guess, thirteen people in two rooms can have some challenges of its own. Here are some musings and tips we have discovered. That way you will know what you can expect next time you find yourself and twelve others in two motel rooms!

1. Those teeny-tiny trash bags they have in motel rooms will never do. Bring a box of those lawn-and-garden bags.

2. Same goes for those pitiful little bars of soap. Since the motel probably won't want to give you a new bar for each person for each bath, come prepared.

3. Call your lender to make sure everything is in place. Let's not make this any longer than we have to.

4. Find a hotel close to a Wal-Mart. They have good deals on soda, bottled juice, cereal and such. They also have cold milk. This will be your daily destination for breakfast since you have no refrigerator. The clerks may even start to know you.

5. Call the realtor so he knows you're still around.

6. Bring your own twelve-pack of toilet paper. Those housekeepers probably have no idea how much toilet paper thirteen people can use in three weeks. They might think you're papering local trees or something. (If twelve isn't enough, you can always get more. You'll be at Wal-Mart today anyway.)

7. Find your local library quick so you can access your email. Your son's free service will let you stay connected about three minutes a day (split up).

8. Find a hotel close to a grocery store. This will also become a daily destination (since you have no fridge) if you want anything fresh and that doesn't come in a box.

9. Call the lender again.

10. Be careful when you make the room assignments. You've never lived *this* close to each other before!

11. Designate one room the arctic circle and the other the temperate zone. This happened by accident for us, but at least this way everyone can find a room temperature that suits them.

12. Watch out for the children and parent (who shall remain nameless) who like to go from room to room changing the A/C settings and thus messing up item #11!

13. Go to your realtor's house so he knows you're still around. (OK, we were actually invited.)

14. Designate one room the food room where the food is stored, eaten, and the dishes are done. The other room can be the "laundry" room. (You decide which is worse.)

15. The preferred place to eat is outside. (No messy carpets.) The other is the bathtub. (Just kidding. Or am I?)

16. When you unpack the U-Haul into storage, find your electric burner and electric oven roaster. If you can't find your pots, get one at Wal-Mart. You'll be there today anyway.

17. Mr. Lender and Mr. Realtor, is everything in place?

18. Never run the electric oven, lights, TV, VCR, computer, and A/C at the same time. You might blow a fuse.

19. Save your quarters. That's all those laundromat machines will take - and they take plenty.

20. Visit all the local attractions in three weeks in order to get out of the motel rooms.

21. Make sure your church clothes are in the suitcases and not in storage. That way, when you are invited to church and to dinner, you can be adequately attired. If you didn't pack your Sunday best, don't worry. You can always get some clothes at Wal-Mart. You'll be there today anyway.

22. When your closing date comes, squeeze everything into the car and van. It's OK if you can't see the children; you'll find them when you take everything back out at the house.

23. When the closing falls through at the last moment and you return to the hotel, just take into the rooms the bare essentials. The new closing date is just two days away.

24. Repeat #22 when the second closing date comes.

25. When the second date falls through, find a new motel. There's a reason why the family has been sarcastically calling the first place "The Happiness Hotel."

26. It's great that the new motel has bigger rooms. Unfortunately the Wal-Mart isn't so close, but at least now you can walk to the laundromat.

27. Don't forget to buy a calling card. These calls to the Lender are way too expensive on the cell phone.

28. Call the Realtor. Really, really, we're so close.

29. Make sure your parents know where you are. No elaboration needed on that.

30. The best place to keep all of your important papers is on the floor in the car – away from roaming toddlers. If your wife gets tired of your filing cabinet being in the way of her feet every time you drive, remind her that it'll be for just a couple of weeks. (Or three or four or five.)

31. The next time you're eating supper on the beds and floor, take turns sharing your *favorite* thing about living in the motel for the last 5-1/2 weeks. Some children may need to be prodded a little more than others, but this is a good exercise. (For adults, too.)

32. This has been way more than you bargained for, but it's been a good growing experience. You can't answer the question, "Why has all this happened?" but it doesn't matter. It's nothing more than an inconvenience in the bigger scheme of things. When you think about it, it sounds worse than it really has been. Share that with your co-workers who ask, yet again, if you're in your house yet.

33. When you get into your new home after five plus weeks, thank the Lord who is always with us no matter where we may be, and provides for us no matter what we may have. We have been safe, together, and healthy. And now He has given us a beautiful home to enjoy. He is a good God.

"The LORD is the portion of my inheritance and my cup; You support my lot. The lines have fallen to me in pleasant places; indeed, my heritage is beautiful to me."
Psalm 16:5-6

Bittersweet: Moving can be such sweet sorrow

Our family went through quite a change this summer. We sold our home in Maryland, packed up our eleven children and belongings, and trekked 1100 miles across the country to settle in a new home in Missouri. That one sentence makes it sound so easy! But the last four months turned out to be much crazier than we had anticipated. We are glad we made the move, but change often has a bittersweet quality to it.

On our last day in Maryland, when the van was finally all packed, we were anticipating our trip and our new home. But there was the final walk-through of the old house. As I went from room to room, checking for missed items and residual dirt, each room sparked some memories. After all, a house can hold a lot of memories after thirteen years.

I started on the front porch. Thirteen years ago my parents took a picture of Jim and I standing here, in front of our brand new home. They had driven out from Wisconsin just to help us on moving day. We walked into this home with four children and today leave with eleven. I didn't know at that time how good God was going to be to us here.

Next I walked into the foyer. Looking up, I remembered the peanut butter stain that had been there. I still don't quite understand the story behind that, but some things are better not to know. Turning right I entered the family room. How much activity this room has seen! The whole family would look forward to fires in the wood stove and hot cocoa on really cold nights. In this room sat the toy box and rocking horse my dad had made. Many issues of SALT were written, edited, and printed here. And every year the discussion would take place as to what room the Christmas tree would be in. As of late, this room didn't win that honor, but it saw its own share of Christmas morning chaos. And, finally, I remember nursing our baby in this empty corner the day we moved in. That baby is now thirteen. Today I nursed our newest baby in the very same place.

As I made my way into the kitchen, I wondered how many floury messes have happened here. The Christmas cookies we decorated and the birthday cakes we baked – all with little helping hands. This dining room barely had enough space for the table that fit us all. Here we enjoyed feasts, talked over dinner, and did many a project. Birthday after birthday the walls were adorned with balloons and crepe paper. Yes, we are a party ourselves.

I glanced out the patio doors and remembered how big the yard looked when we moved in and our oldest was only six. Now the grass is torn up from all the rough-and-tumble football games. I remember making homemade piñatas and the kids bursting them over the patio bricks. Lately they have enjoyed hunting for Easter eggs back here. The trees have grown so big now that they dwarf the house. And I will miss my tulips. They were the first every year to remind me that winter was almost over and that we were stepping into spring.

And now I find myself in the living room. Once upon a time it was called the "green chair" room because the little ones understood that better than calling it the "living room." That green chair is long gone but every once in awhile the name resurfaces. Here we had family devotions, watched movies, homeschooled, and celebrated holidays. I bet someone today found some old Easter grass or New Year's confetti under the couches!

As I wander upstairs and look in and out of the bedrooms, I remember that once upon a time one of these rooms was an office/guest room. But now they are all filled with children. The boys used to call their bedroom the "ugly" room until we painted over the drab gray with a more suitable blue. And how sweet it is to think about how we would set up the bassinet in our bedroom, waiting for our newest little blessing to be born.

You almost hate to leave. But I know that it is not these four walls that have given us so many cherished moments. It is our God who fills our lives with meaning and with joys we surely do not deserve.

But as I go from room to room, I also recall some not so pleasant memories, and moments that I'd rather not live again. Even in those times there are lessons. Lessons of seeing God working, of protecting us, of paving the way and dealing with our problems even before we knew there was a problem. We see how much God loves us and how He fills our lives and days with His grace.

So there is no fear in moving, for God is going with us and He does not change. His presence and kindness will be with us in our new home as well. Not only does He go with us, but He also goes before us – providing for us and preparing our way.

As I close the front door for the last time, I say a prayer to God that He may grant the next inhabitants of this home the same meaning and richness He has so graciously given to us. Only God can make the bittersweet so pleasantly tasteful.

Courtship

There are three things which are too wonderful for me, four which I do not understand: the way of an eagle in the sky, the way of a serpent on a rock, the way of a ship in the middle of the sea, and the way of a man with a maid.

(Proverbs. 30:18-19)

The Birds & the Bees: And the need to know

Recently I heard a Christian teacher – for whom I have great respect – advocating that parents begin explaining the issue of sex to children at six or seven years of age, or perhaps as late as nine years if the child was homeschooled and had little contact with other children. The point was made that the parents should take the initiative with young children to inoculate them from those outside the home who might misinform their children or lead them astray.

I certainly agree that the child should not be getting his information about this subject from the heathen who live in the neighborhood. I also agree that the parents should at some point be the ones who instruct the child on this subject. However, I would like to disagree with the point that it is in the best interest of the child to be taught about this subject at such an early age.

First of all, I think that a parental discussion about this subject or graphic reading from a book supplied by the parents would tend to create powerful memories that would often be replayed in the child's mind and create an interest in the matter that may not have been there otherwise. It is natural for grade school children – and particularly boys – to prefer activities with their own gender and to resist being forced to play with members of the opposite sex. In fact, grade school boys whose interests have not been piqued prematurely are commonly disgusted at the thought of being forced to play with a girl.

That does not mean that young children cannot be trained to dwell on the subject. When I was a substitute teacher in the public schools I confiscated a note in a third grade class that was extremely suggestive in nature and showed that girls were already competing fiercely for the affections of boys. An unfortunate number of sixth graders were already boy or girl crazy and many already had physical relationships.

But things were not always that way. I don't remember any boy in my sixth grade class having a "girlfriend" and any boy accused of liking a girl would have been teased mercilessly. After school I played exclusively with boys and to my knowledge it was the same for the other boys in my neighborhood. There was no rule compelling us to separate from the girls, but there was no need for one because there was no interest. We played ball and climbed trees and raced bikes, and to be honest I don't know what the girls did after school. I think you'll find that many other people grew up similarly.

I guess the teacher I mentioned, recognizing the corruptness of the culture, has decided that negative influences are inevitable and that the best way to combat the problem is to inform his children about the "birds and the bees" about the time they start school. The hope is that the parental talks will give the third grader the ammunition to recognize and avoid inappropriate conversations and to resist the advances that may already be coming her way.

I know that what I'm going to say will be controversial – even among Christians – but I don't agree at all with this approach. Rather than teach an 8-year-old how to handle life in a sexually charged environment – an environment known to have led a significant number of children from Christian households into a lifestyle of immorality – why doesn't the parent simply protect his child and remove him from the harmful exposure? If the problem is in the school, pull the child out of school. If the problem is in the neighborhood, don't allow the children to run around with the kids in the neighborhood. If the problem is in the TV shows, TV commercials, movies, music, computer games, internet, or reading material, then remove the sources of offense.

Paul writes, " 'Therefore, come out from their midst and be separate,' says the Lord. 'And do not touch what is unclean; and I will welcome you.' " (2 Cor. 6:17) He says, "But among you there must not be even a hint of sexual immorality, or of any kind of impurity." (Ephesians 5:3a, NIV) He also says, "Do not be bound together with unbelievers," (2 Cor. 6:14a) and "Do not be deceived: Bad company corrupts good morals.' " (1 Cor. 15:33) James writes, "You adulteresses, do you not know that friendship with the world is hostility toward God?" (James 4:4a) By sending our children to public schools or by allowing them to play with children who threaten their purity, we are teaching them that it is acceptable to be yoked with unbelievers and that it is unnecessary to separate ourselves from the world.

I choose to believe that we are able to protect our children from the negative influences of a godless culture. I don't want to yoke my children with worldly people and run the risk that they will be overly curious about matters not appropriate to their age. I have decided, rather, to teach my children about this topic on a "need to know" basis. Children need to know very little about this subject until they reach the later grade school years. Perhaps young children may be taught to avoid looking at an unclothed body. Eventually, girls need a heads-up and an explanation as to what should be expected regarding monthly cycles before they are frightened by the first one. Boys and girls need to understand that modesty demands that they cover certain parts of their bodies. Teenagers need to understand the family rules for courting and what kind of behavior is unacceptable outside of marriage. A teenager who knows that kissing or any other form of romantic touching is unacceptable outside of marriage should know enough to keep himself out of trouble. Until marriage, however, it is not necessary to be graphic. Things can be explained in general terms. Obviously, when a young man or woman is ready to marry more complete and intimate knowledge is required, but until that time I don't understand the necessity of conveying such information.

What harm do you suppose will befall the young child who doesn't know exactly how babies are made or what human anatomy is involved in the process? The answer offered by the radio host was that a young child left ignorant by his parents is likely to gain knowledge from a source that doesn't share the parents' values. My reply is that young children who are not inappropriately exposed to romantic or immoral influences are not likely to have an insatiable desire to know a lot of detailed information about the reproductive process, and that it is not so difficult to protect a child from inappropriate and immoral influences.

All that is necessary is to get the child out of the school, away from the unbelieving children, and away from offensive media. It may even be necessary to protect the child from the church youth group or from certain family members. If separation seems difficult it is only because we don't like the thought of having to educate our own children, lose the friendship of our unbelieving neighbors, offend our ungodly family members, or give up our immoral media. As uncomfortable as the prospect of separation may make us feel, however, it is simple and easily accomplished by the person undeterred by the disapproval of those he is separating from. Hopefully the spiritual well-being of our children is worth more than the approval of those who may harm them.

Absolute Purity

There is a growing movement among Christians that rejects the custom of dating. Some support "courtship" and others support "betrothal" as more consistent with biblical principles. Others counter that nowhere does Scripture condemn dating. After all, where is the Bible verse that condemns a young man for inviting a young lady to a restaurant for dinner or a cup of coffee?

As for my household, our children will not be dating. Dating is a relatively new custom and, whether you believe it is unscriptural or not, it has a very poor track record for protecting the sexual purity of its participants. Perhaps I was hanging around the wrong crowd, but it seemed that nearly everyone I knew who dated had some sort of intimate physical relationship before they married. For many, this meant "going all the way," but most of the rest were not opposed to long bouts of kissing and hugging. And typically, those who dated had this kind of physical relationship with multiple partners before they decided on a spouse.

Perhaps the Bible does not directly address the issue of dating, but it does directly address the issue of sexual purity. Paul tells the young man Timothy, "Treat ... younger women as sisters, with absolute purity." (1 Tim. 5:2, NIV) Paul wrote to the Corinthians, "Now concerning the things about which you wrote, it is good for a man not to touch a woman." (1 Cor. 7:1) Paul says elsewhere, "Among you there must not be even a hunt of sexual immorality or of any kind of impurity." (Eph. 5:3, NIV) Jesus went even farther: "You have heard that it was said, 'You shall not commit adultery'; but I say to you that everyone who looks at a woman with lust for her has already committed adultery with her in his heart." (Mat 5:27)

We know from these verses that "absolute purity" is the positive command and that "touching a woman" or even looking at her lustfully is forbidden. The young men should be treating the young women as sisters. Any honorable man would be revolted at the prospect of giving his sister a romantic kiss or touch. Therefore, any honorable man should avoid giving any woman who is not his wife any romantic kiss or touch. The biblical standard is uncompromising.

Under the Law of Moses, the consequences of sexual sin were as severe as possible, as adultery and homosexuality carried the death penalty. In addition, a girl who married and was later found not to have been a virgin was dealt with in this way: "Then they shall bring out the girl to the doorway of her father's house, and the men of her city shall stone her to death because she has committed an act of folly in Israel by playing the harlot in her father's house; thus you shall purge the evil from among you." (Deut. 22:21)

This seems harsh to our enlightened modern ears, but these were only temporal punishments. The New Testament describes a much more horrifying punishment for unrepentant sexual sin – horrifying because it is eternal. Paul writes, "Do you not know that the unrighteous will not inherit the kingdom of God? Do not be deceived; neither fornicators ... nor adulterers, nor effeminate, nor homosexuals ... will inherit the kingdom of God." (1 Cor. 6:9-10) The writer to the Hebrews writes, "Marriage is to be held in honor among all, and the marriage bed is to be undefiled; for fornicators and adulterers God will judge." (Heb. 13:4) The Apostle John writes, "But for the cowardly and unbelieving and abominable and murderers and immoral persons and sorcerers and idolaters and all liars, their part will be in the lake that burns with fire and brimstone, which is the second death." (Rev. 21:8) He says something similar in the following chapter: "Blessed are those who wash their robes, so that they may have the right to the tree of life, and may enter by the gates into the city. Outside are the dogs and the sorcerers and the immoral persons and the murderers and the idolaters, and everyone who loves and practices lying." (Rev. 22:14-15) Solomon writes, "For the lips of an adulteress drip honey and smoother than oil is her speech; but in the end she is bitter as wormwood, sharp as a two-edged sword. Her feet go down to death, her steps take hold of Sheol. She does not ponder the path of life; her ways are unstable, she does not know it." (Prov. 5:3-6) Paul adds, "For this you know with certainty, that no immoral or impure person or covetous man, who is an idolater, has an inheritance in the kingdom of Christ and God. Let no one deceive you with empty words, for because of these things the wrath of God comes upon the sons of disobedience." (Eph. 5:5-6)

Because unrepentant sexually immoral people will not inherit the kingdom of God, the Scriptures tell us to avoid impurity at all cost. Paul writes, "Flee immorality. Every other sin that a man commits is outside the body, but the immoral man sins against his own body. Or do you not know that your body is a temple of the Holy Spirit who is in you, whom you have from God, and that you are not your own? For you have been bought with a price: therefore glorify God in your body." (1 Cor. 6:18-20) Jesus, Himself, says this: "You have heard that it was said, 'You shall not commit adultery'; but I say to you that everyone who looks at a woman with lust for her has already committed adultery with her in his heart. If your right eye makes you stumble, tear it out and throw it from you; for it is better for you to lose one of the parts of your body, than for your whole body to be thrown into hell. If your right hand makes you stumble, cut it off and throw it from you; for it is better for you to lose one of the parts of your body, than for your whole body to go into hell." (Matt. 5:27-30)

Of course, sexual immorality may also have awful consequences in the here and now. Some will endure the shame when an adulterous relationship is discovered. Others will experience the pain of divorce. Promiscuity can cloud a man's judgment and cause him to form a romantic relationship he will deeply regret. Immoral behavior may also produce children out of wedlock. This may be embarrassing, of course, but children born out of wedlock may suffer more serious consequences. Some children will grow up without the love or financial support of a father and others will never know the love of the woman who gave them birth. Unfortunately, we also know that millions of children never see the light of day because their mothers would rather kill them than face the consequences of their own sin. In addition, AIDS and a host of other diseases may result from sexual immorality. Even some cancers are more prevalent among promiscuous people. A person who indulges in immoral behavior, therefore, is literally risking his health and his life.

Given the clear biblical standard for absolute purity and the potential for disastrous temporal and eternal consequences for those who do not observe that standard, one can only wonder why dating is so popular among Christian families. Parents know very well – probably from their own dating experiences – that their dating children will experience plenty of romantic hugging and kissing with an indeterminate number of partners before they are married. Parents know there is a very good chance their children will lose their virginity before they reach the altar. Even so, many Christian parents accept all this as an inevitable risk and condemn parents as meddling radicals who would play a role in protecting the purity of their children.

Why have so many Christian parents become so cavalier about their children's purity? Why would a Christian parent scoff at a parent for rejecting dating when participation almost guarantees that the biblical standard of absolute purity will not be observed? Why would a Christian parent scoff at a another parent for adopting courtship or betrothal when perhaps a majority of dating young people will not be virgins on their wedding day?

I will offer an explanation. Most Christians in America have grown up in public or parochial schools, where dating and immorality were commonplace. Coarse humor, lewdness, and immodesty were experienced daily. We grew up on immoral music and immoral TV. Sexually immoral entertainers, athletes, and politicians were idolized – their adulteries never condemned. We looked the other way for the likes of President Kennedy and John Lennon. Since then, the downward trend has only accelerated. In the schools, homosexuals are openly affectionate. Football's Lawrence Taylor writes a book about his exploits, broadcast television has given permission to use the "F" word, and cable and satellite offer pornography to the masses. We Christian Americans have become so desensitized by the immorality around us that we think it unreasonable to expect any normal teenager to abide by the biblical standard. We are so wise to immorality that we have forgotten how to blush.

We have also abdicated our responsibility to protect our children. We just throw them to the wolves and hope they don't get themselves into serious trouble. Again, I realize dating is not directly forbidden in Scripture, but as Christians who are not naïve about these issues we should know that a system that allows young singles unlimited and unsupervised casual romantic relationships will breed immorality. As parents, we need to teach our older children by word and example that the biblical standard is absolute purity (no romantic kissing or touching with anyone but one's spouse). We also need to protect our children from immoral music and videos, and not allow them to run around unsupervised with members of the opposite sex.

This may seem extreme to many believers, but only to Western believers of the last two or three generations. These views would not have seemed extreme in America at the time the Pilgrims landed in 1620 and for the next 300 years. And even if absolute purity were extreme it shouldn't matter. It is the biblical standard and, therefore, it should be our standard no matter how crazy it appears to others.

We are called to witness to the resurrection of Christ and one of the ways we do that is by living as salt and light in a fallen and corrupted world. Living in a thoroughly immoral culture gives Christians an opportunity to witness to the power of the resurrection by living to a higher standard. Instead, we have adopted the immoral practices of the surrounding culture.

"The land which you are entering to possess is an unclean land with the uncleanness of the peoples of the lands, with their abominations which have filled it from end to end and with their impurity. So now do not give your daughters to their sons nor take their daughters to your sons, and never seek their peace or their prosperity, that you may be strong and eat the good things of the land and leave it as an inheritance to your sons forever (Ezra 9:11-12)

Marriageable Age!

When I was growing up, there wasn't a lot of question as to how a boy was to go about finding a wife. He would probably meet the girl of his dreams at school or at work, ask her out on a date, get her to agree to go steady, and then – if he had the means to support a wife and he was so inclined – he would ask the girl to marry him.

As Christians began opting out of the public schools in significant numbers for homeschooling, many were emboldened to question an institution that rose to prominence with the public schools – dating. Many books and articles have been written about the evils of dating. Courtship and betrothal are increasingly familiar words, and in the most radical sectors there is even talk of bringing back arranged marriages.

This debate about how young Christian men and women ought to find marriage partners is long overdue, but it has made finding a mate a little confusing. With some Christians dating, some courting and some betrothing, a young man or young woman may not know at first how to proceed.

With things up in the air, I thought I would add to the confusion by challenging the age at which most people marry.

Recent History of Marriage Age: In 1890 the median age for a first marriage in the U.S., according to the Bureau of the Census, was 26.1 for males and 22.0 for females. In the 1950 and 1960 censuses the age had dropped to 22.8 for men and 20.3 for women. In the 2000 census the age had risen to 26.8 for men and 25.1 for women.

We observe first that marriage ages fell between 1890 and 1950. Urbanization, the trend toward higher education (high school was not universal in 1890 and college was only for the wealthy few), increasingly co-ed schools and workplaces, and economic prosperity gave young men and women greater opportunity to find a mate.

However, the recent trend toward later marriage age doesn't reflect a return to Victorian morality. However, the abandonment of Christian morals in the 1960s (marriage is no longer a prerequisite for sex), contraception, the continual rise in the years of formal education required to prepare for a career, and the perception that girls, too, need to prepare for a career outside the home have caused the marriage age to rise in the last 40 years.

It is interesting, however, that as first marriages are pushed into the mid-twenties, sexual activity begins earlier and earlier. A promiscuous environment, then, has satisfied the drive to mate without the necessity of marriage. The enabler has been the education system, which throws hormonal children together in a values-free environment and keeps them there until they are well into their twenties.

The Christian reaction: It is my experience that most Christians have accepted the belief that it is better to wait to get married. After all, it is difficult to fight the current economic realities. More education is necessary to be competitive in the job market than was the case 40 years ago and young men and women just aren't as mature as they used to be. Most Christians, too, have accepted the belief that girls should wait until they have developed a job skill outside the home before marrying. Christians are worried about their young sons and daughters struggling to survive and tend to think that when their offspring want to marry young it means they have no idea what they're up against or maybe that they have lost their minds.

Is there any biblical help?: Unfortunately, there is no Bible passage that specifically answers the question of marriageable age. We do know that God told Moses to number the men 20 years old and up as eligible for military service so perhaps that gives us some insight into the age a male is considered an adult, but the tie to marriageable age is indirect and uncertain. It also doesn't include women, who traditionally have been considered ready for marriage at a younger age.

We can look to the Scripture verses on marriage to see if there are any clues to marriageable age. The most important passage on marriage is probably found in Genesis and was repeated by Jesus. The Scripture says, "For this reason a man shall leave his father and his mother, and be joined to his wife; and they shall become one flesh."

Leaving father and mother and cleaving to his wife: The first point in this Scripture is that the man should be ready to leave his father and his mother, but what exactly does this mean? It would seem that the man must be physically separated from his parents, but many would add that the man must be financially independent of his parents as well (or how else can he live separated from his parents?). At first glance this seems to make sense, but when different circumstances are considered it becomes more difficult to know what leaving specifically means.

For example, can a man live on his parents' property and still be considered to have left? Is a farmer's son leaving his father and mother if he lives with his new bride in a separate house on his father's farm with the expectation that someday the farm will be his? What if the son's house is connected to his father's house? What if he lives in a room in his father's house that has its own private entrance? What if he lives in separate rooms but does not have his own private entrance?

It seems to me that this leaving the book of Genesis is alluding to is a leaving of his parents' household, which in most cases will result in the son having a different street address than his parents. However, just as multiple independent households may inhabit an apartment building, couldn't two or more households inhabit separate rooms in the same house and live as separate households? Genesis doesn't say how far from his parents the son must be, so it would be legalistic to imply that a man must live in a separate building or on a separate piece of property to have left father and mother. Therefore, if the son's leaving is only as far as the back room of the house – as long as he is treated as the head of his own household and not as a boy under his father's authority – he may be considered to have left.

I am not saying that newlyweds ought to share walls with their parents. Given the choice, most young couples would rather have different living quarters. It is easier for a son to maintain control over his new household when there is significant separation from the parents, for parents sometimes struggle to treat their children as independent adults. Nevertheless, there may be situations that would result in parents and young married couples living in very close proximity to each other. Parents may help sustain their newly married children by allowing them to live on their property for a time. Young married couples may also be needed to help care for their sick or elderly parents or grandparents. As imperfect and undesirable as these arrangements may be, I don't believe they violate the biblical injunction to leave as long as the integrity of each household is maintained.

Now that we have considered the command to leave father and mother, let us consider whether a man must be financially independent to leave his parents and marry. The argument for financial independence is weaker than the argument for leaving, because the command to leave is explicit in Scripture while the idea that he must be financially independent is not addressed.

Tough Cases: Let's say that a wealthy man offers his son and future daughter-in-law a monthly income that would allow them to live independently in another state while the son finishes his medical degree. Should the fact that the son is financially dependent on his wealthy father deter him from marrying his betrothed?

I think most people would say the medical student should be allowed to marry. He would certainly be leaving his father and mother and cleaving to his wife in obedience to the biblical standard. He may be, like the son sharing a wall with his parents, taking the risk that the wealthy father would withdraw his support and leave the young couple in a precarious position. Nevertheless, there is no biblical injunction against a father helping his married children financially.

Let us consider another situation. What if a couple has a 23-year-old son who is a medical school student and he wants to marry a 20-year-old girl. The parents offer the son a room in their home that is to be considered the son's private living quarters. Let us also assume that the couple has agreed to subsidize the son financially until he has graduated from medical school, but to allow the son to govern his own affairs without interference.

If we hold to our previous principles, this too should be acceptable. The son has left his parents – even if it is only across a wall - and financial independence, although certainly desirable, is not required. However, would we change our mind if the son was an engineering student, an MBA candidate, a history major, an electrician's apprentice, a construction worker, or a cook at McDonald's? Should different rules apply for men who are going into different occupations?

The answer, of course, is that a man's occupation should not disqualify him for marriage and it certainly wouldn't change whether we consider him to have left his parents or not. The McDonald's cook may, in fact, have a more difficult time convincing the girl to live a wall away from his parents than the medical student, but that is a separate issue. My point is this: If you agree that the medical student with the backing of his wealthy parents may marry, then you do not believe that financial independence is a requirement for marriage. If you believe a young farmer can get married and live in a house on his father's farm – a farm he expects to inherit, then you do not believe that a married son must leave his parents' property.

Becoming one flesh: Besides leaving father and mother, the other half of our verse in Genesis says the man must cleave to his wife and become one flesh with her. There is at least one reason God commanded this "one flesh" relationship. The Lord commanded the man to be fruitful and multiply. He gets more specific in Malachi by saying, "Has not the Lord made them one? In flesh and spirit they are his. And why one? Because he was seeking godly offspring." (Mal. 2:15, NIV) It seems reasonable, then, to infer that in order that God's purpose for marriage may be fulfilled, those who marry should be old enough to reproduce and to understand that they are making a life-long commitment to their mates. Although the Bible doesn't explicitly say this, I think it would be reasonable to say that those who marry must have reached physical maturity. Until then they are not ready to be fruitful and multiply.

Please allow me to clarify what I mean by physical maturity. One could argue that a 12-year-old girl could be capable of having children, but I don't think God had 12-year-old girls in mind for marriage. Until a girl is fully mature I believe bearing children is dangerous and her ability to live independent of her parents suspect. Marrying before full physical maturity is like eating fruit before it ripens – it is unhealthy. However, physical maturity might be reached anywhere between 15 and 22 depending on the person in question.

It would appear that as long as the young man and woman are capable of leaving their parents and running their own household, and as long as they have attained physical maturity so that they can be fruitful and multiply, Scripture gives no minimum age limitation for either member of the prospective couple.

Other biblical principles that could help determine the marriageable age:

It could be argued that men under the Law of Moses were called into military service at age 20 because that was approximately the age a man reaches physical maturity and could compete on the battlefield. Using 20, then, as a general guideline as an age of male maturity may be acceptable, but it would be presumptuous to assume this was meant to keep 18 or 19-year-old males from marrying.

Another issue in choosing marriageable age is the legal limitations set by the civil government. We are to obey the laws of the land so long as they don't force us to disobey God in the process. A young man and woman are not forced to break a biblical command by waiting until they have reached the legal marriageable age. Most states in the U.S. allow a person to marry without his parents' consent if he is 18 years of age, but according to the Cornell University Legal Issues Institute in 1999 most states allowed marriages to 16-year-olds with parental consent and a few states went even lower.

The bottom line: At what age should people marry: Up to this point we have mainly discussed at what age a person *may* marry. The question so many people want answered, however, is at what age people *should* marry.

First, Paul cautions people who don't feel a need to be married to remain single. Singleness is superior to married life in that a single person can completely devote himself to the Lord. He doesn't have to worry about how to please his spouse and can go wherever the Lord needs him. A person who has no desire to be married should not be pressured into marriage simply because he qualifies as a marriageable person.

However, most people do not have the grace to live a life of singleness. Martin Luther said that such a gift was not possessed by one in one thousand. So, for the 999 out of 1,000, we need to decide when we should marry.

One thing about timing is obvious. A man of marriageable age must not marry until a woman of marriageable age accepts his proposal. In other words, if a boy has no one to propose to or his proposal has been turned down, now is not the time. God will provide when the time is right.

As Christians, we have an added issue in that the person we choose to marry must also be "in the Lord." I don't believe a Christian should even consider a person who does not appear to be in Christ. I have heard of people who build relationships with unbelievers and are just waiting for the potential marriage partner to confess his faith in Christ for the first time. This is dangerous because once a romantic relationship is established the judgment of both parties is often compromised. The Christian may be seeing signs of a conversion that an objective person knows isn't there, and the unbeliever may outwardly become a Christian simply as a means of getting the object of his desire. And even though God makes some such relationships work out in the end, there are many more that end in a life of unhappiness or divorce.

Let's assume, however, that a Christian man is of marriageable age – say 25 years old. He has his own construction business, earns about $125,000 per year, owns his own 6-bedroom house and a few acres with it, and is extremely active in his local church. Let's say the object of his affections is a blossoming single 23-year-old "Proverbs 31" woman. I'm sure most of us would have no problem saying that such a couple should get married if they want to.

Let's say, however, that the boy is a 19-year-old college student and the girl is an 18-year-old high school graduate. Both deeply love the Lord and they both want desperately to be married right away. Should they be married? I would say yes and their families should help them get started.

I understand that most Christians would probably disagree with me on this point, but allow me to humbly explain. The argument against such a marriage must be considered realistically before such a marriage should take place. That argument is economic in nature. The young couple should understand that marrying in this situation will be a financial challenge. Until the young man finishes college, they will probably have lean years. They will live in a room instead of a house, eat beans and rice instead of steak and potatoes, avoid buying new clothes, do without going out to dinner, drive "basic" transportation or even walk, use crates and bean bag chairs for furniture, and vacation for free in their home town or at the homes of relatives. All this assumes everything goes well. If there is sickness or some other unforeseen problem, such a couple would have nothing to fall back on. This is the situation the young people would face and most young people in our culture probably don't truly comprehend the magnitude of their challenges. If the man waits five or ten years he may well be able to avoid such hardships.

Having explored the downside of marrying early, we should also explore the downside of waiting. Perhaps I am biased by my own circumstances, but Cindy and I were married the year before we both were to finish college. Cindy finished college the first year of our marriage and I worked full-time at a restaurant. The following year, I was able to finish my degree in one semester (18 ½ credits). Even after graduation, I was unable to land a decent job with my theology degree so I enlisted in the army to support my family. The truth is that we have struggled financially from the beginning of our marriage and it hasn't always been fun (the financial struggles, not the marriage!).

Had I waited five years to marry, it is likely our financial struggles would have been avoided, but what would we have lost? The first thing we would have lost is the five years we spent together. I would consider that an inestimable loss. However, we would also have had four less children (our fourth child was born less than a month after our fifth anniversary). The question I always ask myself is what would I have done in those 5 years that would have had a greater impact for the kingdom of God than the raising of those four children? Martin Luther said, "But this at least all married people should know. They can do no better work and do nothing more valuable either for God, for Christendom, for all the world, for themselves, and for their children than to bring up their children well." So then, what we would have lost by waiting is infinitely greater than the loss we suffered by marrying.

There is also one other issue relevant to this discussion. As a concession, Paul told his readers at Corinth, "It is better to marry than to burn with passion." (1 Cor. 7:9) Sadly, there is much sexual immorality in the Christian church and one of the primary reasons is that young people who have the drive to be married are told to wait. In other words, we have changed Paul's words into "it is better to wait and burn with passion than it is to marry." In our culture, where most of us have so much contact with members of the opposite sex, it would seem that to avoid immorality we should be marrying younger. Just as it is wrong to pressure a happily single person into marrying, it is also wrong to pressure a young adult Christian couple who have a strong physical attraction for each other to wait. This is an issue many parents overlook when advising their children. It's as if they have forgotten what it was like to be young.

Therefore, my belief is this: When a man meets a suitable helper, if both are physically mature, if the man has the ability to leave father and mother, if they are also obeying the marriage laws of the civil government, and if the man clearly favors married life over singleness, he should marry.

Some young men are probably ready to marry at age 18 and some young women at 16 (notice I didn't say most or all), but the age at which a person is ready to marry will differ from person to person, as will the age at which the right opportunity comes along.

Martin Luther wrote about this topic and I would like to conclude with some relevant excerpts from "Estate of Marriage," written in 1522. Please read them! These excerpts deal with the challenges people who postpone marriage will face and the economics of marrying young and poor.

"Finally, before us one big, strong objection to answer. Yes, they say, it would be a fine thing to be married, but how will I support myself? I have nothing; take a wife and live on that, etc. Undoubtedly, this is the greatest obstacle to marriage; it is this above all which prevents and breaks up marriage and is the chief excuse for fornication. What shall I say to this objection? It shows a lack of faith and doubt of God's goodness and truth. It is therefore no wonder that where faith is lacking, nothing but fornication and all manner of misfortune follow. They are lacking in this, that they want to be sure first of their material resources, where they are to get their food, drink, and clothing. Yes, they want to pull their head out of the noose of Genesis 3, 'In the sweat of your face you shall eat bread.' They want to be lazy, greedy rascals who do not need to work. Therefore, they will get married only if they can get wives who are rich, beautiful, pious, kind – indeed, wait, we'll have a picture of them drawn for you.

"Let such heathen go their way; we will not argue with them. If they should be lucky enough to obtain such wives the marriages would still be un-Christian and without faith. They trust in God as long as they know that they do not need him, and that they are well supplied. He who would enter into wedlock as a Christian must not be ashamed of being poor and despised, and doing insignificant work. He should take satisfaction in this: first, that his status and occupation are pleasing to God; second, that God will most certainly provide for him if only he does his job to the best of his ability, and that, if he cannot be a squire or a prince, he is a manservant or a maidservant.

"God has promised in Matthew 6, 'Do not be anxious about what you shall eat, drink, and put on; seek first the kingdom of God and his righteousness, and all these things shall be yours as well.' Again Psalm 36 says, 'I have been young and now am old, yet I have not seen the righteous forsaken, or his children begging bread.' ... Indeed, God has shown sufficiently in the first chapter of Genesis how he provides for us. He first created and prepared all things in heaven and on earth, together with the beasts and all growing things, before he created man. Thereby he demonstrated how he has laid up for us at all times a sufficient store of food and clothing, even before we ask him for it. All we need to do is to work and avoid idleness; then we shall certainly be fed and clothed. But a pitiful unbelief refuses to admit this. The unbeliever sees, comprehends, and feels all the same that even if he worries himself to death over it, he can neither produce nor maintain a single grain of wheat in the field. He knows too that even though all his storehouses were full to overflowing, he could not make use of a single morsel or thread unless God sustains him in life and health and preserves to him his possessions. Yet this has no effect on him.

"To sum the matter up: whoever finds himself unsuited to the celibate life should see to it right away that he has something to do and to work at; then let him strike out in God's name and get married. A young man should marry at the age of twenty at the latest, a young woman at fifteen to eighteen ... Let God worry about how they and their children are to be fed. God makes children; he will surely also feed them. Should he fail to exalt you and them here on earth, then take satisfaction in the fact that he has granted you a Christian marriage, and know that he will exalt you there; and be thankful to him for his gifts and favors."

Preparing Sons for Marriage

Whoever said boys are the same as girls couldn't have had one of each. Our youngest son is approaching his first birthday and his more aggressive and active nature compared with our sweet little girls is evident. I think God made boys and girls different because boys and girls have different jobs to do and different roles to play. Only girls can bear children and nurse them. Girls tend to be softer, cleaner, more attractive, "nicer," more detail oriented, more verbal, and more intuitive. On the other hand, boys tend to be bigger, stronger, more attracted, dirtier, more aggressive, more active, more competitive, more math oriented, and more interested in machines and technology.

The culture we live in, however, has gone to great lengths to minimize the differences between boys and girls and the significance these differences may have. Schools train boys and girls identically – to the point that gym classes and home economics classes are now coed. They start school at the same age and finish at the same age even though girls and boys develop at different rates. Girls are encouraged to choose a career as if being a wife and raising children are non-issues. There is a radio ad put out by the Girl Scouts, of all people, that laments the fact that many girls lose interest in math at about the 6th grade when they will need math for most future jobs. Girls are also told that male headship is archaic and is a threat to female equality. Men and women are supposed to share everything equally - including the authority in the home.

We all know, however, that the effort to form an androgynous culture has been a failure, because the differences between boys and girls are part of our God-given design and are inescapable. That being said, the culture has been successful in confusing us over what our God-given roles in marriage are and how we can best prepare for those roles.

We must understand, then, as we seek to prepare our sons for marriage that the culture has an anti-biblical agenda for gender roles. Therefore, we need to reject the culture and raise sons who are willing to accept their biblically mandated responsibilities.

What are these? Paul writes, "For the husband is the head of the wife, as Christ also is the head of the church, He Himself being the Savior of the body." (Eph. 5:23) He continues, "Husbands, love your wives, just as Christ also loved the church and gave Himself up for her, so that He might sanctify her, having cleansed her by the washing of water with the word, that He might present to Himself the church in all her glory, having no spot or wrinkle or any such thing; but that she would be holy and blameless. So husbands ought also to love their own wives as their own bodies." (Eph. 5:25-28a) Our sons must understand that they will become the undisputed head of the home, but they are to use their headship for good. They are to love their wives, care for them, and protect them with their lives if necessary. Our sons must learn to be strong, but not to lord it over their families.

Our sons must also take fatherhood very seriously. Paul tells fathers, "Fathers, do not provoke your children to anger, but bring them up in the discipline and instruction of the Lord." (Eph. 6:4) As head of the family, fathers must see that their children understand the commands of our God. Moses writes, "These words, which I am commanding you today, shall be on your heart. You shall teach them diligently to your sons and shall talk of them when you sit in your house and when you walk by the way and when you lie down and when you rise up. You shall bind them as a sign on your hand and they shall be as frontals on your forehead. You shall write them on the doorposts of your house and on your gates." (Deut. 6:6-9) Thus, our sons must understand that they have an obligation to discipline, train, instruct, and teach their children. This is not "women's work."

What should we do, then, to train our sons to be husbands and fathers after the biblical model?

Give them the habit of reading God's word: I have said this before, but I'll say it again. The best thing we have done as parents is to see that all our children read their Bibles daily. They all read through the entire Bible at the rate of 4 chapters per day once they are 9 years old. It takes them until age 9 to read through the Bible once and they read through about once per year after that. Thus, my 17-year-old son has probably read the entire Bible about 9 times.

This is a critical issue, because it is the mechanism through which they come to faith in Jesus Christ. As the Bible says, "Faith comes from hearing, and hearing by the word of Christ." (Rom. 10:17) It is also the best method of teaching character. I may diligently try to mold the character of my son, but the Holy Spirit is much more effective. The more time I allow the Holy Spirit to teach my son through His word, the less difficult my job is and the more sanctified he is likely to become. All the principles my son needs to know to become a godly man are found in the pages of Scripture.

A young man who doesn't know the Scriptures – even if he seems to be a well-behaved believer – is standing on thin ice, indeed. His lack of knowledge and understanding makes him much more susceptible to false teaching and loose living. Unfortunately, his parents may not understand the severity of his shortcomings until he is on his own and free from parental oversight.

Another reason to make sure our sons know the Scriptures is to make them qualified to effectively pass on the faith to their children. How can we expect our sons to pass on what they have never received from us? Taking our sons to church and Sunday school is not enough. They need to know the Bible and know it well.

Discipline them: Having our sons read the Scriptures is critical to their success as husbands and fathers, but it isn't enough. We must discipline them properly so they learn to respect authority and to understand that sin has negative consequences. The book of Proverbs says, "Discipline your son while there is hope, and do not desire his death." (Prov. 19:18) "Foolishness is bound up in the heart of a child; the rod of discipline will remove it far from him." (Prov. 22:15) "Do not hold back discipline from the child, although you strike him with the rod, he will not die. You shall strike him with the rod and rescue his soul from Sheol." (Prov. 23:13-14) And, "He who withholds his rod hates his son, but he who loves him disciplines him diligently." (Prov. 13:24)

Boys tend to be more active and aggressive, so disciplining them may be more of a challenge. Discipline should be firm enough to impose our will over the strong willed child, but not so strict or arbitrary that he is driven to rebel or his spirit is broken. And discipline must come from parents who delight in their son, so it is easier to see that the discipline is done in love and not because his parents dislike their son or enjoy lording it over him. Also, if my son is to be responsible for maintaining godly discipline in his home, he will probably do a better job if he experienced godly discipline in my home.

Teach and model biblical gender roles: Feminism has had a profound impact on our culture and many homes have been negatively affected by it. Most men tend to be too weak and selfish to effectively carry out their God-given responsibilities as husbands and fathers. On the other hand, most women tend to be too unsubmissive and selfish to effectively carry out their responsibilities as wives and mothers. Boys are used to seeing mom run the house, make most decisions, and get her way if there is disagreement. They are not used to seeing strong, sacrificial fathers and strong, but submissive, helpmeets for mothers. Our sons should know from experience how a man is supposed to act and how he is to interact with his wife and children.

Help them get a marketable skill: A young man should be focused on preparing for marriage and a big part of marriage preparation is attaining a skill that will allow him to provide for his family. Boys shouldn't be allowed to waste their late teens and early twenties. Paul said, "When I became a man, I did away with childish things." (1 Cor.

13:11b) Many of us let our young men waste time on computer games, "hanging out" with their friends, watching television, listening to music, going to parties, and chasing girls they have no intention of marrying when they should be studying and working.

I wasted my late teens and early twenties and suffer some of the consequences 20 years later. My sons know I have no intention of allowing them to do the same. My oldest son started college two years ahead of his peers because he knew what he wanted to do and it didn't make sense to wait around. My second son has had trouble deciding what he wants to do, but he will be forced to choose a direction before his 17th birthday. (I think even that is too late.) I don't think it is healthy for a young man of 20 to be trying to figure out what his major should be or what he's going to do when he quits his dead end, minimum wage job. A boy who is serious in his teens will probably be a great blessing to his future family and reap the benefits the rest of his life.

Help them acquire practical home skills: I will admit that this is one of the weaknesses of my own parenting, but I think teaching our sons how to maintain property, a house, and a vehicle would benefit them tremendously. I know that a man can learn these things as the need arises, but he may make many costly mistakes in the process. Or, he may pay someone else a lot of money to do the things he never learned.

A man cannot be blamed for failing to pass knowledge on to his son that he doesn't have, but often information is not shared with our sons because it is easier for us to do the work ourselves. Training our sons will slow us down and he is sure to make mistakes as he learns, but this is an investment well spent.

Teach them to appreciate children: One of my favorite verses is found in Malachi. In it, God says, "Has not the LORD made them one? In flesh and spirit they are his. And why one? Because he was seeking godly offspring." (Mal. 2:15, NIV) One of the primary purposes of marriage is to produce godly offspring for the Lord. Most men believe marriage does not necessarily obligate them to have children, but a man who purposefully remains childless rejects God's purpose for marriage. Our sons should know that a man who won't have children is keeping from God that which He is seeking.

He should also know these Scriptures: "Behold, children are a gift of the LORD, the fruit of the womb is a reward. Like arrows in the hand of a warrior, so are the children of one's youth. How blessed is the man whose quiver is full of them; they will not be ashamed when they speak with their enemies in the gate." (Ps. 127:3-5) And, "How blessed is everyone who fears the LORD, who walks in His ways. When you shall eat of the fruit of your hands, you will be happy and it will be well with you. Your wife shall be like a fruitful vine within your house, your children like olive plants around your table. Behold, for thus shall the man be blessed who fears the LORD." (Ps. 128:1-4)

Therefore any prospective husband who doesn't want children despises God's reward and certainly isn't ready for marriage.

Concluding thoughts: There is a shortage in the world of young men who have a godly vision for marriage. Most young men marry because living with their girl is better than living without her. Most men have children because they would rather have a family than not have a family. Most men leave their wives and their children because they've changed their minds about them. Everything is done for selfish reasons.

We have four sons. Although we are raising them imperfectly, we are striving to make them the best husbands and fathers they can be. But we also have seven daughters. I can only hope and pray there are enough godly young men out there for them. I can't give a good reason for this, but I worry more about my daughters finding godly husbands than I worry about my sons finding godly wives.

Are sons harder to raise than daughters? Are fathers naturally more protective of their daughters than their sons? Perhaps the answer to both questions is yes.

Is Your Daughter Ready for the Wedding?

We have seven daughters. (Are you laughing yet?) Our oldest is 15 and our youngest is 2, so preparing daughters for marriage is something we take very seriously. In a few short years we'll probably be giving daughters away on a fairly regular basis. If our daughters aren't prepared, just think how many young men we can inflict with the consequences. We'll probably have to move and get an unlisted phone number so none of our in-laws can track us down.

When a girl gets engaged in our culture, she spends months getting ready for the wedding. She buys a dress, gets a pastor to officiate the ceremony, chooses bride's maids, chooses bride's maid dresses, rents a hall, chooses the food and drinks that will be served, chooses the music, prepares the invitations, and registers for gifts.

But as we all know, a girl who is ready for the wedding isn't necessarily ready for marriage. Will the bride be ready to respect, honor, and love an imperfect man as long as they both shall live? Will she be a good helper for him? Will she be ready to love, discipline, and raise godly children? Will she be ready to manage a home? Will she be ready to leave her father and mother and transfer her allegiance to her husband? Will she be able to adjust to her in-laws?

We hope our married daughters will be able to answer affirmatively to all these questions, but how can we raise them to make our hope for them a reality?

Helpful Hint #1 – Mothers should be role models: One of the many drawbacks of our educational system is that boys and girls get virtually identical training. That would be fine if boys and girls were training for virtually identical roles in the family, the church, and the workplace, but they are not. Boys need to learn to lead, protect, and provide for their families. They also have greater responsibilities outside the home. Men are to serve as elders and deacons in the church, and as leaders in business and government. On the other hand, women are called to submit to their husbands, bear and raise children, manage a home, care for widows, and "wash the feet of the saints." When boys and girls receive identical training and education, they may have difficulty discerning and accepting the biblical distinctions in their roles.

Many Christian girls don't hear about their God-given role until years of feminist principles have been absorbed. They think women should be doing all the same things men do, and they resent the fact that the Bible gives the headship of the home and church to men. When they get married, the girls often struggle with their husbands to get their own way and do not easily accept their husbands' leadership. They may also shun having children. It is not uncommon for men to say they would have more children but their wives won't go through childbirth again. A girl who resents male leadership and doesn't want children is not ready for Christian marriage.

Girls need to know, accept, and embrace godly womanhood instead of resenting the advantages they believe God gave to men. If a Christian wife and mother is sincerely happy with her calling and she expresses the joys and responsibilities of being a wife and mother to her daughters, her consistency in word and deed will go a long way in training her daughters to be happy with their Scriptural role.

Helpful Hint #2 – Make your daughter's character your first priority: Christian character is more important in a wife and mother than all of the practical parenting and homemaking skills combined. Character can cover a multitude of ignorance. My wife Cindy came into our marriage not knowing how to cook and didn't have much experience with children (she was the baby of the family). However, Cindy was sweet, kind, disciplined, and had a quiet confidence and resolve coming into the marriage. All the practical skills she needed were learned on the job and she has become competent in every area necessary to keep our large household going. In fact, she has excelled at everything she's ever done. Thus, the only truly necessary prerequisite for successful wife- and motherhood is a strong Christian character. Proverbs compares the beautiful woman with poor character to a gold ring in a pig's snout. The girl competent in homemaking skills but lacking in character is no better.

Unfortunately, our culture makes academic education its highest priority for girls (just think how much time and money is spent on educating the average girl), and character is a distant second. We have sowed the wind and reaped the whirlwind. Some of our girls may be entering all kinds of professions once open only to men, but generally they are failures at being wives and mothers. Our emphasis on educating our girls at the expense of cultivating their character is just one of the reasons the divorce rate is so high and children are raised so poorly today. I'm not one of those who say that girls shouldn't be educated, but it's not crucial to succeeding as a Christian wife or mother. Character certainly is.

Helpful Hint #3 – Girls benefit from experience with young children: When my oldest daughter first started watching a younger sister, she would complain that the toddler wouldn't let her dress her or wouldn't let her brush her teeth. We had the opportunity to train her to impose her will on her strong willed younger siblings when it was necessary. Now, she is terrific with our younger children. It's nice that that lesson could be learned before she had children of her own. It amazes me that, given the fact that the vast majority of Christian women will have children, many girls get very little experience to prepare them. For small families and for girls without younger brothers or sisters, it is still possible to gain experience by helping with the children of relatives, church families, and friends.

Helpful Hint #4 – Girls benefit from practical homemaking skills: Modern technology has made housework much faster, less physically demanding, and require less skill. Even so, girls often go into a marriage not knowing how to cook, clean and organize a home, balance a checkbook, or garden. The Proverbs 31 woman had learned all kinds of practical skills that helped her contribute to the welfare of her family.

While my wife has proven that it is possible to learn most practical homemaking skills after the marriage, I think it foolish to enter marriage unprepared if that can be avoided. I think that because most girls are at school all day, evenings become a time for homework and not homemaking work. I also think many mothers have learned to do things efficiently by themselves and don't want to be bothered showing their daughters how to do things. I understand that the more help a mother gets from her young children the more time things take and the less acceptable the results. But it is a mother's duty to train her daughters, and sometimes a mother's desire for efficiency and quality is a mask for selfishness.

In large families, where the workload is too much for the mother to handle by herself, the oldest daughter tends to be very competent in practical housekeeping skills. In the end, a daughter who is trained in practical homemaking skills is a blessing to her parents' household long before she leaves to begin a household of her own. Thus, training a daughter in practical homemaking skills is good for her, but even a selfish mother will find that the investment at the beginning will pay back big dividends in the end.

Concluding remarks: To some extent, no girl is ever prepared for marriage and the best training in the world will not take away all the surprises. On the job training is required no matter how hard we try to get our daughters ready for the wedding. And still, life moves on. One season of life blends into the next and new challenges must be met. We are never fully prepared for them and our daughters won't be either. But the fact that we will never achieve perfection doesn't mean that our best efforts will be in vain. I believe wisdom can be passed on from generation to generation as long as the older generation takes the time to teach and the younger takes the time to listen.

Daughters are a wonderful blessing and God can use them to change the world – even as wives and mothers. We can't wait until the engagement to start getting them ready for the wedding. We start at their birth, cultivating Christian faith and character that will eventually enable them to help their husbands fulfill their purposes in the world, bear children who will advance God's kingdom in the next generation, manage a household that will show good stewardship of the Lord's resources, bless a local congregation of believers, and help the poor and needy.

And all these noble goals require humble work to be accomplished. Diapers must be changed, dishes need to be washed, floors need to be scrubbed, children's arguments need to be refereed, sheets need to be washed, appointments with doctors need to be made, errands need to be run, and babies need to be held. Our daughters should see these tasks in light of what they accomplish in the end and not as curses of womanhood. I have seven daughters. I hope they all grow up happy to be girls and glad to do the beautiful and important work God gave them to do.

Finding a Mate

The Christian teaching on marriage is radically different from what we see in the world. The world says that if you think a girl looks good and is fun to be around, she is a potential marriage partner, significant other, or insignificant other (someone who merely satisfies physical urges). Since the standard is very low and the commitment level open to negotiation, most girls would qualify as a potential match. When this is combined with the fact that the world throws almost all of its teenagers together in coed schools, it is not surprising that high schools and colleges have become little Sodoms and Gomorrahs.

For the Christian, however, things ought to be very different. First, Christians are commanded to marry only "in the Lord." A Christian man, then, can only marry a Christian girl. This in itself should eliminate a majority of the female population as prospective mates. Furthermore, the Bible does not support romantic relationships outside of marriage. Therefore, much of what passes for dating, going steady, and any other extra marital romantic relationship is not supported either. Paul commands Timothy, "Treat the younger women like sisters with absolute purity." (1 Tim. 5:2, NIV) These extra marital relationships are not generally characterized as men treating the young women as sisters with absolute purity. And marriage itself is a life-long commitment – it is not to be broken simply because a man finds his wife difficult or incompatible. This narrows a man's choices even further, because only potential life-long marriage partners would qualify for his attention.

To make a Christian man's search even more difficult, the body of Christ is divided into factions and denominations (some of which have conflicting beliefs that are very difficult to reconcile). The incompatible differences between denominations may be obvious to many, but there are other divisions as well. For example, if the potential husband wants two children and believes his wife should use birth control, he may have problems with a girl who wants a large family and believes birth control is wrong. This requires, then, that the girl either come from the same religious background or be willing to submit to her husband's belief system.

For young men attending Christian schools and large churches, there may still be a large pool of marriageable Christian women. However, many Christian men have much more limited circumstances. Those who are homeschooled into the high school and college years may never have the luxury (or the temptation) of spending most of their days around large numbers of single Christian girls. Also, for those who attend small churches, family integrated churches, or house churches, there may be very limited choices among their Christian acquaintances. Add to this the fact that in many neighborhoods, relationships with like-minded Christian families are limited or non-existent. The young Christian man may be left wondering where he is supposed to find a wife. Our family is one of those families that offers its children very few options when it comes to finding a husband or a wife. We do not have close relationships with the families in our neighborhood, we have homeschooled our children through high school, and we attend a very small church. Even in our little church, not everyone shares our beliefs about important family issues such as education and birth control. Where, then, are our children to find spouses?

First of all, I think it is good to remember that God knows what we need and will provide for us and for our children. Jesus said, "Seek first His kingdom and His righteousness, and all these things will be added to you." (Matt. 6:33) The writer of Proverbs says, "A prudent wife is from the LORD." (Prov. 19:14) Ultimately, it is God who takes responsibility for finding us spouses. If we are separated from our culture because it is immoral and if our children make incompatible spouses for many Christians because we would rather serve the Lord than fit in, we shouldn't worry. God will provide our godly children with suitable spouses.

Second, earthly fathers have a responsibility to see that their children are provided for – and this includes helping to provide a spouse. Some in our enlightened culture believe it is wrong for a father to help his child find a spouse – that it's a meddling in the private affairs of his grown-up children. What do the Scriptures say? Was Abraham, whose believing household was isolated in a heathen land, wrong when he sent his servant (without his adult son Isaac) to his Aramean relatives to find Isaac a wife? Was Isaac wrong when he sent Jacob to Laban's household to find a wife among his relatives instead of allowing him (as he did Esau) to marry a Canaanite woman?

If finding spouses for one's children were wrong, God wouldn't have commanded the Israelite exiles in Babylon to do so. Jeremiah writes, "This is what the LORD Almighty, the God of Israel says ... 'Marry and have sons and daughters; find wives for your sons and give your daughters in marriage, so that they too may have sons and daughters.' " (Jer. 29:4a, 6a, NIV)

As like-minded Christians become more separated, it will become increasingly helpful for fathers to take a more active, biblically sanctioned role in their children's search for a mate. This may scare some young Christian singles, but they would probably be surprised at how helpful a father can be in making the biggest decision they will probably ever make outside their decision to follow the Lord.

We have decided that a young single should look to his God first and then to his father for help in finding a spouse – a stark contrast to the schools and drinking establishments the unbelieving young turn to first. That being said, we know that the young man must meet his potential bride somewhere.

The first place to look for a spouse is in families that belong to the same local church or who share a long-standing friendship. These are the people who are most likely to share our values, our way of raising children, our manners, and our priorities. We also have a better idea as to how the families interact with each other. In this group we are also most likely to discern hidden strengths and flaws that could make or break a marriage. Thus, a man is more likely to make a wise decision concerning a potential mate when he has more knowledge on which to base his decision.

Nevertheless, it is entirely possible that young men and women could find themselves in a position where no suitable mates are apparent. If the Christian single is young or not in a hurry to marry, patience may be the best option. However, if Christian singles are ready to marry they may seek out places where the kind of spouses they want to marry would be. Some may find suitable mates at Christian colleges, church youth groups, Bible studies, or singles ministries.

While this may increase a single's exposure to potential mates, it does have its drawbacks. First, acquaintances who are only recently known and infrequently seen may not be as good as they seem. It is easy for a young man to put his best foot forward at a Bible study (especially when there is a young lady he wants to impress). His past, family background, and even his true current character may all be a mystery. Second, when singles get together outside and apart from the protection of the family, immorality often results – even among Christians. Recently, I heard a Focus on the Family radio broadcast. Dr. Dobson asked his guest, who ministered to college students, whether immorality was rampant on Christian college campuses. Of course, the answer was yes. I would add that immorality is rampant wherever young Christian singles gather regularly apart from their parents.

Most Christian parents will probably take what they consider an unavoidable risk, send their children to Christian schools, youth groups, and Bible studies, and pray that God will protect their children and lead them to godly spouses. This approach has probably worked out well enough for many parents, so they don't see this as a problem. And for the vast majority, this approach will give their children ample opportunities to find a spouse.

I do believe immorality among Christians is avoidable if we make an effort to protect ourselves – and this would apply to married Christians as well as singles. In the case of young singles, the family setting generally and the father specifically should be the first line of protection.

I can hear the objection of those who would say that parents do not choose spouses any better than the child and that a poor decision by the father would potentially cause life-long resentment. However, I am not advocating parental choice. Ultimately, it is the son who must choose to leave his father and mother and cleave to his wife, and ultimately, the daughter must consent to a proposal of marriage.

What I am advocating is parental involvement and parental protection. There can be little disagreement over the statement that marriages decided on the front porch of the girl's father's house are less likely to include sexual immorality than marriages decided on the college campus, movie theater, or any other place where parents are absent. God made the attraction between men and women exceedingly strong and God commanded that fulfillment of this attraction be confined to marriage. Nevertheless, a great many Christians will not be able to control themselves if left alone with a person of the opposite sex with whom there is mutual attraction. It is the job of the parent, then, to protect the children from sexual immorality by supervising courtship. Basically, parents should not allow their courting children to feel so alone that sexual immorality could occur without a realistic fear of being caught. A parent who allows his child to be unchaperoned with a member of the opposite sex should understand that there is a high probability that sexual immorality will result.

For those of us, then, who do not want our children finding a mate without parental involvement or protection, the responsibility lies with the parents to provide the children with adequate opportunities to find a mate. If between the parents and the child there are not adequate associations to realistically find a spouse, the parents should take it upon themselves to expand their associations to include other families that have Christian children approaching marriageable age. I know that in our case, visiting other families is not something we do very often. Now that our oldest three children are teenagers, however, we need to make that a priority.

After being provided with the opportunity to meet girls of marriageable age (the daughter should also be provided with the opportunity to meet boys of marriageable age), the son should choose a suitable helpmeet. The son should seriously consider the advice of his parents before making a final choice and the girl should seriously consider her parents' advice before she accepts.

Paul said that anyone who doesn't provide for the needs of his immediate family is worse than an unbeliever. I doubt Paul had spouses for children in mind when he wrote that, but I think the principle could be applied here. A mate is a physical and emotional need for most – as surely as food and shelter are. God said, "It is not good for the man to be alone," (Gen. 2:18) and He provided Adam with a wife. Likewise, parents have an obligation to see that their children who want to be married can find godly spouses.

For those of you who send your children to schools of respectable size, you have probably provided your child with ample opportunity to find a mate. For those parents who plan to be involved in the process of finding a spouse and in protecting their children from sexual immorality, I hope you have developed relationships with a large number of families that have potential mates for your children. If this is the case you may have done enough already. However, if you are like us and want to protect and be involved but haven't developed many meaningful relationships with like-minded families, you need to make a conscious effort to get out of the house and meet others.

Since our oldest is 16 years of age, we have a little time. But within ten years our eighth child will be sixteen years old. Therefore, finding spouses will fast become a significant part of our parenting effort. Don't pity us, though. Despite the cost of weddings we cannot afford, we are looking forward to seeing our children launch Christian households of their own.

Choosing a Wife

Unbelieving male requests a mate: She should have nice hair, big beautiful eyes, a great smile and an attractive feminine figure – and she must also be fun to be around.

Sadly, beauty and charm are the cultural standards by which potential wives are judged. Even more sadly, the standards for many Christian men are similar. The only alteration many Christian men would make to the world's standard would be this: "Oh, I almost forgot. I am a Christian, so she should also believe in God."

Choosing a wife is the most important decision a man makes except for his decision to accept the Gospel of

Jesus Christ. Who you choose to marry is more important than your career or where you live. The average man changes jobs many times, but once the decision is made, his wife may never be changed. A good wife will always help a man achieve his calling – the purpose God has for his life. A good career, however, will not always help a man achieve a happy marriage. As proof, just look at the tabloid headlines in the grocery store. A bad wife can ruin a man's career, but a poor career will not ruin a godly wife. More important is the fact that a godly wife will bless a man with lifelong companionship and intimacy, which makes his life a pleasure even when other things are going wrong. A bad wife, on the other hand, will be a source of stress all the time.

Since finding a godly wife is so important, why do so many Christian men choose a mate using the same criteria as the unbelievers? I am so blessed to have married a godly woman. Cindy has been my friend and lover for almost 14 years. We have had nine children and lived in four states. Life has been a struggle for us at times. I don't remember how many jobs I've had. Nothing seems to work out the way it's supposed to. This has been the cause of chronic financial struggle. A few years ago we were late getting the water bill paid and I couldn't come up with the money until the last day before our water was to be shut off. I got to the payment center about 20 minutes after the place closed, so for one night and part of the next day we had no water. That night all of our seven children came down with the flu. Trying to clean up the mess without water was an awful experience I will never forget, and I was filled with regret for the mistakes I had made which got us into that mess. But Cindy never criticized me. She never lost her temper. She didn't even get angry. She just helped me clean up the mess and take care of the children. The next day the bill was paid and we got our water back. Cindy could have been bitter for my career failings, but she was above that. My wife has been nothing but a blessing to me since the day I met her.

How did I find a girl like that? I wish I could say I was looking for all the right qualities, but I didn't completely know then what I should have been looking for. But now having observed Cindy for almost 14 years, I will tell you what I would advise my sons to look for.

I would tell them to read Proverbs 31, for Proverbs 31 accurately describes their mother. First, the Proverbs 31 woman had a noble character. A woman of noble character has a quiet and gentle spirit, and she respects and submits to her husband. She is honest, generous, responsible, disciplined, and godly.

Second, the Proverbs 31 woman was competent. Through her excellent work her family and her servants were fed and clothed. She had good judgment in her business and real estate dealings and the Bible says her trading was profitable. She also had the good sense to prepare for the future. That is why she could "smile at the future." She watched over the affairs of her household and earned praise from her husband. She was not weak but strong. She was competent and productive.

Third, I don't know if the Proverbs 31 woman was charming or fun to be around, but I know I have never tired of being with my Proverbs 31 wife. I would tell my sons that charm is a positive attribute in a wife.

Finally, it is preferable for a wife to be pleasing to look at. Cindy is the delight of my eyes and I hope my sons can find girls who attract them as well. Girls are crafted by God to be beautiful, and a good wife should care about her appearance, for her body is also the temple of the Holy Spirit.

In summary, I would say that my sons should concentrate on finding a girl who has a noble character and is competent in her work. These are necessary attributes and should not be compromised. Charm and beauty are preferable, but should not receive the priority of the other two. Character and competence will last a lifetime, but, as the Scriptures say, "Charm is deceitful and beauty is vain." (Prov. 31:30)

The unbeliever, then, prioritizes the attributes he is looking for in a wife in the exact opposite order of their true importance. Beauty is first on his mind and charm is second – some would say a distant second. Competency would be next and character would be last. A wife who is chosen based on beauty and charm will usually be a disappointment. The beauty is temporary and the charm is deceptive. They will not help a man fulfill his calling and they are irrelevant in raising godly offspring. If hard times hit, beauty and charm will not be of much help. The modern songwriter says that he was "looking for love in all the wrong places, looking for love in too many faces." This is true of most men, and perhaps that is one of the reasons a wife of noble character is so hard to find.

Choosing a Husband

Choosing a husband is the most important earthly decision a woman will ever make. God was abundantly good in the spouse that He gave me. I feel that He watched over me and guided me because, in retrospect, I see that there were many things that I did not know. Having seven daughters, there is a potential for a lot of weddings and a lot of son-in-laws in our home. I want to teach my daughters the things that I have learned, in the hope that it will help them choose a mate.

First of all, prayer is a vital part of this process. A woman in a Bible study that I attend told us that even as a young girl she began praying for the type of spouse she wanted – and God did answer her prayer! What a powerful message to tell our daughters – to encourage them to pray for a spouse and for the wisdom necessary in choosing him.

I think that prayer is also important for the parents. I have begun praying for the future spouses of my children, as well as for their parents during these critical growing years. I also pray for my children, that they may be wise in choosing a mate.

Following the Bible's teaching in 2 Corinthians 6 about not being yoked with unbelievers, choosing a Christian man for a spouse is the most important criteria. We must not be fooled. According to the Apostle Paul, we do not have any "fellowship," "harmony," or "agreement" with unbelievers – and this extends to marriage, the closest of all earthly relationships.

Furthermore, a Christian husband should hold to and practice Christian values such as the importance of family, work, honesty, etc. Whoever is not faithful in small matters may very well prove unfaithful in large matters. I don't worry about Jim lying to me, because he has been honest with me in large matters as well as small from the very beginning of our relationship. Watching how a person deals with the everyday situations of life will give one a good indication of their value system. Does he cheat on tests, lie to his parents, avoid family functions or call out of work a lot? Those things can tell you a lot about a person.

I think it is also very important to see in your future spouse a person who will help you grow, both personally and spiritually. The husband is supposed to lead the family in such growth, not the wife. The wife should not be dragging the husband to church or prodding him to read his Bible. Our husbands should bring out the best in us, and encourage us to grow to our potential.

Closely related is the characteristic of self-improvement. Is your future spouse trying to grow spiritually himself? Is he leading by his example? The first summer after I met Jim he was living and working on the college campus. He was hundreds of miles away from his family and we probably saw each other only once a week. He had a lot of free time to fill, and he spent hours and hours reading his Bible. This had quite an effect on me. I knew that I would be encouraged to grow simply by watching his example. I could see him being a leader who was submissive to God.

I'm not saying that one's future spouse needs to be a perfectly cut, polished diamond. We all continue (or at least should) to grow throughout our lives. But the potential and desire for growth needs to be evident in the men we marry.

One of our roles as wives is to be submissive to our husbands. We are not given the choice of whether to be submissive to our husbands or not, but we are given the choice of *who* we will submit to as our husband. Are you willing to submit to this man? Do you trust his motives, his priorities, his judgment, his character? At the same time, are you willing to let him try, and to fail?

It is necessary before marriage to talk about issues that will affect your life together. I remember that one discussion Jim and I had was about disciplining children. (Considering our life now, that was a pretty important talk!) Do you agree on important issues? If not, how will you handle those differences? Are some differences just too important to compromise on? Better to find out before marriage than after.

Do you have similar interests? It is not necessary to be alike in every way, because those differences can teach us new things and broaden our horizons. But you still need to be able to decide what to do together on your day off. Being together and doing things together is necessary to keep a relationship strong and growing.

I hope I am not misunderstood, but I think there is something to be said for the "spark" and the "chemistry" between two people. That is not the only reason to marry, but without it there may be many men who would fit the other criteria, men you wouldn't want to spend the rest of your life with. Do you like being with him? Do you miss him when you're apart? Are you excited when you hear the phone ring? Finally, would you be proud to introduce him to your family, your friends, your pastor, the people you respect most? If not, there may be something about him that you need to take another look at. Maybe something you haven't realized yet.

How do you know when you're ready to get married? I've heard a lot of people ask that question, so perhaps my daughters will ask it, too. Like any decision, we need to talk to God about it in prayer. James chapter one tells us God will give wisdom to those who confidently ask Him for it. Second, being ready to marry means being ready to completely commit yourself to this person and choosing to be completely happy with him, forsaking all others as well as the search to find any other. This is a serious oath. Third, the intended spouse must pass any criteria for a husband that you have set up beforehand. And, last of all, I think that a good test of readiness for marriage is this: does marriage feel like the next natural step in your relationship? Are you beginning to see and feel yourselves as being married? If the decision to marry is fraught with fear and indecision, it is probably best to wait. There is no hurry.

Marriage is a wonderful gift of God, and should my children marry, I hope they will know its joys in the fullest. Talking to them about choosing a mate is an important step in that direction.

"But from the beginning of creation, God made them male and female. For this reason a man shall leave his father and mother and the two shall become one flesh; so they are no longer two, but one flesh. What therefore God has joined together, let no man separate." (Mark 10:6-9)

Who Should Pay for the Wedding?

Growing up in this culture, it never occurred to me that it should be any different: The bride and her mother plan the wedding and the bride's parents pay for it. I was intrigued, however, when I read an article by John Thompson ("God's Design for Scriptural Romance, part 9: The Wedding Stage") that stated that the biblical norm was the opposite: The groom and his father were responsible for the wedding.

Naturally, since I have 7 daughters and 4 sons, you may suspect my motives in bringing up this issue. Just think how much money I could save if the groom's family has to pay! Hopefully, you'll overlook my financial stake in the outcome of this debate and enjoy the process of trying to apply biblical principles to this issue. (All of you with potential grooms for my daughters, read especially carefully.) All kidding aside, what do the Scriptures say about weddings and does this help us know who should pay for the wedding feast?

The first thing we must acknowledge is that there are no clear commands that outline specifically how weddings are to be conducted. So there is room for individual preferences. I don't think you need to turn to the Scriptures to decide whether you are going to have chicken or beef, Coke or Pepsi, or linen or paper or plastic plates.

There are a number of marriages described in the Bible. Adam & Eve, Isaac & Rebecca, Jacob & Leah, Rachel, and their maidservants, Samson & the Philistine woman, Boaz & Ruth, David & Abigail, David & Michal, Solomon & 700 wives and 300 concubines, Esther & the Persian king, Hosea & Gomer, and the wedding at Cana that Jesus attended. Jesus used parables about weddings to describe truths about the kingdom of God, and the Scriptures also used wedding language to describe God's relationship with Israel and Christ's relationship with the church.

However, just because a wedding involved a godly person or is mentioned in the Bible doesn't mean we should use it as an example. In other words, we have to discern what in the Bible is descriptive and what is prescriptive. David was a godly man, but I don't think we should require our prospective son-in-law to kill a hundred

Philistines and deliver us their foreskins. I'm not sure I need to give every prospective daughter-in-law a gold nose ring because Abraham gave one to Rebekah. I don't think my son should marry a prostitute because God told Hosea to marry Gomer. These events are described in the Bible, but using them as precedents we need to follow would be unnecessary in some cases and sinful in others.

That being said, I do believe that we can glean principles from the Scriptures that can give us some guidance on finding a spouse and conducting a wedding. I think the wedding between Adam & Eve is a great place to begin because this is where marriage began and God was the father of the bride, father of the groom, and matchmaker – all rolled into one.

The first principle that strikes me – and which until recently would have been unnecessary to mention – is that God established marriage as the union of one man and one woman. God said, "For this reason a man shall leave his father and his mother, and be joined to his wife; and they shall become one flesh." (Genesis 2:24) A man means one man; a wife means one woman. Homosexuality is called an abomination throughout the Scriptures and God made homosexuality a capital offense in Israel. If the wedding ceremony you're planning is between two men or two women it is an abomination in the eyes of God.

The second principle is that the woman is given to the man. God made the woman because no suitable helper was found for the man. As the Apostle Paul wrote, "Man does not originate from woman, but woman from man; for indeed man was not created for the woman's sake, but woman for the man's sake." (1 Cor. 11:8-9) God says in Jeremiah 29, "Find wives for your sons and give your daughters in marriage." (Jer. 29:6, NIV) God himself gave the first bride away. Genesis 2 states, "Then the Lord God made a woman from the rib he had taken out of the man, and he brought her to the man." Paul writes, "I betrothed you to one husband, so that to Christ I might present you as a pure virgin." (2 Cor. 11:2b) The bride, then, is presented or given at the wedding. It is interesting how the traditional wedding ceremony explicitly recognizes this fact. The father of the bride brings his daughter down the isle and acknowledges that he is responsible for giving her away.

The next wedding I'd like to look to for guidance is the wedding of Jesus Christ to His bride, the Church. Although this wedding isn't really a wedding in the strict sense of the word, I'd like to assume that the bridegroom Jesus Christ would serve as an example that all bridegrooms would want to emulate, and His bride, the Church, would serve as an example that all brides would want to emulate.

Here are some biblical descriptions of the wedding of Christ and His church. " 'Let us rejoice and be glad and give the glory to Him, for the marriage of the Lamb has come and His bride has made herself ready.' It was given to her to clothe herself in fine linen, bright and clean; for the fine linen is the righteous acts of the saints. Then he said to me, 'Write, "Blessed are those who are invited to the marriage supper of the Lamb." ' And he said to me, 'These are true words of God.' " (Rev. 19:7-9) "And I saw the holy city, new Jerusalem, coming down out of heaven from God, made ready as a bride adorned for her husband." (Rev. 21:2)

From these passages we see that the bride is beautifully clothed for her husband. The clothes are "bright and clean" which symbolizes a purity that goes much deeper than the wedding dress. For the church it represented the righteous acts of the saints. Paul, too, said he wanted to present his bride as a pure virgin. Here we see how the traditional wedding ceremony copies the biblical model. (Although for many today, the white dress is mere tradition and mocks the idea of purity.)

We also notice the mention of a marriage supper. The parable of the Ten Virgins calls it a "wedding banquet." It is interesting how feasting was associated with special days. The feasts prescribed by God for the Israelites included Passover, First Fruits and Booths. Feasting has also been historically associated with weddings in almost every culture. It is interesting that Jesus not only attended the wedding at Cana, but turned about 150 gallons of water into wine as well.

Do the Scriptures give us any clue as to where the wedding feast is to be held? This is where John Thompson's article was so illuminating for me. He lists a number of biblical weddings and the pattern is clear. The bride of Christ prepares herself for the wedding, but it is Christ who prepares the feast. At the "marriage of the

Lamb," the church leaves this world and lives forever in the place God and His Son have prepared for her to live. Indeed, we call this wedding the "marriage of the Lamb" and not the marriage of the church.

Jesus, in the parable of the wedding banquet, says, "The kingdom of heaven may be compared to a king who gave a wedding feast for his son." (Matt. 22:2) Here, the father of the groom prepares the banquet. The Wedding Psalm says, "She will be led to the King in embroidered work; the virgins, her companions who follow her, will be brought to You. They will be led forth with gladness and rejoicing; they will enter into the King's palace." (Psalm 45:14-15) Note that the wedding takes place in the residence of the groom and not in the home of the bride. Likewise, Rebekah left her home and was brought to Isaac. When Jesus attended the wedding at Cana, the bridegroom was in charge of providing the refreshments. John writes, "The headwaiter called the bridegroom, and said to him, 'Every man serves the good wine first, and when the people have drunk freely, then he serves the poorer wine; but you have kept the good wine until now.' " (John 2:9b-10) We conclude, then, that the Scriptural norm is that wedding banquets be prepared by the groom and his father and held at the residence of the groom or his father. You would be hard pressed to find biblical precedence for a wedding prepared by the bride and her mother.

And although we aren't told who actually pays for the wedding, it seems reasonable to assume that the groom and/or his father would bear the burden. It seems unlikely that the wedding banquet – hosted by the groom and his father – would be financed by the bride's family. Likewise, God redeemed Israel to become her husband and Christ redeemed the Church. At the marriage feast of the Lamb, we the Church – the bride of Christ – will not be paying. I conclude, therefore, that the groom and his father should be responsible for hosting and financing the wedding.

Concluding Remarks: How many people do you think – if any – will be convinced that the groom and his father should host and finance the wedding? I was convinced by John Thompson's article, so I know I'm not alone. But this issue is just one of many that challenge us to rethink the things we took for granted as we were growing up. You know, it's hard to believe that when Cindy and I met 20 years ago our views were much more mainstream. Then we were confronted with the birth control issue, then homeschooling, then home-based businesses, then dating, then modest dressing, then family integrated churches, then church meetings.

The consequences have been life-changing and life-defining. We're known by many as the homeschoolers with 11 kids. We spend more on food than I ever dreamed. We need a 15 passenger van to go anywhere as a family. Our perspective and our experiences are so different from the typical two-child, public school family that we are in many respects foreigners to each other. Certainly, we are members of completely different cultures.

And this has caused us to be isolated, but not just from the heathen culture that surrounds us. We are outsiders in most churches because our views are considered extreme and divisive.

In the movie "Fiddler on the Roof," Tevye says, "And because of our traditions, each one of us knows who he is and what God expects him to do." When the traditions are toppled we don't always know how to act and interact with others. When everyone was dating, everyone knew the rules and it eliminated confusion. Now, everyone has a different take on courtship. Who should pay for the wedding? What do you do if the bride and her mother want to plan the wedding when you think it is more appropriate if the groom and his family pay for the wedding? You may have problems your parents didn't have.

The answer to this problem, of course, is for Christians to look to the Scriptures to guide them in these matters. All Christians share the same guidebook and are led by the same Spirit. There is hope, then, that this is a time of transition for us and that believers who are sincerely seeking God's truth will achieve greater unity with the passage of time.

Counter Culture

In essence, the church has left the world. Contrary to the first century church and the Reformation-era church, the 20th century church has abandoned a biblical world and life view. The church offers only a personalized and pietistic religion. The message received by young people is one of how to get to heaven when they die (something which none of them are thinking about!) but not how to live while on earth. With no comprehensive philosophy of life being offered by church leaders (at least in the majority of our churches), it's little wonder that young people find the church irrelevant.

Dan Smithwick, "Why Do Our Youths Depart," www.nehemiahinstitute.com

Garbage In – Garbage Out

"WARNING ABOUT COURSE CONTENT: Due to the expressive nature of some of the readings that are used in this course, some students may be offended by the content of this course. If you are one of them, please contact me to discuss the possible need for your withdrawing from the course."

Our son started his college studies just recently and the above quote was printed in the syllabus for his composition/literature class. It wasn't just a footnote, tucked way back in the pages no one reads. During the first class the professor told the students that the novels they would be reading contained adult themes and bad language. He advised those students who might feel offended to contact him and consider dropping his class. The next day Michael was out of that class and enrolled in another. We shouldn't have to compromise our principles for three credits. We had definite reservations about Michael participating in a class where he would not only spend hours reading unwholesome material, but then spend hours discussing it as well. At best, it provides no benefit whatsoever. At worst, there is real spiritual danger involved.

Paul wrote, "Do not be deceived: Bad company corrupts good morals." (1 Cor. 15:33) If we spend a lot of time around people who engage in regular, deliberate, and sinful behavior, we are more likely to become like them. Likewise, if our entertainment or topics of discussion center on sinful thoughts and behaviors, we are more likely to have a greater interest in such things and our consciences become less sensitive to evil. In the process we are putting distance between ourselves and God and jeopardizing our relationship with Him.

Michael is sixteen years old and so is younger than most college students. That is not the issue, however. Whether we are sixteen or sixty, we are admonished to dwell on those things that are true and right. We read in Philippians 4:8: "Finally, brethren, whatever is true, whatever is honorable, whatever is right, whatever is pure, whatever is lovely, whatever is of good repute, if there is any excellence and if anything worthy of praise, dwell on these things." This is a call to all Christians – not just the young or the new believers. We are no longer what we were – those who love sin. Paul writes: "Therefore if you have been raised up with Christ, keep seeking the things above, where Christ is, seated at the right hand of God. Set your mind on the things above, not on the things that are on earth. For you have died and your life is hidden with Christ in God." (Colossians 3:1-3)

We are different now because we have been redeemed by the blood of Christ according to God's grace. We will stand out as being different compared to those around us. Also in Philippians we read, "For many walk, of whom I often told you, and now tell you even weeping, that they are enemies of the cross of Christ, whose end is destruction, whose god is their appetite, and whose glory is in their shame, who set their minds on earthly things. For our citizenship is in heaven." (Phil. 3:18-20a)

Your personal beliefs on these things will affect many issues. It is easy to say we shouldn't dwell on evil, but how do we apply that to our daily lives? It should affect the materials we read and the shows and movies we watch. In our house we have a uniform standard for acceptable entertainment. You will not find Jim and I watching movies after our kids go to bed that we won't allow them to see.

The younger children aren't regulated to another room in the house so the teenagers and adults can watch sitcoms of a more mature nature. Neither the young nor old in our house may read materials that take God's name in vain or have multiple curse words or are violent, sexual, or unwholesome. If it is not good for my children's spiritual lives, it is not good for mine, either. It doesn't have to do with being more spiritually mature and able to avoid temptation. That's not what the Bible is saying. It has to do with concentrating on those things which are wholesome and pure. This means everybody!

Believing these things will set us apart from the world around us, and will even set us apart from many Christians. There have been times I've had to return movies unwatched that were lent to us by my well-meaning co-workers. I know there have been many popular movies (such as "Titanic") that we haven't seen. I'm sure we've seemed a little odd or strict more than once. But we even survived it. We're really not missing out on anything. Our walk with God should be the most important thing to us.

I am grateful that the professor was forthright about the content of his course. It saved us from having to deal with a more complicated situation later. Personally, I think all the students should drop that course and the professor throw his books away. He doesn't need to read that stuff, either.

What About Harry Potter?

Harry Potter has taken the world by storm and Christians are divided over whether that's a bad thing or not. In our house, none of us had ever read a Harry Potter book or seen the movies. Then my teenagers' theologically conservative Sunday school teacher said in class that he didn't think there was anything wrong with Harry Potter.

First, this teacher defined magic as anything supernatural and said that magic (supernatural power) could be either good or bad. He pointed out that the Bible is full of supernatural events and so are a lot of other books most Christians have no problem reading. He concluded by saying that if parents give their children a right understanding of supernatural power before they read the book, no child who reads Harry Potter would ever be drawn to Satanism or the occult. Thus, the blame for any child who might be led astray by reading a Harry Potter book was placed on the parents, not on the author of the books.

Even though I had no knowledge of what was inside a Harry Potter book, I took issue with two of his statements and the first was his definition of magic. Remember, he defined magic as any supernatural power. As the Bible uses the term, magic and God's power would never be lumped together in the same category. God's mighty power is always good and magic is always bad. In my NIV concordance I found that the word "magic" was used eight times.

Isaiah writes, "Disaster will come upon you and you will not know how to conjure it away. A calamity will fall upon you that you cannot ward off with a ransom; a catastrophe you cannot foresee will suddenly come upon you. Keep on, then, with your magic spells and with your many sorceries, which you have labored at since childhood. Perhaps you will succeed, perhaps you will cause terror. All the counsel you have received has only worn you out! Let your astrologers come forward, those stargazers who make predictions month by month, let them save you from what is coming upon you. Surely they are like stubble; the fire will burn them up. They cannot even save themselves from the power of the flame. Here are not coals to warm anyone; here is no fire to sit by. That is all they can do for you – these you have labored with and trafficked with since childhood." (Is. 47:11-15a, NIV)

The prophet Ezekiel says, "This is what the sovereign LORD says: 'Woe to the women who sew magic charms on all their wrists and make veils of various lengths for their heads in order to ensnare people. Will you ensnare the lives of my people but preserve your own? You have profaned me among my people for a few handfuls of barley and scraps of bread. By lying to my people, who listen to lies, you have killed those who should not have died and have spared those who should not have lived.' Therefore this is what the sovereign LORD says: 'I am against your magic charms with which you ensnare people like birds and I will tear them from your arms; I will set free the people that you ensnare like birds. I will tear off your veils and save my people from your hands, and they will no longer fall prey to your power.' " (Eze. 13:18-21a,

NIV)

Luke writes, "Now for some time a man name Simon had practiced sorcery in the city and amazed all the people of Samaria. He boasted that he was someone great, and all the people, both high and low, gave him their attention and exclaimed, 'This man is the divine power known as the Great Power.' They followed him because he had amazed them for a long time with his magic. ... When Simon saw that the Spirit was given at the laying on of the apostles' hands, he offered them money and said, 'Give me this ability so that everyone on whom I lay my hands may receive the Holy Spirit.' Peter answered, 'May your money perish with you because you thought you could buy the gift of God with money!' "(Acts 8:9-11, 18-20, NIV)

John writes, "The rest of mankind that were not killed by these plagues still did not repent of the works of their hands; they did not stop worshiping demons, and idols of gold, silver, bronze, stone and wood – idols that cannot see or hear or walk. Nor did they repent of their murders, their magic arts, their sexual immorality or their thefts." (Rev. 9:20-21, NIV)

"By your magic spell all the nations were led astray." (Rev. 18:23b, NIV)

"But the cowardly, the unbelieving, the vile, the murderers, the sexually immoral, those who practice magic arts, the idolaters and all liars – their place will be in the fiery lake of burning sulfur. This is the second death." (Rev. 21:8, NIV)

"Blessed are those who wash their robes, that they may have the right to the tree of life and may go through the gates into the city. Outside are the dogs, those who practice magic arts, the sexually immoral, the murderers, the idolaters and everyone who loves and practices falsehood." (Rev. 22:14-15, NIV)

As you can see, the Bible does not claim neutrality when it comes to magic. Magic is always evil and those who continue to practice magic will all spend an eternity in hell.

I also disagree with the argument that understanding the truth about magic will inoculate the reader against being drawn into occultism. Understanding the truth about anything will not necessarily keep us from succumbing to temptation. We can understand the evils of pornographic magazines or books that glorify violence, but if we read that kind of literature on a regular basis we are much more likely to be seduced into immorality or violence. Paul said, "Do not be deceived: Bad company corrupts good morals." (1 Cor. 15:33) And there can be no mistaking the fact that reading a Harry Potter book is keeping the company of its author, Ms. Rowling, just as if she were sitting at your kitchen table. In fact, reading a book is probably company of a more potent nature than if she was in your home, for in a book she has a chance to prepare her thoughts ahead of time and speak uninterrupted for hours.

So I disagreed with the teacher, but I recalled an article written by a former pastor of mine who also defended Harry Potter. When I went home and started to research the subject I found that Chuck Colson and *World Magazine*, too, had written articles supportive of Harry Potter books. Colson wrote (Break Point, www.pfm.org, Nov. 2, 1999), "The books are enormously inventive, and include the kind of humor that makes many parents want to borrow the books from their kids. But if you're the parent of a Harry Potter fan, you may be concerned about the elements of witchcraft in these books. It may relieve you to know that the magic in these books is purely mechanical, as opposed to occultic. That is, Harry and his friends cast spells, read crystal balls, and turn themselves into animals - but they don't make contact with a supernatural world." Ron Maynard in *World Magazine* (May 29, 1999) wrote, "Rowling... keeps it safe, inoffensive, and non-occult. This is the realm of Gandalf and the Wizard of Id, not witchcraft. There is a fairy-tale order to it all in which, as Chesterton and Tolkien pointed out, magic must have rules, and good does not – cannot - mix with bad."

Given the fact that so many Christians I respected had condoned Harry Potter I decided to read the first book and judge for myself. I read about 60% of the book and set it aside for good. My mind was made up – my first dose of Harry Potter would be my last and no one in my family would be reading it either.

The biggest problem with Harry Potter is that Rowling blurs the line between right and wrong and between good and evil. Magic is one issue, but there are other related issues. Dr. Neil Chadwick wrote,

"Say what you will about the literary genius of the Harry Potter books; the problem with them is simply this, they promote the very things God forbids. Listen to the Scriptures:

" 'There shall not be found among you anyone who... practices witchcraft, or a soothsayer, or one who interprets omens, or a sorcerer, or one who conjures spells, or a medium, or a spiritist, or one who calls up the dead. For all who do these things are an abomination to the Lord.' (Deuteronomy 18:9-12) 'And the soul that turneth after such as have familiar spirits, and after wizards, to go a whoring after them, I will even set my face against that soul, and will cut him off from among his people. Sanctify yourselves therefore, and be ye holy: for I am the LORD your God.' (Leviticus 20:6,7)

"In case you are among those who have decided that the Old Testament is only for Jews, listen to what the New Testament says, 'Now the works of the flesh are manifest, which are these; Adultery, fornication, uncleanness, lasciviousness, idolatry, witchcraft, hatred, variance, emulations, wrath, strife, seditions, heresies, envyings, murders, drunkenness, revellings, and such like: of the which I tell you before, as I have also told you in time past, that they which do such things shall not inherit the kingdom of God.' (Galatians 5:19-21)

"We must not turn away from the fact that the obvious evil practices listed in these Scriptures are encouraged in the Potter series, such practices as witchcraft, sorcery, spellcasting, divination, calling up the dead, etc." (www.webedelic.com/church/hpotter.htm)

I would add one more verse to Dr. Chadwick's list. Exodus 22:18 says, "You shall not allow a sorceress to live." The Harry Potter story, then, is about a boy's experiences at a school that trains sorcerers and sorceresses – people God did not even allow to live under the Mosaic Law. If the book made any other Mosaic Law capital offense sin into an adventure, Christians would be unanimous in condemning it. Can you imagine a book about a boy's adventures as he learns about murder, adultery, or homosexuality?

You may be wondering – as I did – why so many believers support a book series that makes behavior which God considers abominable seem like harmless fun.

Although I'm not sure I understand, I came up with three potential reasons. The first reason is that this wickedness is packaged as a children's story. Rowling hasn't written an essay condoning occult behavior, but has masked that message in a venue we think of as cute. The fact that it seems cute and harmless at first glance, however, should not surprise us because we know that Satan masquerades as an angel of light. The second reason is that the books are so well written and entertaining that we want them to be all right for us to read. I'm sure many of us have mistaken our own will for God's when it concerned something we really wanted. The third reason is that we have been desensitized to the dangers of witchcraft and sorcery. We have been influenced by the naturalism of our culture that says if a thing can't be grasped with at least one of the five senses, it isn't real. Many in our culture, therefore, consider anything "supernatural" (such as witchcraft or the miracles of Jesus) as fairytales and make-believe. We have also been desensitized by fairy tales, Disney cartoons, Halloween celebrations, and television shows such as "Bewitched." These give us the idea that casting spells, and engaging in witchcraft and sorcery, can be used for good just as easily as they can for evil. It's hard to think of Samantha Stevens or Cinderella's fairy godmother as being bad or wrong. But once we've embraced "Bewitched" it isn't a major leap for us to embrace Harry Potter as well.

Many Christians have survived this leap seemingly unscathed (I imagine Chuck Colson is one), but some people have not been so fortunate. One newspaper article entitled "Potter fans turning to witchcraft" reports, "The Pagan Federation has appointed a youth officer to deal with a flood of inquiries following the success of the Harry Potter books which describe magic and wizardry." (*Associated Newspapers Ltd.*, Aug 4, 2000) Ten-year-old Gloria Bishop, speaking about the beginning of the book *The Goblet of Fire*, said, "I was eager to get to Hogwarts first because I like what they learned there and I want to be a witch." ("What readers think about the Goblet?" *San Francisco Chronicle*, July 26, 2000)

It could be that your child will not be one of those the Harry Potter books turns toward the occult, but I'm not taking a chance with my kids. And any book that makes sin look like an adventure isn't for me either.

On the Feminine Side

"Boys have it better."

One day one of my daughters uttered these words. I wasn't sure where they came from. I always have it in my heart to be a good role model of a Christian wife and mother. I feel this includes embracing with joy the position which God has given me as a woman. I want my girls to be happy God made them as they are. I want my daughters to know why it is good to be a girl!

God has put us women in a wonderful position because we are protected. It begins when we are children and in the home of our fathers. Our fathers protect us from the normal childhood dangers: accident, sickness, injury. They protect us from people, ideas, and events. This continues into the teenage and early adult, single years when daughters venture out more on their own and as the "threat" of boys increases. I believe fathers have a special inclination towards protecting their girls. Fathers have even been known to worry about their adult, married, established daughters – even though these ladies now have their husbands to protect them. Yes, we get married and then we also have husbands to protect us. My husband has protected me from potential dangers, bad situations, and unpleasant tasks. I'd rather not have to walk six blocks carrying a gas can through a bad neighborhood in the middle of January. I don't care what age I am – I like that protection!

We are not only protected, but cherished, cared, and provided for. Before the feminist movement, society treated its women members, married or not, with care and respect. Men opened doors for women, teenagers gave up their seats on the bus for mothers and grandmothers, and it was always "women first." Now men are in danger of receiving rude looks and snide remarks if they offer to open doors or surrender their place in line to a woman. But generally we are still afforded extra kindnesses as women, and this is especially true if we are married. "You husbands in the same way, live with your wives in an understanding way, as with someone weaker, since she is a woman; and show her honor as a fellow heir of the grace of life, so that your prayers will not be hindered." (1 Peter 3:7) It is a precious thing to be loved by a person for life.

As wives we have a role of helper and follower. This position is vital in maintaining a household and raising children. We can take joy and pride in the contributions we make to our noble calling as a couple (whatever that calling may be). And while we have a degree of authority, our husbands take the ultimate responsibility before God for the direction which our household takes. Our husbands must answer to God for the priorities that are chosen, the decisions that are made, and the spiritual condition of the home. This is also a place of shelter for us.

I love being a mother. Some of it doesn't make sense from a rational point of view. The bond that develops between a mother and her baby even before the baby's birth is difficult to understand. The joy we receive from raising and being around our children and watching them grow and mature is pretty incredible. I think God has placed the desire to nurture within the hearts of women. This gift of nurturing can be used in other roles besides mothering. It is a very gratifying thing, and I am glad that I can experience it.

Finally, I think the thing I like most about being a girl is that that is what God made me. I don't believe in probabilities or chances when it comes to that. I believe that I'm a female by God's choice, decision, and design. He has a certain job for me to do in this place and in this place of time, and in order to fulfill that purpose it was necessary for me to be a girl. I am here by His plan and intent. God knows best. He is not only infinite in wisdom, but in love. He lovingly and purposely created me. Why would I desire to be something different than what God made me?

Maybe some women, old and young alike, would argue with me that being female isn't all that it's cracked up to be. It's just not that good. People aren't that kind. Our husbands don't treat us that well. Bearing children is difficult and painful. Raising children is hard, unending, and carries little reward. You get stuck with a lot of work. You give up a lot in order to help others. It's not easy to be the one who follows rather than the one who leads. And so forth. It is true that in a sinful world we cannot experience the plan the way God originally intended it. We may have bad experiences. We are bombarded with the message that a woman's role is not a worthwhile or rewarding one. But it is not only the fault of the sinfulness of those around us; it is also the fault of our own selfish and discontented tendencies. We cannot allow ourselves to be deceived. There is great joy and fulfillment in doing the work in the role in which God has placed us.

I wonder how I can better impart to my daughters the joy of being a woman. I can strive to make sure that my words, actions, and attitudes are consistent and positive. I can watch for and counter the negative influences they may meet. I can pray that they embrace their womanhood with joy and passion and that they will enjoy the labor and fruits of their work. Boys don't have it better; just different. We women have it good. I'll make sure my daughters know it.

The next three articles deal with our struggle with some of the negative aspects of television programming. It also shows how our policy has slowly and progressively become more restrictive. To be honest, we continue to struggle to find a satisfactory solution to eliminating negative television images and dialogue. But a standard that works today may not work tomorrow because television itself continues to change (or should I say devolve) over time.

The Doofus

Lately, I've been noticing a trend in commercials. I don't think it's my imagination; I'm noticing it far too often now. Men are made to look like a bunch of doofuses. (The editor appreciates any letters regarding how to spell doofus!) Have you ever seen those commercials? The man and woman are driving in the car and they keep changing the radio channel back and forth to the station that each wants to hear. Then the woman says, all sweet like, "Honey, do you *enjoy* sleeping on the couch?" With a look of terror on his face, the husband quickly changes the radio back to her station. Then there's the one where a couple set out to buy a car. The husband becomes exhausted going from place to place while the woman goes to one place and finds the deal of a lifetime. And lest we think the trend has to do with married couples only, we can remember the one where two business associates are driving and the driver (a man) swerves to avoid a deer, which the woman says she never saw. All the while the man is looking and talking rather wimp-like. I'm a woman, but I find these commercials offensive. The men are made to look unintelligent and powerless, while the women are made to look superior and in control. Is this a purposeful portrayal? For what reason?

I also saw a commercial with the woman driving and the man in the passenger seat. There's nothing wrong with this, and some couples prefer it, and I honestly don't care. But it is probably not the norm, so why did they purposely make the commercial that way? What statement are they trying to make? These commercials bother me because I believe they are doing one of two things: they are either catering to a generation where male-female relationships are becoming increasingly unbiblical (and thus endorsing them), or they are telling us the way they think male-female relationships should be. Women do not need to be kicked around in commercials, but neither do men. Marriage is not to be a power struggle, but a relationship where each strives to serve the other. Intimacy is not to be withheld from one another and thus be a power-wielding tool.

Biblically, the man is the head of a household. And neither gender is intellectually superior to the other, although you might not know that from watching commercials. The feminist movement calls for equal treatment with men and for respect from men. But why should women expect respect from men in general and their husbands in particular when they don't respect the men in return? If we respect our husbands and try to serve them, we will be treated likewise. (Kind of like the Golden Rule!) We should model our relationships from the guidelines we see in the Bible and not be influenced by the poor models we see in our society. These influences may be obvious or they may be subtle. See enough of either one and it will affect your belief on things, whether you realize it or not. You can be sure that by the time my children leave our house, they (both the girls and the boys) will know what their God-given role is and how to treat everyone with respect. We may be considered old-fashioned, but it's a tradition whose origin is second to none.

The TV Commercial Dilemma

By the culture's standards, our family has a restrictive policy for TV and movie viewing. Our family is allowed to watch most G-rated shows, but we do not watch most PG-rated shows or anything that uses "God" or "Lord" in vain even once. We also censor shows that use what we consider "bad words" more than three times. This may seem arbitrary and legalistic, but we decided we needed an understandable and enforceable standard. So far, we have been satisfied enough with how these rules have worked for us. We have noticed that by eliminating shows with offensive language, we have eliminated most shows with questionable content.

We do, however, make exceptions to the rules. For example, the movie Chariots of Fire is a PG movie and the characters use God's name in vain a number of times, but because of the Christian message we not only allow but encourage our kids to watch that movie. On the other hand, the movie Pocahontas is rated G and contains no offensive language, but in our opinion the anti-Christian message is so strong we do not watch it.

At the onset of our family policy, we didn't have cable, so our potential TV viewing was limited to some sporting events, news, some PBS programming, and some reruns of old shows. Because our TV selections were so limited, we often went to Blockbuster to rent a video. Most of our movie selections were either Disney animated movies or movies that were over thirty years old.

While your standard may be different than ours, we were satisfied because our kids had been trained to the point that they would turn off "bad shows" even when we weren't able to watch with them. When we were at a Bible study recently, another parent brought the movie Shrek to entertain the kids while the adults were upstairs. Without a word of complaint from them or prompting from us, our kids went upstairs to another room and stayed there the entire time the movie was on.

We found that we were comfortable in our system, except for the problem of TV commercials. Our standards didn't take into account the commercials that came with the shows. Our first experience with censoring a TV show for the commercials came a few years back when the I Love Lucy show was sponsored by a psychic network. Every day the show was on, there were multiple appeals for the viewer to call the psychic. Our children were told they could not watch Lucy because of those commercials. Next, we censored Star Trek because of the terrible shows the UPN network repeatedly promoted. We had the same experience with NFL football on the FOX network. At this point, we were down to news – which promoted a liberal, godless worldview to go along with the offensive commercials – and PBS kids shows, which were always a danger to promote evolution. This almost eliminated our ability to watch TV, and new movies we were able to watch came so infrequently that our resource of old movies at the video stores was starting to run dry.

About this time we were hooked up to cable – not because we wanted cable TV but because we needed cable internet access for our home business. Along with the cable internet access came an opportunity to get cable TV at a significantly reduced rate. I figured that part of the remaining cost would be reduced by not going to the video store so frequently. I knew there would be a lot of garbage we would never watch, but I thought The History Channel, TV Land, Nick-at-Nite, and The Disney Channel would give us a fair amount of programming we could watch without the bad commercials. We were also looking forward to getting our news from the FOX News Channel instead of ABC.

Our hope that cable TV would give us wholesome programming without the bad commercials has not been fully realized. On the one hand, the kids have enjoyed old shows like Zorro, The Cosby Show, and Gomer Pyle. We have also seen some very good programming on The History Channel. On the other hand, we have had to turn off offensive commercials on networks like TV Land and Nick-at-Nite. I can't even watch Leave it to Beaver without wondering if a commercial break will contain an advertisement for an R-rated movie or show an immodestly dressed young woman. It seems ridiculous to censor violence and sexually suggestive shows but allow violent and sexually suggestive commercials.

It was obvious that our TV watching policy wasn't complete. Whether we get rid of the cable TV is yet to be decided, but our new standards must account for the commercials. So the bottom line here now is no commercials at all. The minute the commercials start, the

TV is turned off. We may miss a few seconds of the show when it comes back on, but we are happy to be missing the commercials altogether.

Commercials have evolved much like the TV shows and movies. Every year they are just a little more offensive than the year before. The change is so slow that we are liable to accept this year's commercials because they are only a little worse than last year's. Had today's commercials appeared thirty years ago there would have been an uproar, but we have been conditioned year by year to accept a little more garbage. Now we have been desensitized to the coarse language, the violence, the suggestive humor, and the woman in the bikini.

Some days I'm tempted to throw away the TV set. The television is a powerful entertainment tool, and like almost any tool it can be used for good and for evil. The TV can be used to promote the Gospel and to provide a welcome relief at the end of a hard day's work. However, the TV can also be used by Satan to tempt us into being more accepting of immorality, and to waste our precious time in idleness.

May God grant us all His wisdom to discern the proper TV policy for our families.

The Super Bowl: A new low

Fortunately, no one in my family saw any of the Super Bowl commercials or the half-time show. It's not that we don't watch football. We had company that night, so we saw little of the game. We also have a rule that the channel must be changed or the TV turned off when commercials come on.

That being said, I have heard enough discussion of the game's commercials and half-time entertainment to know that new morality lows were reached for family broadcast TV. As shocking as the half-time incident was, and as raunchy as the show and some of the commercials were, none of this should have been a surprise. Not too long ago, the FCC decided to allow the "F" word on broadcast television for the first time and who knows what firsts will be allowed next year. The moral deterioration of broadcast television, movies, and music has been going on for at least two generations. The addition of cable and satellite TV has done nothing but help pave the way for the airing of previously unthinkable displays of nudity, lewdness, coarse humor, and graphic violence.

The Super Bowl half-time show and commercials were only shocking because they occurred during the Super Bowl. Most people in our culture – and I'm sad to say that includes a great many Christians – watch and allow their children to watch more graphic nudity and immorality on an ongoing basis than what was shown at the Super Bowl.

Media immorality, then, is much bigger than the Super Bowl fiasco and has been going on for decades. The problem is much bigger than Janet Jackson. If the trend continues, people will look back a few years from now at the Janet Jackson Super Bowl and marvel at how such a mildly suggestive program could have caused such an uproar. Unless God intervenes, there will be new shocking incidents, new uproars, and new accommodation for immorality, profane language, and violence.

Given the present state of affairs, what is a Christian to do? It seems to me that the majority of Christians feign protest at the increasing immorality and violence in the media, but soon lower their standards right along with the popular culture. The "D" word may have shocked Christians who heard it uttered in Gone with the Wind in 1939, but they continued to go to the movies. Based on my experiences as a teacher in a homeschool cooperative, in a classical Christian school, and as a member of a variety of evangelical churches, it is my opinion that most Christians are watching most of the popular PG and PG-13 movies with their children, and a very large number will watch R-rated movies as well. I also believe most Christian children are listening to popular music and watching popular television programs on a regular basis. If that is true, then the uproar over the Super Bowl incident involves a fair amount of hypocrisy.

I think modern music, TV, and movies are poison for our minds that Satan uses to desensitize us to sin. This poison is like liquor in that the more a person consumes the more he tolerates. The Devil, therefore, slowly increases the potency of the poison until we tolerate and even crave all manner of filth. We get used to a few bad words, and then we accept a little sexual innuendo, and then a little blood and before you know it we are hooked on the same garbage all the heathen in Canaan are watching. And the buzz we experience from immoral music and media is so strong that we go into withdrawal if our TV and radio are taken away from us. We are bored without it.

Yet, most of us would think it scandalous if someone were to invite to his home live entertainers who performed sex scenes, used foul language, took God's name in vain, and displayed grotesque and graphic violence. We may want to throw him in jail if he had these entertainers perform for his children. But millions who claim the name of Christ are perfectly comfortable watching the realistic images of such entertainers with their children.

Paul wrote, "Finally, brethren, whatever is true, whatever is honorable, whatever is right, whatever is pure, whatever is lovely, whatever is of good repute, if there is any excellence and if anything worthy of praise, dwell on these things." (Phil. 4:8) "But immorality or any impurity or greed must not even be named among you, as is proper among saints; and there must be no filthiness and silly talk, or coarse jesting, which are not fitting." (Ephesians 5:3-4a) How, then, can we justify the garbage we subject ourselves to? If this Super Bowl has done anything for me, it has crystallized my realization that the body of Christ must do more than simply shake their heads while continuing to watch and listen.

The option we've adopted the last few years has become increasingly difficult to maintain. I have always been of the opinion that we don't need to throw out the baby with the bath water. Television is not good or bad; it's just a way of communicating pictures and sound. I have always liked good movies and good music, so I decided that our family would edit out most of the offensive material.

For many years we turned off shows that used three bad words or used God's name in vain once. We banned shows that we considered to have immoral or violent themes, and we also banned most PG movies. (No one in our family has ever seen a PG-13 movie.) We have cable and almost everything we watch comes from TV Land, classic movies, Fox News, or NFL football. When a psychic sponsored the I Love Lucy show, we started taping shows and skipping the commercials or turning off live TV during commercials.

However, this hasn't been working very well either. Graphic violence and tabloid journalism are ruining the news, cut-ins to cheerleaders are ruining football, and my increasing sensitivity to immodesty and coarse humor is ruining TV Land. I am now even offended by the immodesty in I Dream of Jeannie.

My point is that it's getting almost impossible to be moderate on this issue. Many of the "family" oriented shows on cable TV were pushing the envelope a generation ago. The last vestiges of inoffensive news and entertainment television programming will probably be swept away with the passage of a decade or two. Perhaps in the past a discriminating viewer could avoid nudity, profanity, coarse humor, violence, and liberal propaganda, but that is becoming increasingly difficult, if not impossible. You will either lower your standards and accept increasing amounts of immorality and violence, or you will turn off the TV.

Many valiant Christians have not accepted defeat in this area. For years, messages of complaint have been sent and boycotts have been organized. I'm sure successes could be cited to prove the effectiveness of these tactics, but the trend toward more and more offensive programming has not been changed. If Christians didn't continue to watch offensive programming, they wouldn't continue to be offended. Next year the Super Bowl half-time show may not be as bad, but five years from now television is likely to be noticeably more risqué than it is now

I think we are better off disconnecting ourselves from popular culture. We shouldn't be surprised when depraved heathen produce television shows that appeal to depraved heathen. And contrary to what some would like to admit, most of the people in America are depraved heathen.

We can produce our own news, our own video entertainment and our own music. If Christians would turn off Friends, Frazier, Seinfeld, and CNN – and support our own enterprises – things would change. I wouldn't be surprised, however, if Christians spend more time and money supporting the decadent heathen media than they spend supporting wholesome Christian alternatives. But as long as we're hooked on their filth, Satan has succeeded in tempting, weakening, compromising, and distracting us.

So for me, the Super Bowl was the last straw – at least as far as television is concerned. I guess if I want to watch something I'll have to buy or rent a video. This is hard for me because I really enjoy TV entertainment. I guess turning off the TV will free up a few minutes every day. Maybe I can put the time to better use anyway. I could converse with my family or read challenging and entertaining Christian literature (such as that excellent publication called SALT Magazine I've heard about!). What you do is up to you, but I think many of you will agree that what we see and hear makes us uncomfortable and that we tend to tolerate more garbage as time goes on. The Janet Jackson affair is just the latest marker on a long and well-traveled path that is quickly approaching Sodom. Whether you stay on the path or get off is your decision to make. I've got to get off.

Therefore God gave them over in the lusts of their hearts to impurity, so that their bodies would be dishonored among them. (Rom. 1:24)

Modesty is the Best Policy

Well, summer is upon us and so is summer attire. Short sleeves and T-shirts have replaced long sleeves and sweaters, and shorts are as common as dandelions. American women are trying to lose weight so they can look good in summer fashions and American men are enjoying the view. Nowhere is this truer than on the beach, where form fitting one-piece bathing suits are considered conservative and where girls who look good wear bikinis.

If we grew up in the 1960s or later, nothing may seem wrong or abnormal about summer clothing. Our definition of modest dress may be fitting sleeveless shirts and shorts, and our definition of modest swimwear may include less revealing two-piece suits. Most of us know that the 60s were supposed to have been culturally revolutionary, but having grown up after it was all over, the sexual revolution is the ho-hum status quo. We may vaguely sense that standards of modesty are eroding, but it happens so slowly it doesn't elicit more than an occasional sigh. Sure, Janet Jackson's Super Bowl stunt got our attention, but not for long. We have returned to our lives and our indifference.

Christians, too, generally share this cultural indifference towards immodesty. Our fashions have continued to reflect the changing fashions of popular culture, but no one ever talks about why. Most of us just go along with the flow without giving it a second thought. An author I read recently observed, "We can therefore walk into most churches on any given Sunday and behold a parade of young women pass by in tight tee-shirts, low-slung jeans, form-fitting skirts and other curve-and flesh-revealing styles. Church youth groups participate in mixed-sex pool parties without a second thought, everyone coming in their skivvies and no one batting an eyelash." (Mrs. M.L. Chancey, "Modesty and the Christian Woman")

Imagine what girls wore to church in America in 1904. How many girls do you think came to church in pants? How many came in shorts? How low do you think the hemlines of their dresses were? How high do you think their necklines were? How many of our young Christian women would be arrested for indecency if they were transported to 1904 wearing the clothes they wore to church last Sunday? What would be the reaction in 1904 to one of our church pool or beach parties?

Standards of dress have changed considerably over the last 100 years, but fortunately we'll never have to worry about offending the people of another time. However, we should still be worried about offending God, and fortunately, the Bible does speak a little to the issue of dress.

Consider what Paul and Peter had to say: "I want women to adorn themselves with proper clothing, modestly and discreetly, not with braided hair and gold or pearls or costly garments." (1 Tim. 2:9) "Your adornment must not be merely external – braiding the hair, and wearing gold jewelry, or putting on dresses; but let it be the hidden person of the heart, with the imperishable quality of a gentle and quiet spirit, which is precious in the sight of God." (1 Peter 3:3-4)

The main principle we get from these verses is that a woman's outer covering should reflect the same unpretentious purity the Lord seeks in a woman's character. Specifically, Paul mentions modesty and discreetness, while Peter points to gentleness and quietness. At the very least, we should be able to conclude from these verses that a woman's clothing should not draw attention to herself. If a girl wears something that turns heads and gains compliments wherever she goes or if she chooses her clothing to be noticed, she is not being discreet no matter how much skin the outfit covers. Do the clothes our wives and daughters wear reflect modesty, discreetness, gentleness, and quietness, or are they attention getters?

Modest dress, therefore, is certainly about covering the body adequately and in such a way that the eyes of others aren't drawn to admire the "outer excellencies" of the female form, but modesty is more than that. A girl who shocks people by the multitude of her earrings, the ring in her tongue, her green and purple hair, and her bulky black clothes is being just as immodest and just as indiscreet.

Most of us understand that modesty, discreetness, and quietness in dress would mean that a girl shouldn't draw attention to herself, but that only solves part of the problem. For even if a woman resolves to dress so as not to draw attention to herself, she will still have to contend with the fact that fashions change. As I have already pointed out, standards of modesty may change considerably over time.

Does the Bible offer any objective, unchanging standards to help us know what to wear? The answer you get, of course, depends on whom you ask. Some Christians, in an effort to comply with biblical principles, dress like 16th century Europeans, some dress Victorian, some women only wear dresses, some blend into the culture, and a few compete in beauty competitions in their bathing suits. There is controversy because the Bible doesn't give a great deal of detail on how long, high, or loose a modest garment must be. But we do know a few principles that can help us out.

One thing we can say with certainty is that nakedness is shameful. Although Adam and Eve were naked in the Garden before the fall, sin changed that forever. After the fall, God himself clothed the first couple. The Bible says, "The LORD God made garments of skin for Adam and his wife, and clothed them." (Gen. 3:21) (Apparently the fig leaf aprons Adam and Eve made weren't adequate.) Noah was shamed when his youngest son saw his nakedness and he showed his displeasure by cursing Canaan. The prophets graphically illustrated a harlot having her nakedness exposed to show the Israelites how utterly shameful their unfaithfulness to God was. For example, Isaiah writes, "Take the millstones and grind meal. Remove your veil, strip off the skirt, uncover the leg, cross the rivers. Your nakedness will be uncovered, your shame also will be exposed; I will take vengeance and will not spare a man." (Is. 47:2-3) The shame of nakedness was also part of the humiliation of going into captivity. Isaiah also writes, "So the king of Assyria will lead away the captives of Egypt and the exiles of Cush, young and old, naked and barefoot with buttocks uncovered, to the shame of Egypt." (Is. 20:4) In the New Testament, also, it is written, "Because you say, 'I am rich, and have become wealthy, and have need of nothing,' and you do not know that you are wretched and miserable and poor and blind and naked, I advise you to buy from Me gold refined by fire so that you may become rich, and white garments so that you may clothe yourself, and that the shame of your nakedness will not be revealed; and eye salve to anoint your eyes so that you may see." (Rev. 3:17-18)

Most of our readers do not go out without clothes on, but many watch movies and television shows, read magazines, and look at art that exposes the body. The ungodly like to point out that the body is beautiful, but to expose the body publicly is a disgrace whether the venue is an immoral movie, a National Geographic special, or a Greek statue.

Another principle the Scripture makes clear is this: "A woman shall not wear man's clothing, nor shall a man put on a woman's clothing; for whoever does these things is an abomination to the LORD your God." (Deut. 22:5) We should take no pleasure in cross dressers, drag queens, and the like. We should find no humor in something God condemns as an abomination.

Application of principles: If a girl covers her body, wears clothing appropriate to her gender, and dresses modestly and discreetly, she is satisfying the biblical principles of dress. However, how these principles are specifically applied is the cause of great controversy. Let's take a look at a few of the most commonly disputed applications:

Can a woman wear pants? Those who say a woman should not wear pants believe pants are men's clothing; Since women aren't supposed to wear men's clothing they're not supposed to wear pants. I think it's hard to make the case from Scripture that pants are the prescribed clothing for men and that dresses are the prescribed clothing for women. Men and women in Bible times apparently wore robes of some sort over their undergarments. Perhaps these robes resembled dresses more than they resembled pants. Because the Scriptures don't specify what exactly distinguishes men's from women's clothing, I think we should not judge women who wear pants.

On the other hand, there can be no doubt that for hundreds of years men have worn pants and for thousands of years women have worn dresses. I don't think it's a coincidence that gender clothing distinctions have been diminished just as biblically sanctioned roles have been erased. It is true that pants may be widely recognized today as appropriate attire for women, but the fashion designers who developed pants for women and the women who first started wearing pants were not known as the godliest bunch. And the men and women who resisted the change from dresses to pants were more likely to be Christians who took God's word seriously.

Having grown up in a time when girls generally wore pants and reserved dress wearing for special occasions, it's hard for me to think of pants as uniquely male. Perhaps we Christians don't fully appreciate the spiritual battle that led women to abandon dresses and embrace pants, and we also may not appreciate the fact that for some the battle isn't over. Therefore, we should admire any woman who is willing to risk criticism and wear only dresses because she is trying to obey the Lord's commands.

Can a woman wear shorts? If pants are forbidden, then short pants would be forbidden also. However, shorts bare the legs and a Christian who may condone women wearing pants may still reject shorts as shameful and immodest. Isaiah wrote, "Remove your veil, strip off the skirt, uncover the leg, cross the rivers. Your nakedness will be uncovered, your shame also will be exposed." There can be no doubt, therefore, that to "uncover the leg" was shameful. I also understand that the Hebrew word used to describe the garments God made Adam and Eve refers to a tunic or coat that went from the neck to the lower leg.

Many who reject shorts will cite these verses. Of course, bare attractive female legs are also sure to grab the attention of male onlookers. If baring the leg is shameful, if it is liable to gain the attention and admiration of men, and if the admiration of some of those men may turn to lust, perhaps shorts aren't such a good idea.

I understand that shorts are more comfortable on a hot day. I also understand that God never commanded that the clothes He made for Adam and Eve serve as eternal and unchanging clothing patterns. The truth is, the people who base their standard for the length of their garments on the length of the coats God made for Adam and Eve are usually not also willing to limit their clothing to animal skins. And we really don't know exactly how long the coats were or what gender differences there may have been. I understand, too, that most of the people who cite Isaiah 47 as biblical proof that an "uncovered leg" is shameful are inconsistent in that most do not also hold that a removed veil (part of the same verse) is shameful.

Even so, I think the argument that shorts are modest is less compelling. Just because there isn't a Bible verse that gives specific measurement standards for clothing doesn't mean that all garments are modest. And just because those who reject shorts may not always be consistent in their application of the Scriptures doesn't mean their point is necessarily wrong. It seems clear from the verses we have cited that bare legs and bare buttocks (Is. 20:4) are shameful and most of us know from experience that bare legs get a man's attention and, therefore, could not be called discreet or modest.

What about bathing suits? I am convinced in my mind that modern swimwear is inherently immodest. The most modest bathing suits that could be considered culturally normal bare everything but the torso, but even the torso is wrapped in thin, stretchy material, which leaves little to the imagination. Many two-piece bathing suits cover less than the undergarments a woman wears. Most women would be appalled at the thought of going to the grocery store in their underwear, but many wouldn't flinch at going to a public beach or pool in clothes that cover less. If bathing suits are modest dress, what could we describe as immodest?

Conclusion: I know this issue is a very emotional one for Christians. We disagree about what biblical principles come into play and how those principles apply. How, then, can we get along? If we implement the principles we can be sure of (modesty, discreetness, covering the body, and dressing according to gender), if we reserve judgment against our fellow Christians on disputable matters, and if we dress for the good of others and not just ourselves, we will go a long way toward reaching unity.

In this decadent culture we always seem to be asking ourselves the wrong questions. "Many times we seem to be asking, 'How much can I get away with before it is considered sin? How many articles of clothing may I shed before it's considered wrong? How tight is too tight? How short is too short? How low is too low?' Instead my question to you today is, 'What is God's best?' " (Stacy McDonald, "Let's Talk Modesty," www.patriarchspath.org)

I grew up giving modesty very little thought. Short shorts, short skirts and dresses, tight shirts and sweaters, and two-piece bathing suits were normal. As my Christian life progresses I am becoming more and more sensitive to the issue of modesty. I would still consider our family's dress as culturally normal, but I'm sure my older children are covering a bit more skin and wearing their clothes a bit looser than me and the people I grew up with did. As my views on modesty change, however, I am compelled to lead my family in the direction I believe God wants us to go. One of the most difficult things a parent can do is to set new standards after the first have been accepted. But we need to be concerned about what God's best is and not what's less trouble.

For the Men

Modesty may be a bigger issue for women than for men, but men ought to be modest, too. Some men unbutton their shirts to show off their hairy chests, some wear their pants too tight, some wear their pants so low their underwear is visible, some are covered with tattoos, and some have disgusting words and pictures printed on their T-shirts. Men should consider the message they send by the way they dress. A man also must protect the purity of his family and make sure his wife and his children are not stumbling blocks to the purity of others.

For the Ladies, From a Lady

In the previous article Jim spent some time discussing what modesty is and the principles Christians can apply to their lives. While the concern for modesty is not for ladies only (men also can choose to dress modestly or immodestly), I would like to consider some specific questions that women can ask themselves when they stand in front of their closets each morning:

"Is this clothing modest in all ways?" As mentioned, immodesty is not just showing too much skin. It can be showing too much shape and form. It can be teasing the viewer or giving substance to his imaginings. And while that is the way we usually define immodesty, it can be anything that draws attention to ourselves. So, is my outfit tasteful, clean, well-fitting without drawing attention to myself to boost my ego or satisfy my desire for attention? Is there any way in which this clothing is not modest?

"What are the possible consequences of wearing this clothing?" This is another way of asking the previous question. Will it cause me to be proud? Will it make me feel like I'm better than others? Will I tempt someone? Will I be a poor witness for Christ? Questionable clothing will most likely produce questionable results.

"What am I hoping to achieve by wearing this article of clothing?" Does this outfit come from a gentle and quiet spirit? Or do I want to wear this clothing to show off or gain attention? Do I strive to glorify God and be a good witness by the clothes that I wear?

"Why does this clothing make me feel good? Why do I like it?" This, too, is another way of asking the previous question. What exactly is my motive? If my motive is questionable, I would do well to find something else to wear.

"Would I want my husband to look at women dressed like this?" Now, this is a good question. We may think it's pretty innocent to capture a man's look, but how would that make his wife feel? How would I feel if a woman wore clothing which made my husband look twice? I know I sure wouldn't appreciate her choice of wardrobe.

Likewise, for the sake of marriages out there and the purity of men's thoughts, I will also be careful in my selection.

"Would I want my sons to look at women dressed like this?" We shouldn't wear something we would be embarrassed for our sons to see us in, or that we wouldn't want them to see other women wear. If we really desire our sons and our sons-in-law to remain pure before and after their weddings, we need to be modest in our clothing and teach our daughters to do the same. Furthermore, we should dress in a way that trains our sons to know what is modest, what is not, what is acceptable to view, and what they must turn away from. As a mothers, sisters, aunts, cousins, etc., we are role models and teachers of the males around us regarding modesty.

"Would I feel embarrassed to stand before Christ wearing this?" Whatever we do is before Christ. Would He approve?

"By wearing this clothing, am I willing to bear the responsibility for the reactions of others?" While each person is undoubtedly responsible for his or her own actions, I do believe we bear some responsibility if our clothing causes others to sin. We shouldn't purposefully wear something knowing that it may be a source of temptation to someone else. We are not to be stumbling blocks to those around us, but ambassadors for Christ, leading people to Him. How horrible it would be to stand before Christ knowing that we were the cause of someone's sin, when we could have easily prevented it. Our dress and actions should encourage purity in others' thoughts and actions. In its simplest form, it is the Golden Rule. I would not want a woman to tempt my husband or son by what she wears, so I won't either. I would not want someone to do something knowing that it could very well tempt me, so I won't do the same.

The question of modesty does concern the type of clothing we wear, but even more importantly it concerns our hearts and motives. If our hearts are right, most likely our clothing will be right. We need to squelch our pride and desire for attention. We need to be willing to be a little different than the culture around us. We should desire to wear clothing that is modest, proper and discreet; clothing which is beautiful because of our quiet and gentle spirits. That is very precious in God's sight.

Friends Unequally Yoked

It seems to me that most Christians live as fish out of water. Because of the mobile society in which we live, many of us find ourselves living, working, shopping, and recreating in a largely unchristian environment. The result is that we often have friendships with unbelievers because we share many common experiences and interests. Is this a good thing? What does the Bible say about our relationships with unbelievers?

Let us begin by observing Jesus' life on earth. Jesus was well known and criticized for associating with tax collectors, prostitutes, Samaritans, and other "sinners" – people the religious leaders would have nothing to do with. He even broke bread with them. Jesus explained His conduct by saying, "It is not those who are healthy who need a physician ... I did not come to call the righteous, but sinners." (Matt. 9:12, 13b) Again, Jesus says, "The Son of Man has come to seek and to save that which was lost." (Luke 19:10) After His death and resurrection, Christ passed on to us the task of preaching the Good News and making disciples. It would be very difficult, indeed, to fulfill our commission without associating with unbelievers. We can say, therefore, that we may certainly associate with unbelievers for the purpose of calling sinners to repentance and to share the Gospel with them.

In fact, the people we are called to separate ourselves from completely are not the great sinners outside the church, but the great sinners inside the church. Paul writes, "I wrote you in my letter not to associate with immoral people; I did not at all mean with the immoral people of this world, or with the covetous and swindlers, or with idolaters, for then you would have to go out of the world. But actually, I wrote to you not to associate with any so-called brother if he is an immoral person, or covetous, or an idolater, or a reviler, or a drunkard, or a swindler--not even to eat with such a one." (1 Cor. 5:9-11)

The command to disassociate from those who live like godless heathen but claim to be brothers in Christ is easy enough to understand. However, what guidance do the Scriptures give regarding our relationships with unbelievers who are outside the church? Paul writes, "Do not be bound together with unbelievers." (2 Cor. 6:14a) Paul's point is that the believer and unbeliever have too little in common to be yoked together. He continues, "What partnership have righteousness and lawlessness, or what fellowship has light with darkness? Or what harmony has Christ with Belial, or what has a believer in common with an unbeliever? Or what agreement has the temple of God with idols? For we are the temple of the living God; just as God said, 'I will dwell in them and walk among them; and I will be their God, and they shall be my people.' Therefore, 'Come out from their midst and be separate,' says the Lord. 'And do not touch what is unclean; and I will welcome you.' 'And I will be a father to you, and you shall be sons and daughters to Me,' says the Lord Almighty."

Paul sees believers and unbelievers as extreme contrasts. But many of us look at our unbelieving friends and see them as basically good people. However, we must not be deceived. Christians have their minds on the things of God; unbelievers have their minds on the things of men. Paul warns us, "Do not be deceived: Bad company corrupts good morals." (1 Cor. 15:33)

To some, the way Jesus associated with unbelievers may seem to contradict what Paul is telling us here. That is not the case. Paul preached the good news to unbelievers, just as Jesus did. Paul associated with unbelievers, just as Jesus did. Paul isn't telling us to stay away from unbelievers, but to avoid being yoked with them.

Marriage is the most obvious and common application of this principle, but we may be tempted to be yoked with unbelievers in other types of relationships as well. I think we should make all effort to avoid making unbelievers our business partners, our advisors, and our closest friends. It would seem that Jesus' most intimate relationships were with His disciples. It would seem that Jesus spent the bulk of His time with His disciples. It would also seem that Christ's primary purpose in associating with unbelievers was to save their souls, not to simply have fun and fellowship.

Our motivation to spread the Gospel, then, should compel us to associate with unbelievers, but our desire to be holy compels us to separate from them. We should be in the world, but not of the world. We should be with unbelievers, without being yoked with them.

The Difficult People at the End of the Bell Curve

I've read somewhere that between one and two percent of the population homeschools. We are among them. I read on a U.S. Census Bureau report that less than one percent of women have seven children or more. We have eleven. I don't know how many people reject unsupervised courtship (dating, for example) or think the government should make adultery and homosexuality capital offenses, but I know these views are held by a very small fraction of the population.

So I now find myself sitting out here at the end of the bell curve and I've been sitting here long enough to observe myself and the other oddballs sitting with me. There is much to admire in the people I've observed, but, to be honest, we tend to be difficult. This message, then, is an attempt to encourage and admonish those who travel a narrow, more difficult road that few people travel.

But before you stop reading (because this message isn't for you), allow me to say that every Christian should be at the end of the bell curve. Jesus Himself said that many are called but few are chosen. Many travel the road that leads to hell, but few travel the road that leads to eternal life. The Scriptures are clear that only a remnant will be saved. Therefore, if you bear the name of Christ and are so much like everyone else in the middle of the curve, perhaps you need to examine yourself.

For my fellow oddballs I have some good news and some bad news. The good news is that going against the flow for a long time shapes our character. The bad news is that going against the flow for a long time shapes our character. Allow me to give you some examples to show you what I mean. People at the end of the bell curve generally ...

Have a strong, independent nature: A person has to be thinking independently to say to himself, "You know, everyone else believes this, but I'm going to believe something else." It takes strength of character to teach your children at home when the vast majority of people think your children will be socially handicapped the rest of their lives. It takes strength of character to tell your children they cannot watch most movies and TV shows, cannot listen to most of what's on the radio, cannot dress immodestly at the beach, and cannot go out on a date. It takes strength of character to be ostracized in the church because you don't believe building magnificent buildings and offering a multitude of programs are the same as spreading the Gospel and making disciples. It takes strength of character to have a faith that compels you to condemn the world of sin and share the truth that salvation can only be found in Jesus Christ when the world and many who profess Christ think it rude to say anything that offends people. Yes, people at the end of the bell curve think for themselves and have been toughened by the time they've spent going against the current and journeying the road less traveled.

That being said, the people at the end of the bell curve generally ...

Have a stubborn, independent nature: Perhaps the strength that allows a man to stand immoveable against the tide of cultural evil tends to make him unyielding in all things. A Christian man who was visiting our unbelieving neighbor came across the street to introduce himself to us. He started talking about the end times and had ideas that, according to his own words, made his presence at his old church untenable. He presented his ideas, which we disagreed with, in such a way that an exchange of ideas was not worth the effort. In his eyes the Bible clearly supported his views and that fact was supposed to be obvious and unquestionable once he recited his supporting Scriptures. From our perspective, the visit was unpleasant, which stood as an interesting contrast to the unbelieving neighbor who has done more than anyone to make us feel welcome in the neighborhood we just moved into. I'm sure many of us oddballs have become more trouble than we're worth in the church because we are never pleased unless it's done our way. We may be aloof (fighting with silence) or we may be constantly pushing for a better way (ours, of course), but it seems we are the fly in the ointment in most groups of people we associate with.

Do we get so used to fighting the enemy that fighting becomes a way of life? Have we lost our ability to discern what battles are worth fighting and what battles are best avoided? Does the guerilla warfare we feel compelled to fight make us unusable in an organized unit that requires discipline and cohesion (such as the body of Christ)? Many of us at the end of the bell curve have become so independent and so sure of ourselves that we are impossible to teach and impossible to lead. I don't fit into the fat part of the bell curve because I'm a committed Christian and part of the remnant. I don't fit in anywhere at all because I'm unyielding and stubborn.

On the other hand, the people at the end of the bell curve usually ...

Act out of principle instead of pragmatism when it concerns their own affairs: The people I know at the end of the bell curve are commendable because they are much more likely to make difficult decisions based on the application of biblical principles and less likely to make difficult decisions based on what seems to work out best for them personally. The person at the end of the bell curve is more likely to suffer shame and loss for the sake of Christ. He is more likely to quit his job if it demands he be dishonest or immoral. He is more likely to share the Gospel when others are afraid. He is more likely to make decisions that seem to cost him financially or that make life more difficult for him when everyone else is cutting corners and breaking the rules. Principled living is important because we cannot be the salt of the earth without it. And in this culture where Christians often go along with the reigning philosophies of relativism and compromise, we need a lot more salt. Praise God for the salt at the end of the bell curve.

However, the people at the end of the bell curve often ...

Apply their principles in an overly judgmental way when it comes to others: I'm certain God wants us to apply biblical principles in every area of our lives without compromise, but we are supposed to give latitude to others. Paul says, "Accept him whose faith is weak, without passing judgment on disputable matters." (Rom. 14:1, NIV)

But those of us at the end of the bell curve divide the body of Christ over all sorts of disputable matters. Is the presence of the Lord in the Lord's Supper physical, spiritual, or symbolic? Is wine or grape juice used? Was I baptized as an infant or as an adult? Was my entire body covered when I was baptized? Are tongues real or not? What day, if any, is the Sabbath? May I have a beer, play cards, or dance? Is the Lord coming pre-tribulation, mid-tribulation, or post-tribulation? What translation of the Bible do we use? Can women wear pants? And it only gets worse.

None of these issues are essential to the Christian message. Indeed, heaven will contain Christians from many denominations. Sadly, those of us at the end of the bell curve are probably most responsible for dividing the body of Christ over secondary issues. Just as we need to learn to discern when to fight and when to hold our peace, so, too, we need to discern when our principles may not be compromised and when to be gracious – not passing judgment on disputable matters.

Concluding Thoughts: It isn't bad to be different and being different doesn't mean we need to be difficult. The Gospel should send all believers to the end of the bell curve, but we need to make sure that the years of fighting lonely battles against an exceedingly numerous enemy don't harden us to the point of being insensitive, unyielding, or ungracious. Courage, strength, independence from the evil culture, principled living, and a willingness to suffer shame and persecution for the Gospel are commendable and necessary for us to be effective in our work for the Kingdom of Christ, but we need discernment and a loving heart to go along with our willingness to be different. We need to continue to be uncompromising on the essentials of the faith and to be hard on ourselves, but to reserve judgment on disputable matters with our brothers in Christ and to love unbelievers. If we are offensive it shouldn't be because we are difficult, but in spite of the fact that we are not difficult. The Gospel *message* should divide and offend people, not the Gospel *messengers* – us oddballs at the end of the bell curve.

Keeping the Family Together

Why is staying together such a struggle for American families? Divorce is rampant, but it is only the most obvious example of family separation. For most of us the problem is much more subtle. In our culture, it can be hard even for loving Christian couples to develop family togetherness. Why is this so? Some of the challenges are obvious, but others may surprise you.

Challenge #1 – Modern technology: Before modern appliances, supermarkets, electricity, plumbing, and automobiles, managing a household took a lot of work. Imagine having to keep a fire going every day of the year and having to cut enough wood to keep that fire going. Imagine having to keep a cow to have milk and cheese, having to hunt and raise livestock to eat meat, and having to grow all your own fruits and vegetables. Imagine having to make your own cloth so you can hand sew your own clothes. Imagine having to keep horses to get anywhere too far to walk. There was so much work to do at home that survival required the help of every able-bodied man, woman, and child. Families needed to work hard and work together.

Struggling together as a team builds cohesion and loyalty. That's why the bond between war comrades or athletic teammates can be so strong. Today families are not forced to work together. Most routine household jobs are easily done by one person. This should allow for more leisure time, but modern technology has even turned leisure into a solitary endeavor. Most people would agree that the television and the computer do not promote family togetherness. They keep us from interacting with each other, even when we sit in the same room.

Challenge #2 – Education: American prosperity has allowed a system that keeps most kids out of the house full-time from age five. Many of us do everything we can to keep our children in that system until they graduate from college at age 22. It's hard to keep a family together when the children spend most of their day somewhere else, but the effect of school on family togetherness extends beyond the end of the school day. When the children come home from a long day at school, they want to relax or play. This doesn't usually mean spending time with parents or siblings, but with friends made at school. School friends share many experiences which are not shared by family members. After the school day and play with school friends, the child must still do homework. Thus, a child's entire day may be dominated by schooling, even when the child isn't in the school building. Yet, there is significant support for extending the role education plays in the life of the child. The National Education Association (NEA) and many politicians believe universal public education should begin at age three and that every child should attend college.

Challenge #3 – Working Outside the Home: Education takes the kids out of the house. Work takes the parents out. Have you noticed that many neighborhoods are like ghost towns during business hours? For many years it has become increasingly common for mothers to work outside the home. This is a disturbing trend, but why do so few seem to care that the father can't be home either? The industrial revolution took men off their farms and out of their homes, and put them in factories and offices. Now, women are leaving home as well. The result is that the home is no longer the center of human activity. People no longer work there, they no longer educate their children there, and they don't even entertain each other there (the entertainment is really done somewhere else and broadcast, or cabled, or telephoned into your home). And because we are all working outside the house, we don't even eat together. How many people eat lunch with their families at home? How many families eat breakfast together?

Challenge #4 – Extracurricular Activities: You would think that all the time we spend outside the home at school and work would compel us to be together as much as possible, but that is often not the case. We run our children to soccer practice, piano lessons, ballet dancing, football practice, art lessons, Girl Scouts, and school clubs. Some parents feel like they run a taxi service for their kids. Parents, however, are managing to throw in some extracurricular activities of their own. Golf anyone? How about a membership at the fitness club? It is interesting that as little time as we spend in our homes and as little as we see our children, we still feel like we need more time away. Honey, how about dinner and a movie?

Challenge #5 – Church: Scripture clearly commands Christians to be in the habit of meeting together, but church activities normally split families apart. The youth group meets Friday night and the grade school girls meet Tuesday. The singles meet at Sally's house on Tuesday and the divorced couples meet at Rob's house on Thursday. Newly married couples meet together, but married couples with small children meet someplace else. Parents with teenagers have their own group and there is another group for the elderly. Of course, we need to provide a nursery so the parents can join their assigned group. We even require our little ones to leave during the worship service. We think it awful that parents of old thought a child should be seen and not heard – and I agree – but we have not improved things by making a child heard but not seen. Churches also tend to see ministry as something that happens outside the home. Rather than helping people raise better children, church ministry becomes one more activity that keeps families apart.

Challenge #6 – Lack of Commitment to Extended Family: If we are having trouble keeping the nuclear family together, it shouldn't surprise us that we share loose ties with our extended family. We have decided career is more important than family. We'll chase a good job all over the country and leave our family for almost any promotion or pay-raise. It's hard to foster togetherness with family when you live thousands of miles apart. And it's hard to break the cycle the way our kids train for careers. They're off to college – perhaps out of state – and when they finish they get job offers that could take them anywhere in the world. Very few people, Christians included, will make family and church a greater priority than career.

How can we overcome these challenges?

Modern culture: We don't need to renounce modern technology to bring our families together. Technology benefits us in many ways. Modern medicine has greatly reduced the number of parents who must bury their children. Modern farming has produced an abundance of food. We wouldn't want to go back to a time when plague and hunger were widespread. In addition, modern communication and transportation have allowed the Gospel to be preached all over the world. Besides, if we want to reach our own countrymen with the Gospel, we need to figure out how to live principled, holy lives in this modern culture. Paul said he became all things to all men, that he might save some. We, too, should have the same attitude. Technology may have helped to break families apart, but it doesn't have to be that way for us. We shouldn't need a struggle for physical survival to force us to work together. We have an infinitely more challenging struggle against the forces of darkness that wage war against God and against every human soul. If our family members believe we don't need each other, it is because we haven't made them understand the awesome nature of our mission, what is at stake if we are ineffective, and the power of the opposition. When we live as if we have a mission and when we diligently explain that mission to our children and include them in it, we will be able to work hard together and keep the TV and the computer in proper perspective.

Education: Many of the challenges of modern education relating to family togetherness can be overcome if parents raise and educate their children at home. What can be better for keeping the family together than having the children at home and forcing a parent to be there with them.

Working outside the home: For some, having both parents work outside the home is at least a short-term necessity. Others can afford to bring one parent home by giving up some luxuries. Others are working toward having both parents work from home. What a parent should be doing is different in each case. However, parents who spend more time living and working with their children are more likely to keep their families together. Some Christians are called to occupations that require them to be away from home a lot. For example, the Christian soldiers fighting overseas cannot be with their wives and children. In such cases it is more critical to have the wife at home as much as possible. We have to be honest with ourselves and ask whether the time we spend away from home is motivated by the necessity of our calling, or by selfish ambition and greed. Many Christians could and should make being home a higher priority.

Extracurricular activities: This is an easy one. Extracurricular activities are unnecessary. No one needs to play football or learn how to ice skate. That is not to say that all extracurricular activities are wrong, it's just that no one should ruin family cohesion for the sake of the Girl Scouts and soccer practice. Extracurricular activities are like dessert: a little goes a long way.

Church: Attending a church regularly should be the goal of every Christian family. Christian parents, however, must balance church activities with the needs of the family. Our first ministry must be to our spouses and children. Church pastors sometimes spend so much time trying to save others they lose the souls in their own homes. We can have the same problem if we aren't careful. Church wouldn't be so hard on the family if church activities involved the entire family. Perhaps some of us are in a position to influence our churches to be more family friendly, but for the rest of us, we just have to resist the temptation to allow church activities to be a vehicle for family neglect. I understand and believe the church is God's instrument to organize Christians and to spread the Gospel, but those of us with spouses and children must be mindful that the church is a body and everyone has a different role to play. Those who are called to full time ministry, single adults, those whose children are grown, and those too young to be married should be expected to spend more time running church activities than parents with children at home. Each season of life has its purpose and its emphasis. Those raising children should give those children priority over other activities. Someday the children will be gone and then comes the time when the wisdom gained can be shared with the membership of the church. That doesn't mean parents of small children can't teach a Sunday school class or serve on a committee, but they should be careful not to spend so much time at church that the spiritual needs of their own families are neglected. Meeting those needs demands the family spend some time together.

Lack of Commitment to Extended Family: When we have practiced selfish independence for many years, it may be impossible for us to form a close extended family in our generation. Nothing is ever hopeless, however, for with God all things are possible. The cycle can be broken. Even if the commitment to extended family has to begin with us, it should still be done. We can instill in our children a commitment to family that our generation never had. Over time, a close, extended family is a real blessing. We can all help carry the load when someone struggles. We can help each other launch a career, a household, or a business. Our children must understand that we are truly committed to them and will sacrifice our opportunities to give them a better life. Isn't this the kind of servant leadership Jesus showed us? Our children can learn to do the same for us, for their siblings, and for their children. We should make a greater effort to live near each other and to spend some time together. Of course, extended family – like anything else – can be abused. Closeness and caring can become gossip and meddling. My guess is, however, that most Christians would be blessed by closer relationships with the Christians in their extended families.

Final thought: Our modern culture has given us many blessings, but family togetherness isn't one of them. Our lack of commitment to family togetherness is certainly reflected by high divorce rates, but it goes way beyond that. Many of us seem unable to keep our kids from adopting the destructive lifestyle rampant in the culture because we have allowed others to raise our children. We have so little family unity because we are selfishly gratifying our own desires at the expense of our children's more pressing needs. The godless families around us are imploding, but for some reason we Christians are trying desperately to emulate their lifestyle. We want so badly to fit in. The result is that the problems that dominate godless families also dominate those who call themselves Christians. This is a poor witness for Christ. We need to take a different approach. If we sincerely and diligently apply Christian principles to our lives, we can transcend the problems of the culture. Our families can be examples of unity, peace and fulfillment – witnesses for Christ in a world of brokenness.

Just Leave Me Alone

"Well, I take a shower every day."

That's my favorite response when people ask me if I get any time for myself. It usually makes them smile, and they probably wonder how serious I am. People don't expect that you have much extra time when you have eleven children, and they're right. But that doesn't concern me as much as it seems to concern them. I think personal time is overrated.

Our culture has become very "me" oriented. We look at the younger generation and wonder how they can be so preoccupied with themselves. Immediate gratification is the word, and the truth is that they are probably learning a lot of it from our generation. This self-centeredness is the exact opposite, however, of what the Bible teaches us. We read, "Do nothing from selfishness or empty conceit, but with humility of mind regard one another as more important than yourselves; do not merely look out for your own personal interests, but also for the interests of others. Have this attitude in yourselves which was also in Christ Jesus, who, although He existed in the form of God, did not regard equality with God a thing to be grasped, but emptied Himself, taking the form of a bond-servant, and being made in the likeness of men. Being found in appearance as a man, He humbled Himself by becoming obedient to the point of death, even death on a cross." (Philippians 2:3-8) Jesus did nothing out of selfishness. He became a man to save sinful men. He spent His earthly life drawing people to God, and then suffered the punishment that we deserve and that we can't fathom. To say that He looked out for the interests of others is an understatement. We are told to have the same attitude that Christ did.

Not only are we to do away with selfishness but also with our desire to get what we want – now. "Therefore if you have been raised up with Christ, keep seeking the things above, where Christ is, seated at the right hand of God. Set your mind on the things above, not on the things that are on earth." (Colossians 3:1-2) We are to look at everything from an eternal perspective. We are not to concentrate on earthly matters nor the desires of our flesh. God's purposes should be our purposes and we should be willing to take up our cross daily and follow Him.

How does this apply to my situation as a mother? It helps me to remember that I am not here to serve myself but to serve God and my family. I think we tend to "glamorize" this idea of carrying our cross or suffering for Christ. We say, "Yes, I'm willing to die for Christ!" and then seem to forget or not understand that giving up our lives for Him entails much more than our physical being. In order to raise godly children we may be required to carry the crosses of limited finances, being misunderstood by those around us, and loss of personal time and freedom. We should count these losses as insignificant because of the eternal work we are doing. We should be like Mary who said, "Behold, the bondslave of the Lord; may it be done to me according to your word." (Luke 1:38)

Let's return to Christ's example. His earthly ministry was spent entirely in the presence of those He was training (His disciples) and teaching (the multitudes). I don't recall Christ trying to "get away" by himself for awhile except when He went alone to pray. The Gospels record times when He didn't even have time to eat. Even when Jesus called His disciples to come away and rest awhile, He was still in the role of leader. (And remember that they didn't get rest at that time – the crowds followed them and out of compassion Christ ministered to them.) Jesus was generous in sharing His entire life with those around Him, even though they were difficult, ignorant, ungrateful, and numerous.

I'm not saying that it is wrong to desire or enjoy some time alone. We absolutely need to be alone daily with God. Time to enjoy personal interests or hobbies can be refreshing for us. I'm just saying that everything should be in proper balance – and by that I don't mean 50-50. The same thing goes for couples taking time together away from their children. We should not overemphasize the need to get away or be alone. A little of it goes a long way.

In the midst of our service to our families we can take time to be alone with our spouses or alone with ourselves. We just need to keep our priorities balanced. We have important, eternal work to do and our time is short. Maybe the next time someone asks me if I get any time to myself I should say, "Yes, just a little and that's just enough. Cause I can't wait to get back to my children."

Please, Come in

Awhile ago we invited some acquaintances over to our house, in order to get to know them better. Our preparations were coming along fine, and it was almost time for me to get the dinner into the oven. Suddenly the doorbell rang; unexpected company had stopped by. We knew each other, but not well. We exchanged a few words in the doorway. At the same time I was debating with myself about inviting this person in. After all, I had company to get ready for! That was some horrible thinking! I knew that God wants us to show hospitality to everyone. I invited her in and those few minutes provided an opportunity for our relationship to grow. Who knows what the true importance of those few minutes was.

Hospitality is listed as a good trait that is characteristic of the people of God. When Paul was telling Timothy who may be put on the list of widows, he included these character traits as necessary prerequisites: the women must have "a reputation for good works; and if she has brought up children, if she has shown hospitality to strangers, if she has washed the saints' feet, if she has assisted those in distress, and if she has devoted herself to every good work [she could be added to the list]." (1 Timothy 5:10) Although we may think of hospitality as "women's work," men are not excluded. In Romans 16 Gaius is commended for his hospitality to Paul and to the church. Being hospitable is also listed as one of the qualities of an overseer. The overseer must be "hospitable, loving what is good, sensible, just, devout, self-controlled." (Titus 1:8. See also 1 Timothy 3)

Although showing mercy, serving, and contributing to the needs of others are listed as gifts of the Spirit (see Romans 12), hospitality is not. Hospitality may come easier for some than for others, but I believe it is biblical to say that all Christians should practice hospitality. Romans 12:13 says, "Share with God's people who are in need. Practice hospitality." (NIV)

Towards whom should we show hospitality? I think it's clear from the above verses that we should be happy to invite fellow Christians into our homes. We should also include the couple who are always inviting people to their house and the woman who makes such a "great hostess." These people, too, deserve an opportunity to be on the receiving end of someone else's hospitality. I think it is also safe to say that our hospitality should extend to those outside our faith. The Bible says, "Do not neglect to show hospitality to strangers, for by this some have entertained angels without knowing it." (Hebrews 13:2) This is a very practical way to show love and concern for others. It helps us to develop friendships with people and will lend itself to the sharing of our faith and our lives, in the hopes that at some time they will come to believe in God as well.

As in all aspects of our service to God, we should do it with a proper attitude. We should do it happily and to the best of our ability, since we are really serving Christ and not man. "Above all, keep fervent in your love for one another, because love covers a multitude of sins. Be hospitable to one another without complaint." (1 Peter 4:8-9)

Hospitality requires time, effort, and resources. Planning and preparation take time. We invest ourselves into our company when we could be relaxing or playing with our families. Under most circumstances it will also cost us money for food and drink. We may feel frustrated if we feel that *we* are the ones who are usually doing the entertaining. But God does not want us to keep score. He wants us to willingly invite others into our homes, regardless of the costs to us and regardless of whether our actions are reciprocated. Luke tells the story of when Jesus went to a Pharisee's house to eat. "He also went on to say to the one who had invited Him, 'When you give a luncheon or a dinner, do not invite your friends or your brothers or your relatives or rich neighbors, otherwise they may also invite you in return and that will be your repayment. But when you give a reception, invite the poor, the crippled, the lame, the blind, and you will be blessed, since they do not have the means to repay you; for you will be repaid at the resurrection of the righteous.' " (Luke 14:12-14)

There are plenty of books and resources to help with entertaining, so I don't need to get into all that. I do want to say, though, that we shouldn't feel like we need to set out a huge spread of food with lively entertainment. Most important of all is to make our guests feel welcomed.

A clean house, smiling faces, listening ears, and interesting conversation are all that's really necessary. I remember one family in particular who invited our large crew over to their house. We came after church. She had almost everything prepared ahead of time, so she didn't have to spend much time in the kitchen away from her guests. The food was simple, but it was tasty and there was plenty of it. Their kids showed our kids around while we adults talked. Nothing spectacular. But we felt more than welcomed.

It is good for us as parents to practice hospitality so that our children can learn both how and why we do it. They should see us do it with a joyful attitude. Our children should learn how, and be expected to, interact with our invited adults. They should be the ones to entertain any children who have come. They should be taught to think ahead of time as to how to entertain their peers and how to make them feel welcome. They may then feel more appreciation towards the hospitality that others show us. And when they grow up and establish households of their own, showing hospitality won't seem so overwhelming, but rather something they do quite naturally.

God has been good to us, so we can freely give as we have freely received. You are welcomed in our home. So, please, come in.

Inspiration

Behold, the tabernacle of God is among men, and He will dwell among them, and they shall be His people, and God Himself will be among them, and He will wipe away every tear from their eyes; and there will no longer be any death; there will no longer be any mourning, or crying, or pain; the first things have passed away.

(Revelation 21:3b-4)

The Urgency of Eternity

I stand by the bedside of my patient and watch her take her last breath. These last couple of minutes have gone so slowly. How quietly death overcomes and life ebbs away. How many times have I found myself at just such a bedside. Yet each time it is an overwhelming spiritual experience.

Death is merely the absence of life. Life is intangible. Though we feel it, we cannot grasp it. Though we possess it, we cannot hold onto it. I have seen death come suddenly and unexpectedly. As we force a person's heart to beat and push air into his lungs, we are not imparting life. Only God can give the breath of life, and it is His to take away.

But now as I see death creep in and life slowly drift away, it causes me a great deal of contemplation. I grieve for this person's family and friends; their lives have been forever changed in this moment. I'm reminded of my own loved ones' mortality – as well as my own. I see again how horrible this world is compared to what heaven is like. And I realize quite profoundly that this soul before me has begun its eternity, though I am not sure where. How many times have I heard co-workers say, "She looks so peaceful." How many times have I heard them utter, "At least she is not suffering anymore." Do they not understand? Have they not heard? The body is a shell. Death is a beginning. Religion is not a philosophical exercise. What a person believes about Jesus Christ will determine his eternal destiny. I wish I could shake them into understanding. I have often spoken with patients and co-workers, yet I know the urgency is not always there. Eternity gets clouded by the temporal. We get distracted by the earthly priorities of the day. We can't hear our heavenly calling through the din of our fallen world. Our feet get entangled by the sin and worries in our lives and we forget the race we are running. And while our citizenship is in heaven, we forget the responsibilities which that involves. Not only do we risk the compromise of our own spiritual health, but our neighbors' as well. Let us not forget the urgency and inevitability of eternity. May it affect what we do today.

"Therefore, my beloved brethren, be steadfast, immovable, always abounding in the work of the Lord, knowing that your toil is not in vain in the Lord." (1 Cor. 15:58)

Stressed!

"210 – medium susceptibility to stress-related illness"

"250 – overstressed" (just barely)

These were the results I received from two stress tests I did online. I thought it would be fun to see how they would rate my stress level from the crazy year we just finished. During the past year I was pregnant, had a new baby, moved into a new home with a new mortgage 1100 miles away, changed my personal routines, and had changes in social, church, and work activities. (Oh, yes, Christmas. You get 10-12 points every year just for that!) Tests like that don't really mean anything to me. Their categories and number ratings seem pretty arbitrary. We don't need an exercise like this to let us know that daily we face pressures that can affect our mood, health, and faith. As I compared where we are at the beginning of this new year to where we were one year ago, I saw that largely we are in a completely different place. And most of it we didn't anticipate. That's the way things seem to go – we have few guarantees and our whole lives can change in a moment. There is often little that we can anticipate and little that we can control. Under those reassuring circumstances, how can we remain calm, full of Christian joy, and most productive for God?

One of those websites gave me an answer on how to manage my stress. It told me to "learn and practice relaxation and stress management skills and a healthy well lifestyle." Of course, the website also had lots of aids for me to buy to help me in that endeavor. As Christians, though, those things are just second-rate substitutions to help us along our way. Instead we can go directly to the ultimate source of peace and power. The Bible is the best stress-management book we can read. If we read the Bible with that in mind, we see it has a lot of things that have to do with being truly peaceful, stress free, and productive.

We feel stress sometimes because we aren't focused, or because our focus isn't correct. We may become preoccupied with advancing in our jobs or achieving other personal goals. Sometimes we wonder what it all means and if it is really important. The Bible helps us to keep correct focus. "Therefore if you have been raised up with Christ, keep seeking the things above, where Christ is, seated at the right hand of God. Set your mind on the things above, not on the things that are on earth. For you have died and your life is hidden with Christ in God." (Colossians 3:1-3) The Bible tells us to be concerned with the things of God and with those things that are eternal. The rest is temporary and of little eternal value.

We also learn from the Bible that we are working for the Lord, not for our bosses or our husbands or even for ourselves. "Whatever you do, do your work heartily, as for the Lord rather than for men." (Colossians 3:23) We are working to fulfill His will and to please Him. We find out what His will is and how we please Him by reading the Bible!

We also feel stressed sometimes because we worry about things that don't really matter. For instance, we get anxious around holidays because we want to get everything done and we want it just right. We may get too concerned about how our house looks to others – and even to ourselves, and so on. We remember the story of Jesus visiting the house of Martha. "She had a sister called Mary, who was seated at the Lord's feet, listening to His word. But Martha was distracted with all her preparations; and she came up to Him and said, 'Lord, do You not care that my sister has left me to do all the serving alone? Then tell her to help me.' But the Lord answered and said to her, 'Martha, Martha, you are worried and bothered about so many things; but only one thing is necessary, for Mary has chosen the good part, which shall not be taken away from her.' " (Luke 10:39-42) Martha was *distracted*. She was stressed over the things that didn't matter so much. How often do we do that?

All of these verses have direct influence on our behavior and our goals. Our stress will be reduced because we are focused. We know how to spend our time. We know that what we are doing is important.

Stress also comes in the form of confusion as to what is right or wrong in certain situations. "Therefore consider the members of your earthly body as dead to immorality, impurity, passion, evil desire, and greed, which amounts to idolatry. For it is because of these things that the wrath of God will come upon the sons of disobedience, and in them you also once walked, when you were living in them. But now you also, put them all aside: anger, wrath, malice, slander, and abusive speech from your mouth. Do not lie to one another, since you laid aside the old self with its evil practices, and have put on the new self who is being renewed to a true knowledge according to the image of the One who created him – renewal in which there is no distinction between Greek and Jew, circumcised and uncircumcised, barbarian, Scythian, slave and freeman, but Christ is all, and in all. So, as those who have been chosen of God, holy and beloved, put on a heart of compassion, kindness, humility, gentleness and patience." (Colossians 3:5-12) The Bible is obviously our best source for learning to make godly choices in our behavior. No, it does not spell out every situation we encounter, but it gives us principles and examples for us to apply to the events in our lives. Forget the ethics committee and your college ethics book. You already have what you need.

Tension (stress) can also arise in our lives when past errors weigh down our relationship with God or with others. The Bible shows us that true forgiveness restores peace to our relationships. We have peace with God through Jesus Christ. "I [God], even I, am the one who wipes out your transgressions for My own sake, and I will not remember your sins." (Isaiah 43:25) We have peace with others as we forgive their wrongs against us. "Bearing with one another, and forgiving each other, whoever has a complaint against anyone; just as the Lord forgave you, so also should you. Beyond all these things put on love, which is the perfect bond of unity." (Colossians 3:13-14) "Above all, keep fervent in your love for one another, because love covers a multitude of sins." (1 Peter 4:8) God can help us forgive those who have hurt us. He is our Counselor! Finally, we have peace with ourselves as we accept God's grace and forgive ourselves, so to speak. “But one thing I do: forgetting what lies behind and reaching forward to what lies ahead.” (Philippians 3:13b)

We may have peaceful relationships and godly aspirations and still feel the strains of day-to-day life. It is easy to become worried that we may lose our job or that the physical needs of our family may not be met. “For this reason I say to you, do not be worried about your life, as to what you will eat or what you will drink; nor for your body, as to what you will put on. Is not life more than food, and the body more than clothing? Look at the birds of the air, that they do not sow, nor reap nor gather into barns, and yet your heavenly Father feeds them. Are you not worth much more than they? And who of you by being worried can add a single hour to his life? And why are you worried about clothing? Observe how the lilies of the field grow; they do not toil nor do they spin, yet I say to you that not even Solomon in all his glory clothed himself like one of these. But if God so clothes the grass of the field, which is alive today and tomorrow is thrown into the furnace, will He not much more clothe you? You of little faith! Do not worry then, saying, ‘What will we eat?’ or ‘What will we drink?’ or ‘What will we wear for clothing?’ For the Gentiles eagerly seek all these things; for your heavenly Father knows that you need all these things. But seek first His kingdom and His righteousness, and all these things will be added to you. So do not worry about tomorrow; for tomorrow will care for itself. Each day has enough trouble of its own.” (Matthew 6:25-34) We worry in vain – first of all because it achieves nothing, and second because God has promised to supply all of our daily needs. “Blessed be the Lord, who daily bears our burden, the God who is our salvation.” (Psalm 68:19)

We also need not be weighed down with concerns for our future. God has given us great promises. He will protect us through this life and bring us to heaven to live with Him for eternity. “Blessed be the God and Father of our Lord Jesus Christ, who according to His great mercy has caused us to be born again to a living hope through the resurrection of Jesus Christ from the dead, to obtain an inheritance which is imperishable and undefiled and will not fade away, reserved in heaven for you, who are protected by the power of God through faith for a salvation ready to be revealed in the last time.” (1 Peter 1:3-5) He loves us and wants the best for us. " 'For the mountains may be removed and the hills may shake, but My lovingkindness will not be removed from you, and My covenant of peace will not be shaken,' says the LORD who has compassion on you." (Isaiah 54:10) Jesus himself said, "And lo, I am with you always, even to the end of the age." (Matthew 28:20b)

But sometimes this earthly road is long and we become weary. Let us remember that God sees all that we do for Him. "Let us not lose heart in doing good, for in due time we will reap if we do not grow weary." (Galatians 6:9) We should count ourselves blessed if we suffer for His name. "But if anyone suffers as a Christian, he is not to be ashamed, but is to glorify God in this name." (1 Peter 4:16) And He gives us strength when we feel we have none. "He gives strength to the weary, and to him who lacks might He increases power. Though youths grow weary and tired, and vigorous young men stumble badly, yet those who wait for the LORD will gain new strength; they will mount up with wings like eagles, they will run and not get tired, they will walk and not become weary." (Isaiah 40:29-31) The strain of feeling tired and discouraged need not be ours.

The truth is that we don't know what's ahead of us. The prospects can almost be frightening! But the other, deeper truth is that God loves us and has all things under His control. The Lord reigns! And He loves me! That's the greatest stress-reducer of all.

No More Locusts

" 'For I know the plans that I have for you,' declares the LORD, 'plans for welfare and not for calamity to give you a future and a hope.' " (Jeremiah 29: 11)

This seems to be a popular verse of Scripture. We hear it quoted in sermons and on the radio and we see it printed in greeting cards. It is a verse of encouragement, reminding us of the love of the Lord. It is warming and reassuring as we repeat it, but pulled from its context its full meaning and impact are diminished.

This verse is actually part of a letter which Jeremiah the prophet sent to those who had been carried into exile from Jerusalem to Babylon by King Nebuchadnezzar. Jerusalem and its people were not defeated by chance because Babylon was so much superior and stronger. Jerusalem was defeated as a punishment for the people's sins. For years God had warned His people through the prophets about their coming destruction if they refused to repent and turn to God. They refused to repent, and so they found Jerusalem defeated and many of themselves in captivity. Those who were left in Jerusalem faced "sword, famine and plague." " 'Because they have not listened to My words,' declares the LORD, 'which I sent to them again and again by My servants the prophets; but you did not listen,' declares the LORD." (Jeremiah 29:19)

That is the setting for this letter. The people were being punished. Now that they were in exile, God had some words of instruction for them: settle down, plant and eat the harvest, marry and have families, pray for the city of Babylon, and don't listen to the false prophets in their midst. God also had words of encouragement for them: " 'For thus says the LORD, 'When seventy years have been completed for Babylon, I will visit you and fulfill My good word to you, to bring you back to this place. For I know the plans that I have for you...' " (vs.10-11a) This is more than a word of hope – it is a word of forgiveness and restoration. God was speaking to people who had long ignored Him and turned away from Him. This was mercy. God was planning to fulfill His *gracious* promise. It was gracious because the people didn't deserve it. (You can read the entire letter yourself for the rest of God's message.)

Joel also was a prophet in Israel. He was sent to Judah – the Southern Kingdom – many decades before Jeremiah. He told Judah of the coming judgment of God. This judgment is described as a plague of locusts. (This may be a reference to the future invasions by Assyria and Babylon.) Joel called them to repent. If they would repent, "Then the LORD will be zealous for His land and will have pity on His people." (Joel 2:18) The Lord would remove the "army" and restore the land. "Then I will make up to you for the years that the swarming locust has eaten, the creeping locust, the stripping locust and the gnawing locust, my great army which I sent among you. You will have plenty to eat and be satisfied and praise the name of the LORD your God, who has dealt wondrously with you; then My people will never be put to shame." (Joel 2:25-26) Notice that God refers to the locusts as "*my* great army that

I sent among you." The locusts were a punishment directly from God. They deserved what they got; it was their fault. But if they repented, God was ready to forgive and restore them in His great mercy. They suffered because of their sins but God was willing to make up for the losses they suffered. This is grace.

We, too, deserve God's punishment. We are no better than Israel. We also have ignored God and turned away from Him. But God offers us His mercy if we repent and believe in the death and resurrection of Jesus Christ. We have an eternal hope. God not only loves us and wants to be good to us; He loves us in spite of our sinfulness.

Have the locusts devastated crops in your life? Are your trees stripped of their bark and the grain destroyed? God is willing to make your land new and abundant once again. I know we don't deserve it. That's why it's grace.

Consider Job

Did you ever feel like you just couldn't make it anymore? Too many financial difficulties? A great loss? Strained family relations? Long term pain or health problems? One thing after another going wrong? I can remember feeling like that. When we were living in California our oldest children were just toddlers (2 1/2 years and 1 1/2 years) and I was very pregnant. We lived at the doctor's office with ear infection after ear infection. We lived at the pharmacy filling prescriptions. We lived at the emergency room with more asthma attacks than I could count. We lived at the hospital when the boys were admitted to gain control over this beast called asthma. We had no family nearby to help. I returned late one night from yet another emergency room visit, put my now easy-breathing son to bed, and slumped into a chair. I told God I just couldn't do this anymore. I felt the same years later at the threat of a third miscarriage. I couldn't stand to go through it again. Human emotions are funny, deceiving things, making us foolishly brave or unnecessarily cowardly. We run into things without really looking or we avoid necessary or worthy causes because we wrongly deem ourselves weak. We become victims in our own eyes and thus make ourselves unable to serve. We are ineffective because we sell ourselves short. We become haughty for lack of a rightful assessment of ourselves. We feel weak and alone when God calls us to persevere.

I wonder if Job felt overwhelmed and defeated. Was it when the Sabeans carried off his oxen and donkeys? Was it when his sheep were destroyed? Was it when the Chaldeans took his camels? How about upon hearing that his servants were destroyed? Did he begin to wonder what else could go wrong? Did he cringe when he saw yet another messenger running to him? Was it when every one of his children perished? Did it happen when he was covered with sores and in persistent pain?

There is a verse in James (5:11), which states, "We count those blessed who endured. You have heard of the endurance of Job and have seen the outcome of the Lord's dealings, that the Lord is full of compassion and is merciful." Imagine those watching Job from a distance. They probably thought there was no hope for him. Here he was – alone, forlorn, and in physical suffering. He was thought to be abandoned or punished by God. But they were wrong. God knew exactly what was happening. He was watching it all. He knew what was to become of the situation, and He had it under His control. Job persevered and refused to curse or blame God. God sustained him and brought about great blessing for him, plus a lesson to anyone who was or is willing to listen. The ending of this verse is so powerful. God brought about wonderful things for Job because He is so full of compassion and mercy. Even in the midst of Job's suffering God was committed to him. God loved Job in the midst of the lowest, most difficult time of his life. God's love didn't go away and then resume after it was all over. God's love for him never stopped. His love brought wonderful things to Job.

I have learned three things so far in my years. One, with God's help, I can do more than I ever thought I could. Two, despite my feelings, I know that by God I can endure any circumstance I find myself in. Three, God knows our limitations and He brings about relief when we need it, and never too late.

Is life careening around you? Be strong. God knows. Watch what God will bring about. Whatever it is, He is full of compassion and mercy. God loves *you*!

"He will not fear evil tidings; his heart is steadfast, trusting in the LORD. His heart is upheld, he will not fear, until he looks with satisfaction on his adversaries." (Psalm 112:7-8)

All Things Are Possible

When hard times hit and things aren't going our way, we all react in different ways. God knows all things, so He understands our situation but we often doubt His help. We remember the Scripture that says, "The effective prayer of a righteous man can accomplish much." (James 5: 16b) And we know the verse that says, "With God all things are possible," (Matthew 19:26) but we are often quick to shake our heads in discouragement and say, "Your will be done." Yet, extraordinary men and women of the Bible had faith that God would help them out of what we would consider hopeless situations. Battles were won against overwhelming odds, the dead were raised, the sick were miraculously healed, and the poor were given sustenance.

When circumstances turn against us, we need to remember that a man of faith can say to the tree and the mountain, "Be uprooted and thrown into the sea," and it will be done. All things are possible for those who believe. Can we accept it?

Some of us suffer from physical problems that limit and discourage us. In the Bible, we read of many people with terrible sicknesses and handicaps who received complete healing. Demon possession, blindness, leprosy, lameness - all cured. Some were sought out by the Lord, but others knew that the Lord was able and willing to act on their behalf. "Your faith has made you well" was said by Jesus more than once. That is not to say that everyone will be healed and that all your problems are the result of a lack of faith. Jesus was persecuted even to death, and so were many of His followers throughout the ages. Sometimes, then, "all things are possible" may mean that despite our sicknesses and physical limitations, God's grace is evident in us. In fact, our physical infirmities may make it easier for others to see that the power within us is of God. As Paul said, "But we have this treasure in earthen vessels, so that the surpassing greatness of the power will be of God and not from ourselves." (2 Cor. 4:7) Paul himself struggled with some sort of "thorn in the flesh" and he prayed three times to God for healing. God's answer was,

"My grace is sufficient for you, for my power is made perfect in weakness." (2 Cor. 12:9, NIV) Therefore, Paul says, "I will rather boast about my weaknesses, so that the power of Christ may dwell in me. Therefore I am well content with weaknesses, with insults, with distresses, with persecutions, with difficulties, for Christ's sake; for when I am weak, then I am strong." (2 Cor. 12:9b-10) So then, "all things are possible" may mean God can and will heal us even though it is medically impossible, and it may mean that our sickness or handicap is an opportunity to show the world that our strength and our joy do not come from good health, but from God.

Others, however, face relational struggles. Their families or work environments have become a painful prison just as real as a sick body. With God, though, all things are possible. We must never forget God's power to change lives. Paul was changed from a zealous church persecutor and violent man to perhaps the greatest missionary the world has ever seen. A profane slave trader would one day pen the words, "Amazing grace, how sweet the sound, that saved a wretch like me." And if the truth were known, every Christian could have penned that song because without the grace of God we would all be wretches. Every Christian, then, is a testimony to the world that God is willing and able to change wretches into saints. Therefore, no matter how difficult, or violent, or flawed you or the people in your life are, God can change you all. With God all things are possible. Maybe, though, God will use our struggle and loneliness to honor Him. We think we are limited by a difficult spouse or an irrational boss, but God is not limited by those things. When others see that our joy is not quenched by difficult people or loneliness, when they see that we not only tolerate our enemies, but love them, when we pray for them and forgive them, will they not wonder what power would enable us to do such things? With God all things are possible.

Others struggle with finances. Meeting basic needs consumes them. They worry about where the money will come from to pay the medical bills and the mortgage. They don't know how to get the car fixed. They work hard at jobs that don't seem to pay enough to live on, or perhaps they don't have jobs at all. With God, however, finances are nothing to worry about. God made the entire universe in six days and owns it all. Jesus fed five thousand men with five loaves and two fish. There is no scarcity of resources in the Kingdom of God. In fact, God promised every Christian that He would provide for his needs. God made Abraham, Isaac, Joseph, David, Solomon, and many others wealthy, and He could do the same for you. Do you believe it? With God, all things are possible.

Some, however, are poor in order to reach those who are poor with the good news about Jesus. Jesus Himself, "Who, although He existed in the form of God, did not regard equality with God a thing to be grasped, but emptied Himself, taking the form of a bond-servant, and being made in the likeness of men. Being found in appearance as a man, He humbled Himself by becoming obedient to the point of death, even death on a cross. For this reason also, God highly exalted Him, and bestowed on Him the name which is above every name." (Phi. 2:6-9) Maybe God humbles us financially to be an example to others in need and to show them that our joy does not come from the abundance of our possessions, but from our relationship with God. Besides, we know as Christians we will inherit all things some day. The world will be ours. Why, then, should we be concerned about money? Even if we seem poor, we are children and heirs of the King!

So we live our lives with great faith, knowing that God could change our circumstances this second. God has used His great power to help more people than we could possibly count and He will continue to help people in the future. It is God's nature to be gracious. We live our lives, then, with the expectation that God will certainly help us, and that He may deliver us from our troubles even today. However, if the end of the day finds us with the same problems we began the day with, we need to remember that our trials are only temporary and that God can use our troubles to bring honor to His name. He will certainly reward us if only we are faithful. With God, all things are possible.

I Have a Dream, Too

Those words "I have a dream" were spoken by Martin Luther King in his famous speech at the Lincoln Memorial in 1963. This article has nothing at all to do with the subject he was addressing at that time, but there is one similarity. King dreamed for an America different from the one he saw, and I do the same.

When God saved me (quite abruptly) from my youthful foolishness, I was determined to live the rest of my life for Him. I have been quite unable to fulfill that desire to the degree I would like. But after twenty years of trying, my views about a lot of things have changed to the point where most Christians would consider my views a little eccentric. I now long for great change – that millions of unbelievers in our nation would turn to the Lord, that the priorities of Christian families and churches would change, and that God would help us to walk more faithfully before Him.

With family hundreds of miles away and most church members ambivalent to our views, we have felt at times that we are alone and separated from the rest of humanity. However, when we read a really good article, hear a like- minded person on the radio, or get an encouraging message from one of our readers, we are reminded again that somewhere out there are others who share our vision. We want that dream to spread and it would even be nice if a few like-minded families would move near us and attend the same church that we do.

So then, what is this dream? I would tell you to close your eyes if you could do that and read at the same time, but seeing as that is not going to happen, I ask you simply to dream along with me.

I have a dream. I dream that Christian families would reflect the biblical model. The Christian family begins with a strong and loving husband who leads his family, loves his wife the way Christ loves the church, and sees that his children are raised in the fear and admonition of the Lord – and he doesn't delegate that important responsibility to school teachers and day care providers. It begins with a man who cares more about his God and his family than he cares about his job, his house, his friends, or his entertainments. It begins with a man who is not afraid to protect his family from the influences of a culture that increasingly models itself after Sodom and Gomorrah. It begins with a man who understands that God has given him the responsibility of leadership.

I have a dream. I dream that each family may be adorned with a loving and respectful wife who submits to her husband as unto the Lord, a wife who dresses modestly and who desires to manage her children and her household more than she wants to succeed in a career that takes her away from the home, a wife whose heart's desire is to help her husband in his God-given calling and to raise godly children, a wife who isn't obsessed with her physical appearance, expensive clothes, or nice things, but prefers things that have eternal significance.

I have a dream. I dream that raising godly children would be the focus of every Christian family. I have a dream that families would consider children such a special blessing and reward that they wouldn't try to stop God from giving them more and that they will have faith that God will provide everything necessary to live no matter how many people are sharing the same roof.

I have a dream. I dream that a new generation of godly children will grow up to challenge the godless culture and attack the strongholds of Satan.

I have a dream. I dream that churches would stop tearing families apart and start training parents to raise their own children the way God prescribes in the Scriptures, that churches would be more concerned about spreading the Gospel of Jesus Christ than they are about the size of their church buildings or the multiplication of programs, and that pastors and teachers would be concerned more with teaching the truth than they are about growing their numbers.

I have a dream. I dream that our political leaders would see God as their highest governing authority, that they would punish evildoers instead of funding abortions, illegal drug use, blasphemous art, and homosexual propaganda, that they would no longer steal the fruits of one man's labor to buy the votes of another, that they would treat every person equally under the law regardless of race or political influence, that they would trust in God's protection and not in alliances with ungodly nations, and that they would be sincerely peace loving but ready to use their God-given "power of the sword" to protect us if necessary.

Yes, these are my dreams. I know that the sinful world in which we live cannot be made perfect until God destroys it and puts a permanent end to evil. However, we are called to advance God's kingdom in accordance with the faith and the power He has given us – even in this present evil age. Do any of you share this dream with me?

Also from Jim & Cindy McDermott

SALT Magazine:

You'll get compelling discussion of relevant and sometimes controversial topics, uplifting and encouraging articles, practical advice, and witty, humorous attempts at self-promotion. Get 12 issues of the best home-made magazine this side of the Kansas Expressway for only $24.

You can subscribe online at saltmagazine.com with Visa, MasterCard, or PayPal. You may also mail a check for $24 to SALT Magazine, 2131 W. Republic Rd. #177, Springfield, MO 65807.

Speaking:

If you would like Jim or Cindy to discuss the Christian family at your next radio broadcast, convention, meeting, Bible Study, family dinner, or Frapuccino, contact us at speaking@saltmagazine.com

Need More Books?

You can order more books online at saltchristianpress.com. If you want to order by mail, send $14.99 for each book to SALT Christian Press, 2131 W. Republic Rd. #177, Springfield, MO 65807. Our shipping rates are low. We charge a flat rate of $2.50 per order. So, if you order one book you pay a total shipping cost of $2.50. If you order one hundred books you pay a total shipping cost of $2.50. Please don't be concerned that our low shipping costs will cause us to run out. If people order too many, feel secure in our commitment to print more.

Need a Book and Can't Afford It?

As the Lord provides, we will supply books to anyone who wants one but truly can't afford it. If you need a free book, contact us at info@saltchristianpress.com.